John Cuthbert Hedley

A Retreat

Thirty-Three Discourses with Meditation for the Use of the Clergy, Religious, and Others. Eleventh Edition

John Cuthbert Hedley

A Retreat

*Thirty-Three Discourses with Meditation for the Use of the Clergy, Religious, and Others.
Eleventh Edition*

ISBN/EAN: 9783744653695

Printed in Europe, USA, Canada, Australia, Japan

Cover: Foto ©Lupo / pixelio.de

More available books at **www.hansebooks.com**

A RETREAT

THIRTY-THREE DISCOURSES
WITH MEDITATION FOR THE USE OF THE
CLERGY, RELIGIOUS, AND OTHERS

BY THE RIGHT REV.
JOHN CUTHBERT HEDLEY, O.S.B.
BISHOP OF NEWPORT

ELEVENTH EDITION

LONDON
BURNS, OATES & WASHBOURNE LTD.,
28 ORCHARD STREET, W. & 8-10 PATERNOSTER ROW, E.C.

Imprimatur.

Die 15 Augusti, 1894.

PREFACE.

The following Discourses or Meditations are intended to furnish matter for a Retreat of eight or ten days. Each of them consists of devout considerations, followed by points for mental prayer. The considerations are to be read over slowly and with devotional attention; and the points are to be wrought out with as much fervour of affective acts as may be possible. Each discourse, with its affections, is calculated to afford matter for about an hour's exercise.

The Retreat is intended for priests, religious, and persons in the world. Here and there will be found remarks addressed more especially to one or other of these classes; but the point of view taken is, on the whole, one which concerns the human soul in its relations with its Creator and Redeemer, and which does not depend on any obligation arising from vows or state of life. Even in such meditations as "The Religious Promise,"

"Obedience," and "Poverty," principles are treated which lie at the root of all Christian practice, and aspirations are proposed which will be found natural and useful by every heart which seriously desires to give itself to God.

TABLE OF CONTENTS.

PAGE

I. INTRODUCTORY.—To enter on a Retreat is to pass into a holy silence and retirement—It is the fatherly love of God that gives you this opportunity—You do not know what He is going to say to you—A Retreat is necessary because times of grave thought and special prayer are necessary for every soul—Special reasons which make it necessary in your own case, such as your own drifting, hardening, or listlessness—A Retreat consists of rest, thought, and prayer—Rest from our occupation, even the most excellent and necessary—Thought upon our spiritual condition, our sins, our motives, and above all on the deep fundamental truths of our being—Prayer, with an earnestness that is helped by the silence and solitude, and which deepens as the Retreat goes on—We should begin our Retreat cheerfully and courageously with great belief in the love and solicitude of God, . 1

II. MY SOUL.—The soul is a spirit, and is described in Holy Scripture under the symbols of "fire" and "light"—It is immortal; it lives on for ever when the poor framework of tissue, bone and nerves has fallen to pieces and disappeared—This single thought of immortality gives life its meaning—Death is really an awakening—The soul comes from the Infinite God by a special creative act—Is in His likeness—Hence, whatever men may say or feel, the soul cannot possibly do without God in the long run—Well for us if we awake to this truth before it is too late, ... 15

III. THE VOICE OF GOD.—Being made to God's image, my soul must be in sympathy or accord with God—His voice can be heard gently, sweetly and softly, by those who acquire the habit of listening—There are precious moments when God speaks to us in our interior—He speaks to us also by external nature—The Twenty-eighth Psalm—To hear Him we must "lift up the soul"—Aspirations that He would show us His ways, teach us, and direct us, ... 24

IV. GOD.—The Eighth Psalm—The human words by which we name Almighty God—They are never pure enough—God's causation of the soul and body by creation is as if a wave of the Infinite had passed over them—Creation implies submission to God's will—God's Personality—He and His creatures know one another, and are mutually related, ... 34

V. THE PERSONAL NAMES OF GOD.—More necessary to meditate on "Who" God is than on "What" He is—The Twenty-second Psalm—God always and necessarily a Father to His creatures—The Incarnation has given the word a deeper meaning—God is our most devoted friend—Our pride and sense of safety in having God on our side, ... 43

VI. REDEMPTION AND GRACE.—The reason and origin of Grace lies in the Beatific Vision—Grace, though not substantially the Holy Ghost, is His most immediate effect—It is "life"—It is "beauty"—It makes us "children" and "heirs" of God—and partakers of the Divine Nature—How we have undervalued Grace, . 54

VII. SIN.—A soul in Grace described—The awful change brought about by Mortal Sin—My sins have been many, and aggravated in many ways—Contrition, though resting on fear, should pass on to love—A fourfold exercise recommended: the renewal of Contrition for all past sins; the humbling ourselves for our nearness to Mortal Sin; the acknowledgment of the possibility of Mortal Sin; and the resolution to make Contrition a constant feature of our spiritual life—The Psalm *Miserere*, . . 66

VIII. DEATH.—Death, the great interpreter of life—The mystery and horror of Death to the Pagan and the Jew—A terrifying thought even to a Christian—The circum-

stances of our own death forecast—Physical pain—
Mental trouble and fear—How it comes about that we
are not prepared—Difficulty of conversion and of true
contrition at some death-beds—Resolutions to examine
our conscience, to strive to reduce the power of passion,
and to form strong habits of virtue, ... 78

IX. JUDGMENT.—The seriousness of Death arises from the
inevitableness of Judgment—Every moment of life to
be answered for—The thought of the Judgment helps
us to realise that one day we must come face to face
with the Absolute—My particular Judgment—God
comes as Master—as Rectifier—as Rewarder—as
Avenger—We may look forward with confidence to the
Judgment if we judge not others, study kindness to one
another, and judge ourselves, ... 90

X. HELL.—The thought of everlasting punishment helps
to impress upon us the stern reality of existence—What
Christian sadness is, and its uses—The "anger" of God
—The pit of hell—the fire—the demons—the worm that
never dies—eternity, ... 102

XI. CHRIST OUR LORD.—The Incarnation a great "plan"
of Almighty God to make union with Him more easy—
God in Himself very far removed from us—The Incarnation has enabled us to know and love Him in a
way which would seem impossible—It reveals God as
truly and really loving us—It reveals the value He
places on our immortal souls—Devotional exercise on
the Incarnate God as described in the Old Testament, . 113

XII. LOOKING UPON JESUS.—God became Man in order
to draw or attract men—He came, human, historical,
with a Name and a Mother, poor and carrying the
burden of humanity—The Incarnation makes worship
so much easier—We have only to turn to Bethlehem,
Nazareth, Calvary, and we find the Infinite God—The
Incarnation is intended to transform our beings into
the likeness of Christ—Because the Sacred Humanity
was intended to heal our bruises—and He wishes us to
come to Him to be relieved of our burdens—and devout

contemplation of Jesus tends to reproduce His perfections in our hearts and wills, ... 124

XIII. THE HIDDEN LIFE OF OUR LORD.—The poverty, detachment and humility of the servants of God precisely the forces which have produced such wonderful works—Jesus might have had riches, servants, and influence—Instead of that He went into obscurity, practised obedience, and lived in labour and poverty—Solitude, Obedience, Poverty and Labour, the pillars of the holy house of Nazareth—These are the conditions which make interior love and union most intense and continuous—Hence the Hidden Life means the strenuous endeavour, by means of these conditions, to carry out this union—It means great simplicity of view—The absence of ambition—Indifference to results—A constant watchfulness in small things—Literal "hiddenness"—The predominance of Prayer—Anxious and absorbing occupation no obstacle to the Hidden Life, . 136

XIV. THE PUBLIC LIFE OF OUR LORD.—Exterior work effects nothing of itself—Jesus, before He went out to preach, had (so to speak) thoroughly learnt the Hidden Life—The canticle of Habacuc—External work should be the work of obedience, and intermitted by regular spiritual duties—Failure, disappointment and disgust should be treated rather as pledges of success than as reason for giving up, ... 147

XV. THE SUFFERINGS OF CHRIST.—Why our Lord chose to suffer—How suffering intensifies the acts of the heart—and draws the hearts of men—Our Lord's whole life made up of suffering—The Passion intended to promote the worship of God through compassion—and to facilitate contrition—The Passion and the Holy Mass—The Passion and our own sorrows—Our sufferings purify us, expiate sin, and sanctify us through mortification, ... 161

XVI. THE HOLY SPIRIT.—Spirituality the service of a Father, not a mere system—The Holy Spirit sent to take the place of Jesus as Master and Comforter—What

	PAGE
His Gifts bring to the soul—His intimate companionship with us,	174

XVII. How to Live by the Spirit.—First effect of the indwelling of the Holy Spirit, Fear—Second effect, Divine Love—Third effect, Peace—Do we value the supernatural?—Are we sensitive in regard to sin?—Do we habitually find God in our ordinary actions?—Do we fail in our esteem of the supernatural?—Points in which we may humbly look for the guidance of the Holy Spirit—Three things which may account for our not having His light, ... 186

XVIII. The Religious Promise.—The Religious State a means, not an end—A state of perfection—It was no other than God who called us—He called us to total and absolute sacrifice—How such a state intensifies our love of God—Our feelings when we made our vows—How we fell off—The obligation to aspire to perfection, 200

XIX. Obedience.—Humility the root or source of the spirit of Obedience—Obedience the safeguard of Humility—Obedience a sacrifice—the short cut to perfection, . 212

Reflection on Obedience of the Judgment, . . 223

XX. Poverty.—Our Lord's predilection for Poverty—Evil effects of affluence or possession—Poverty removes temptation—casts the soul upon God—is painful—Our regrets—inordinate attachment—superfluities—murmuring—The degrees of Poverty, ... 228

XXI. Prayer.—Absolutely needful—Mental Prayer—fidelity to its practice—no interior life or success without it—method of Mental Prayer, . . . 242

XXII. The Divine Office.—The Divine Office part of the world's homage to God—the prayer of the Church—a public prayer—its words and forms—it furnishes food for prayer—its devout associations—how to discharge it, 256

XXIII. The Blessed Sacrament.—The Blessed Sacrament the principal means of union with God—powerfully adapted to impress the senses—yet a mystery of Faith—As a Sacrament it acts on the will, producing "devotion," and giving us the Heart of Jesus for our own—

We should prepare for its reception by studying it—by Confession — by actual devotion — Our Communions should not be regulated by the state of our feelings, . 274

XXIV. THE HOLY MASS.—The Blessed Sacrament the great devotion of the Church—The effects of His real Presence depend largely on the use made of it by the faithful—The Mass brings the Precious Blood to individual souls—Ways of hearing Mass, ... 283

XXV. THE LOVE OF GOD ABOVE ALL THINGS.—The life of Charity—Direct and explicit acts of Love—Growth in Charity—Four means of promoting this growth in the soul, ... 302

XXVI. THE LOVE OF ONE ANOTHER.—We must love our neighbour because he is dear to God—The philanthropy of the day—The good effects of kindness—In order to practise the love of one another we require Intelligence, Devotedness, and restraint of the Tongue, . . . 316

XXVII. WORK AND APOSTLESHIP.—Best kind of work is work for others—Apostolic work—Work as Duty—Penitential work—Mental work, ... 330

XXVIII. OUR LIFE AND ITS SURROUNDINGS.—Essential to reconcile our manifold life with the one thing needful—How to use things necessary—how to use things not absolutely necessary—how to see Christ in all persons and things—How to rise from our falls—We should lead a life which fosters humility, ... 344

XXIX. LITTLE SINS.—Deliberate venial sin—Habitual venial sin—Generosity—Consequences of habitual or deliberate venial sin—Sins of frailty and surprise, . 357

XXX. SPIRITUAL READING.—Spiritual Reading is listening to the Voice of God—Its necessity—Its advantages, *viz.*, illumination, purity, tranquillity, nourishment, stimulation, and strength—Kinds of Spiritual Reading—Holy Scriptures—Spiritual instruction—Exhortatory—the Fathers—the Lives of the Saints, . . . 370

XXXI. OUR BLESSED LADY.—Mary's special power to keep before us God's tenderness—She repeats and re-echoes Jesus.—She is the grand triumph of the Precious Blood

—She is the minister of His Grace—How to keep up and practise devotion to her—We should invoke her in temptation, ... 385

XXXII. HEAVEN.—It is right to look forward to happiness—The Beatific Vision—Heaven described by the five words of St. Thomas, viz., Light, Satiety, Joy, Pleasure, and Happiness, ... 399

XXXIII. PERSEVERANCE.—We can merit final Perseverance as suppliants, with reasonable certainty—The root of Perseverance is loving trust in God—Its elements: Careful performance of each day's spiritual duty; Dread of sin and avoidance of its occasions; the Sacraments; and the proper use of our falls, ... 413

I. INTRODUCTORY.

To begin a retreat is to retire within the precincts of a holy silence in order to draw nearer to God. Retirement and silence are more or less familiar to every servant of God. They are the essential conditions of profitable prayer. The more completely a man withdraws from external dissipation or occupation —the more thoroughly he restrains himself from communicating with other men—the more attentive and devout must be his intercourse with his Creator. The time has now come for you to begin a longer silence, a more continuous retirement.

The building of the Temple of Sion went on without the sound of axe or hammer.[1] But the silence was filled with strenuous effort; and day by day the house of the Lord rose higher and higher. It would be a great mistake to look forward to an empty and barren silence. God is in this silence of the retreat. You enter into the "courts" of the Lord; that is, you enter those cloisters which surround the house where He dwelleth and which lead to His Holy of Holies. You go out into the wilderness with Moses; and there, when the cities of Egypt have been left far behind, and when even the tents of travellers have been lost

[1] *3 Kings* vi. 7.

to sight, the fire of God's presence and the sweet majesty of His voice reveal themselves. You seek, as did the saints of old, the solitudes of the sandy desert, and there in the unbroken quiet, your immortal soul will hear God nigh at hand, and will find words in which to address Him Who created you.

It is the fatherly love and solicitude of your God that give you this special opportunity. It is His way always to draw men into silence and solitude when He wishes to bring them nearer to Himself. Thus did He act with His chosen people "in the day of provocation in the wilderness,"[1] where they tried Him and saw His works. Thus did He deal with His prophets and His saints. This manner of acting did He also sanctify by His own example in His human life. If you could only know how He longs to make you know Him and love Him! This is what He is thinking of. You may know Him and love Him already; but He is never content. You might be so much better. Your past life has not been satisfactory, even to yourself. There has been much sin, much negligence, much indifference. Perhaps mortal sins have left weakness and the seeds of death; venial sins have tended to harden into habit; love of the world has occupied your heart; and there are many things in which you feel that you ought to make a sacrifice for God's sake, but in which you neglect to yield to His inspirations, and

[1] *Ps.* xciv. 9.

thus allow your life to slip away in tepidity and much peril of your eternal salvation. Oh for light! Oh for fervour! Oh for a real conversion!

The essential point in entering upon a retreat is to be convinced that it is God Who "draws" us to it, and Who wills to speak to us therein. When we listen, under any circumstance, to the word of God, it is necessary to try to feel that it is not man who speaks, but that Heavenly Father Who loved us from the beginning and of Whose love there is no end. This can be done; and a great step is taken in our spiritual life when we begin to do it habitually. But in a retreat it is more essential than elsewhere. A retreat is something unusual. It is as if God not only spoke to us, but prepared the time and place for His communication. A retreat is like the silence and attention which the king's officers secure before the king speaks himself. As all the graces in our lives—and how many they are we shall never be able to count—are from Him Who loves us, so this marked grace of a retreat is a most marked exercise of His love. Be sure of this. No friend who seeks you out, or helps you, or gives you strength and serenity of heart, has ever planned anything for you that is so strong a grace as this retreat.

What is He going to say to you? You do not know. But you know this, that when this retreat is finished you will be better, or you will be worse; you cannot continue the same. You will either be lifted up, or you will slip down lower than ever. A man does not come into the nigh neighbourhood of his God without having to answer for grace.

The necessity of a retreat is partly general, and partly special. First of all, the most regular life is apt to become relaxed, to lose its true direction, and to grow mechanical. The very means which the man of regular life uses to serve his God withal, not unfrequently obscure the view of God, and fail to lead us to Him. Then, the mere cessation of habitual thought on the fundamental and grave truths and facts of human existence tends to betray the soul by degrees into that easiness, softness, self-gratification and laziness which never can be washed out of human nature. The effect of this is what St. Peter Damian calls the "dust of worldly conversation". Enter a room which has been carefully shut up for months,—you find every polished surface thick with dust. The doors were closed and so were the windows; but nothing can keep out the dust. There is no help for it but to go in at regular times and brush and sweep. Every day must we think and pray. But the time comes regularly round when we must think with a greater effort, and to a greater depth. The time comes when the soul, like that of him who "remembered God and was delighted," must give its most grave attention to solitary consideration: "I thought upon the days of old; and I had in my mind the eternal years; and I meditated in the night with my own heart; and I was exercised and I swept my spirit".[1] The "days of old" are the days of my beginning, when God created my immortal soul for Himself. The "eternal years" are the years of God and the years of my own immortality. The "night" is the silent solitude in which I shut myself up for a time. O holy exercises of the spirit, by which I learn to know myself, to know my God, and to make certain of my path to heaven!

Moreover, there are many reasons special to myself why I require a retreat. I have changed since my last retreat. No man is the same for twelve months at a time—much less for a longer period. Since my last retreat my body and my mind have moved. I see things differently; I understand differently; I am older, and perhaps wiser. Since my last retreat I have had a thousand lights, graces and calls—which have left me better—or worse. Very likely I serve God better in some respects. But in others—in many—I have drifted from my moorings; I have got some way on a downward path; my habits of self-restraint have weakened; I am approaching to a certain hardening of the heart. There is an awful power in unchecked worldliness. It destroys the soul's delicacy of surface as the wet gales of the winter wear down the edges of square stone towers and spread a stain and a growth over them. How heedless may a man become of sin! How reckless of sensual indulgence! How unconcerned as to the

[1] *Ps.* lxxvi. 6

inner and deeper spirituality of life! How neglectful in prayer, and how mechanical in its exercise! We may have even mortal sins not properly confessed. We may have one or two evil habits, like a deadly growth, feeding upon us to kill us. We may have more than one defect which is a source of scandal to our neighbour, a hindrance to our work, and a fruitful root of innumerable failings and venial sins. "Thou hast forsaken Me," saith the Lord; "thou art gone backward."[1] "O children, how long will you love childishness; and fools covet those things which are hurtful to themselves; and the unwise hate knowledge? Turn ye, at My reproof! Behold, I will utter My spirit to you, and will show you My words."[2] It is thus that your Heavenly Father addresses you at the beginning of a retreat; or, rather, He has been reproaching you in words like these ever since you began to fall away from your fervour; but you have not heeded Him, perhaps, until this hour. Will you turn to Him? Will you resolve to do your best to understand what He requires of you, and what is keeping you away from Him? He promises to "utter His spirit" to you; that is, to let you hear that voice which alone of all voices enlightens the intelligence, moves the will, stirs the heart. The opportunity is afforded to you. Do you resolve to accept it?

A retreat chiefly consists of three things: rest, thought, and prayer.

[1] *Jer.* xv. 16.   [2] *Prov.* i. 22, 23.

The rest which the soul requires, and which she obtains in a retreat, is the opposite of that labour and weariness which is the lot of most of us; that is to say, the constant pressure of work or duty, or even of worldly satisfaction. The weariness arises from the struggle to serve God and the world at the same time; and if we are not conscious of a struggle, but have given in to the world and acquiesced in the neglect of spiritual things, our weariness and weakness are still more real and more deadly. We require these days of cessation of profane occupation, even of innocent occupation,—even of good and excellent work. We need to become, for a brief space, like one of those ancient solitaries of the Nile valley or the Syrian desert, who buried themselves in a life of silence and loneliness in order to have nothing to do but to commune with God. Even good work —even God's own work—leads the weak and unstable spirit of men from complete devotion to the God Who made it. A time when, without being guilty of neglecting God's will, we can cease to labour, to plan, and to expect, is a precious gift of God. In a retreat, ordinary occupation ceases; the busy world knows us not; souls go on their way without us; our eyes and ears cease to take note of things external. As did the lawgiver and the high priest of the Israelites, we have fled from the outward tumult to the tabernacle of the Covenant, and as it was then—" When they were gone into it, the cloud covered it, and the glory of the Lord appeared"[1]—so it will be with thee. The cloud brings recollection; the glory will give us light and grace.

Next, a retreat is a time of thought. On looking into our life we cannot fail to see that there is in it very little serious thought. Yet thought is required for conversion, for spirituality, for perseverance. The spiritual life is not really complex; but its very simplicity is not attained without much consideration; just as it may need much consideration to find, or to choose, the broad high road which is to lead us home. Past sins need thought. They are not to be dwelt upon in detail; but they are to be reckoned with, and our repentance made sure of. Motive and intention need thought; for on these things depend the force and direction of our spiritual aids. The will of God needs thought; and there are many who do not see it with sufficient clearness because they do not reflect. Occasions of sin need thought; for the soul has probably grown so familiar with certain dangerous occasions, that one must get a little way off from them in order to feel how really dangerous they are. The orderly arrangement of our devotional and ascetical life needs thought; our mental prayer, spiritual reading, frequentation of the sacraments, practice of mortification, and the rest. Above all, the deep and fundamental truths of existence, and of the perfect life—God, sin, heaven, hell; obedience, suffering, charity; Jesus Christ, and the ministry of His Holy

[1] *Num.* xvi. 48.

Spirit—these grand principles must be well thought out; thought out earnestly, painfully, and with a certain continuousness. On such thought depends the advance of our spiritual well-being, as the advancing line of the waves on the shore depends upon the mysterious impulse which causes the tide. In a retreat we have time to think; and we should look forward to thinking. One by one, in order, and with various help from preaching and from books, the subjects which make up life's responsibility will come before our faculties. "I will meditate on Thy commandments, and I will consider Thy ways; I will think of Thy justifications; I will not forget Thy words. . . . Open Thou my eyes, and I will consider the wondrous things of Thy law."[1]

Rest and thought would be of little avail without prayer; and this is the third advantage offered by a retreat. Prayer is a duty of every day of our lives. But the prayer of a retreat has several characteristics of its own. It is a prayer which is deepened by silence and the cessation of ordinary work. That which plays havoc with our daily prayers is the preoccupation of our mind and heart with business, employment, or amusement. We have now a chance of real, genuine, fervent prayer. The mere interruption of our usual habits—the sudden hush which falls on the house when the first bell of the retreat sounds—the unnatural quiet of the hours and days which succeed one another—this novel environ-

[1] *Ps.* cxviii. 15, 18, 20.

ment strikes the spirit with unwonted attention. The Lord is in His holy temple; let all the earth keep silence before Him.[1]

Yes, in this holy silence the Lord is found. Thy prayer shall not be like ordinary prayer. Moreover, the holy thought of the retreat will intensify its prayer. Now, as always, but with even greater suitableness, the great lesson must be practised—that all thought must be impregnated with prayer, and end in prayer. "In my meditation a fire shall flame out. I spoke with my tongue; O Lord, make me know my end, and what is the number of my days, that I may know what is wanting to me."[2]

The prayer of the retreat will deepen as the days go on; and it may be that, before the end of it, some secret may be whispered to the heart; some step may be taken, never to be lost, in that Divine science of union with God; some degree may be acquired which will bring us nearer to Him than a thousand years of laborious travelling on a lower level.

Each meditation of consideration, then, during the retreat should include a good proportion of affective, petitional or intercessory prayer; and it should be arranged that such prayer may be opportunely made. Our spiritual reading should be vivified with flashes of prayer. Our examination of life and conscience should lead us to earnest contrition. The whole of the long-drawn silence of the time

[1] *Hab.* ii. 20.   [2] *Ps.* xxxviii. 4, 5.

should be made intelligent and spiritual by the continual lifting up of the heart.

Finally, we should begin our retreat cheerfully, and should sincerely accept whatever may seem hard, troublesome, or unpleasant. The mortifications of the retreat are the surest pledges of its success. The retreat, in spite of the rebellion of natural feeling, will be a happy time. "Taste and see!" But be courageous, and give Almighty God your whole heart. Trust in Him. You do not know what He intends to do for you during these days of grace. You feel discouraged, perhaps, because former retreats have not been productive of much permanent benefit to your soul. You do not know this. You do not know—perhaps you will never know—what they have done for you. But even if they have all been failures, what is the only reason? It is that you have not entered into them with your whole heart. Begin, then, as one who looks to God, and to God alone, and who knows that God has designs in your regard; designs that are as yet hidden, but, beyond all doubt, designs of conversion, progress, and union with Himself.

Points for Mental Prayer.

1. First of all, as you kneel in the presence of the Blessed Sacrament, *greet your Lord* and God dwelling silently there for your sake. Many times you have visited Him—but this is a visit which is to

have an influence upon your whole life. Make acts of *adoration*. O Lord Jesus Christ, born of the Virgin Mary, here present for our salvation, I prostrate myself before Thee as my sovereign Lord and Creator, my only Good, my End, my All! *Offer yourself* wholly to Him, and offer your retreat: Accept, O my Saviour, the offering of my whole being, with all my powers and faculties! To Thee do I belong; to Thee belong all the things that I call my own! To Thee do I now consecrate myself, more especially during the retreat which is now beginning; to Thee do I dedicate, during these days, my thoughts, my aspirations, my actions, my strength, my time! Thou dost even deign to ask me to make this consecration! With all my force I make it, O my only Lord! Give me **grace** and strength to carry it through to the end!

2. Next, glance at your life, so far as it has gone. One thing is clear—your life has not been wholly given to God. O my Creator, my life is passing away! So far, it has been full of sin, full of levity, full of self, full of indulgence! How long is this to go on? Till the summons of death? Except by Thy grace, so long it will go on! I resolve to place myself in genuine solitude, in order that I may the better hear the voice of Thy Holy Will. By Thy help *I will observe the rules* of the retreat, and will keep to the spirit of the retreat. I will not only refrain my tongue from speech, but I will cease, as far as possible, to think on external things, and to

feel the excitation of external interests. I will not indulge my sloth, (or even take lawful recreation—) that I may draw nearer to Thee! I will urge my faculties and push my powers to do their utmost to take hold on Thee and the things of Thy Spirit. I will not be afraid of trouble or fatigue. I will make the exercises to the best of my ability; listening— then praying earnestly with acts, petitions and resolutions; devoutly reciting the vocal prayers, whether in private or in common; entering into the scrutiny and settlement of my conscience; reading and lifting up my heart. ("Solitudo mihi Paradisus," said one of Thy saints.) Will not my solitude be a true Paradise if therein I find Thy light, Thy help, and Thyself!

3. For *I hope and trust in Thee*, O my best and truest Friend! Why dost Thou draw me? why dost Thou give me this grace of a retreat? It can only be because Thou lovest me with an eternal love; because Thou hast pity on me; because Thou wouldst make me thine own! I know of some things in which I sadly fail; of some things that I stand in need of; of some, O my Lord, but not of all! Nevertheless Thou knowest! and if I know not even what to ask for, or what to look for, I believe and know that Thou wilt direct me in the right way! I firmly trust that Thou, in the treasures of Thy loving mercy, hast ready the precious gift of which my poverty is most of all in want. I enter this retreat poor and needy; poor and needy I shall always be, till my

life's end; but still, O my God, Thou holdest in Thy hand graces—I know not what or how great—and they are meant to be mine before this consecrated silence shall again be broken. In Thee, O Lord, have I hoped; **let me not be confounded for ever!**

II. MY SOUL.

In the solitude and rest of the retreat our first thought may be ourselves. Doubtless it is God and not ourselves that we have most to try to know; but, as we shall see, to know ourselves is only a way of knowing God better. It is very wonderful how little we know of ourselves; I do not mean our faults, or our capabilities; but our nature, destiny, position. We mostly look out of windows all our life. That is the reason why so many of us are frivolous, curious, averse from serious thought, and selfish. No one can be dignified, solid and unselfish without the habit of thinking on what lies at the root of his being.

A human being may be said to *be* his soul. Not that we are pure spirits; the body most really modifies our spiritual nature, and makes the human soul different from any other spirit. But it is the soul which is highest and noblest in us which explains our destiny, and which creates our most essential needs. We must live up to our soul, or else we must be failures.

It is not easy to make for ourselves a clear idea of a spirit. Holy Scripture, in describing the Infinite Spirit and His angels, makes use of the ideas of "fire," and of "light". The prophet Daniel[1] saw

[1] *Dan.* vii. 9.

the Ancient of Days clad in garments white as snow, seated on a throne which was like flames of fire, the wheels of it like a burning fire; a swift stream of fire issued forth before Him. Fire, with its brightness, its power, and its immateriality, seems to be a fitting symbol or analogy of the awful strength and incomprehensible nature of a spirit. Your soul is a spirit. It is not measurable like your frame; not limited by place; not liable to weariness or fatigue; not to be touched or handled; but it has an elastic unquenchable vitality which neither weight nor muscle can affect, nor any chance of elemental violence extinguish.

It has the prerogative of immortality. In this world where we live, there is death everywhere. Death is dissolution. The flower springs, blooms, withers, and falls to pieces. The living and breathing animal is born and lives its allotted time; then it falls upon the earth, dissolves into its elements, and is mingled with the earth again. That which we call a man, passes from childhood to youth, from youth to maturity, from maturity to age, and then seems to fall to pieces, like the animals and plants. But it is not so. Go to the chamber of the dead. Perhaps it is a little child, whom you saw but a short time ago in all the grace of living childhood; breathing, sporting, talking, laughing; its eye bright, its cheek rosy, its limbs full of motion and vitality. Now, what a contrast! Its body is motionless and rigid, its face drawn and white, the light of its eyes extinguished; and all is as silent and unresponsive as the stone wall. Something has certainly departed; some principle of movement, colour and vital heat. Yes; and that poor little framework of tissue, bone and nerves, for want of that potent principle, will soon turn into forms of commonest matter. But the principle itself is far away—safe, strong, immortal. Or rather "far" and "near" are not words that you can now use about it; for it is in the other world, where space is not as earthly space or time as earthly time. But it is living on—somewhere—and will live. Its vesture of clay will have long become indistinguishable from the earthy bed in which it was laid; the generations will have sprung up from the earth's surface and returned to her again, for as many ages as God may permit—and the soul will be living on as ever. And a day will come when the elements of her body will again, by God's power, be assumed by her; and the moment she touches those long scattered and confused materials of a human being, they will again take their form and their actuality, and leap into being—new and gracious being if she be fortunate—that 'spiritual body" of which the apostle prophesies. And this will only be the beginning of her immortal life.

So true and vital a thought is this of your immortality, that, by itself, it seems a sufficient explanation of your whole life here below. Your real life is all to come after the dissolution which you call death. To live, therefore, for these few years called mortal life, must be a mistake, and a disastrous mistake. You must only live, if you are wise, for the real life. There is no use in grasping what your fingers must one day drop for ever, when all your frame dissolves. There is no use in acquiring a name or a fame which may possibly survive you in this world when you yourself will be in the other world, but which will be nothing to your advantage then. It is most unprofitable to spend time and endeavour in securing a good place at a show which will be over in a few hours, when you will find yourself outside in the dark night, to get through it as you may. Oh! for the understanding of the saints! Oh! for the wise resolution of those self-denying servants of God who have counted all dross which profited not to life eternal! To the Holy Scripture death is not a sleep but an awakening—an awakening, too often, from dreams of abundance, to the reality of famine; when the men of riches find nothing in their hands, when the richly clad see themselves to be in the meanest rags, and the proud are worse than beggars. O my Lord and God, Who hast given me an immortal soul, let me live for the immortal life! Let me scorn and despise all that is less than eternity! Give me the grace to know and value my gift and prerogative of never dying, that I may live for that life for which Thou dost intend me—that life which is heaven, and Thyself!

That your soul is a spirit, and an immortal spirit, is, then, a serious and vital thought. But your value and your dignity are greater still. There was a captive once imprisoned in a tower, and his prison was almost dark, save for one opening where a ray of light came in. He loved that tiny spot of brightness, and he used to watch for its appearance, and follow it with loving affection as it moved along his dungeon wall till it disappeared. But one day, in siege or earthquake, the tower was rent from battlement to foundation. Then the prisoner found himself in a flood of light, and he saw that the little luminous disc which so long had cheered his tedious hours was nothing less than the rays of the glorious sun himself. And your soul, though you call it yours, comes from the Infinite God, and is in His likeness. He made it. It comes from His hand—not by virtue of that general *fiat* which moves the laws and sequences of the universe. He has made it by a special creative act—as if a sovereign placed a golden circle on the head of one beloved; thus setting up between you and your God a primary and most intimate relation, nearer than generation, dearer than parentage. He created you; and He created you a spirit. He Himself is a Spirit. There is this common to all spiritual natures that they cannot be bounded or limited. This does not mean that Almighty God is not Infinite and all other beings finite. But in God boundlessness is something positive; that is, He is the abyss of all that is. Other spirits are without limits, but in a different sense. They never can reach a bound or limit beyond which they cannot see, or know, or advance. To be spiritual is to be eternally progressive, unquenchably active, insatiable in knowledge, and unlimited in aspiration. This must be so; and if we do not always feel it, we can see it on reflection; and, being spiritual, must understand that our present sphere is not our complete destiny. It is this—we may briefly call it reason—which gives us our natural likeness, not only to the angelic choirs, but also to the Supreme Spirit. God cannot make anything higher than a spirit. We are not, it is true, a part of God. That would be a stupidly pantheistic expression. We are finite beings and He is the Infinite. But there is a most true sense in which we are made to His image.

Does not this explain why we cannot do without God? Men say they *can* do without Him. They cheat, blindfold, degrade and trample on their souls. They assert that they are satisfied and happy with earthly knowledge and earthly enjoyments. Is this true? We must not deny that it is, in a certain sense. A spirit has the power to prevent itself from seeing; to look in this direction or in that; to shut out light; to attach itself to darkness. The pleasures of the sense, of the affections, of ease and well-being, and of pride are real pleasures; and they have power to satisfy—for a time. Men are often really happy—that is, sufficiently satisfied and contented and even sometimes joyful and intoxicated—without God. This may be true even of wretches who contemn Almighty God and formally defy Him. It is still more often true of those who only have false views of God and of religion, and whose easy lot in this life blinds them to their immortal destiny. But it is certain that this happiness is only partial and temporary. The soul has a long life before it—a life long enough to awake from every dream and to exhaust every finite satisfaction. This much a reasonable man could prove on merely natural ground. What really happens is this. The soul may be cheated and blindfolded for a time, but she wakes up at last— and when she wakes, the whole man wakes with a terrible awakening. Sometimes these awakenings occur in the midst of sin and indifference— awakenings of mercy. It may be in some moment of silence, some sleepless midnight hour, that the soul—the real soul—speaks to her oppressor, and warns him he must make God his friend, or be for ever lost. It may be when sorrow or pain has awakened conscious thought that the question starts up like a phantom—"What am I living for? Am I prepared to die?" Or it may be that God sends his preacher Death, and that we meet him in our passing, as one might meet a slow funeral in some country lane, and the soul cries out: "To-day for this one, to-morrow for you!" God send us all an awakening of this kind, when an awakening is a mercy, and it is not too late to amend one's life! The awakening may be put off till it is a judgment. It may be deferred--if we are obstinate—to that dread moment when death shall be past, and we shall stand before our God. Then man's being will wake never to sleep again. Then, for one moment, we shall see what was our destiny, what was necessary for our happiness, what this soul of ours must have or must be altogether wrecked. Then we shall see for an instant the God Who is our only End and happiness—but only to be torn from His face for ever!

Shall not my soul be subject to God?[1] Yes,—to Him and to Him alone! Vain are the sons of men; vain is the earth, vain is earthly satisfaction, vain is all that the world can give! Trust not in iniquity! set not your heart on riches! beware of cheating your immortal soul! Resolve to live for immortality—for eternity!

Points for Mental Prayer.

1. My soul is myself—mysterious, real, serious, awful, strong, pure. Its life is to live for ever. Its nature is like unto God's. Its end is none other than God Himself.

Acts. Accept this immortal gift from the hands of your Creator. Pour forth *thanks*. *Promise* to live up to this terrible responsibility.

2. *Regret* how in your past life you have blindfolded, degraded and defiled your immortal spirit, God's image.

[1] *Ps.* lxi. 1.

3. Give the rein to aspirations of immortality.
No joy in creatures!
No rest except in God!
All that is earthly passeth away;
Let me labour for heaven alone!
Time can never satisfy my immortal soul;
May I live only for eternity!

III. THE VOICE OF GOD.

As my soul is made by God's hand, and made to His likeness, it must be somehow in sympathy, or accord, with God. This is true, even from the natural point of view, and leaving grace out of the question. We can hear God's voice; and God has words and a mode of communication for us. If we give our soul fair-play, and do not cheat or blind it, we can hear—fitfully, at least, if not continuously— Divine teachings and Divine exhortations.

We have, all of us, intuitions or intellectual light. Truth, justice, morality and beauty, in their general principles, are part of the light of our soul. The possession of these principles and their use make up the living soul. And if we had no other proof of the existence of God, we should have one in the constant shining of this intellectual light in our soul. For, if it shines in every human heart, one and the same in its nature, whence can it come except from a source outside of us all—outside of the created universe? Whence can it come except from Thee, O my God, Who in creating me to Thine image, causeth Thy radiance to shine upon me and givest me a participated likeness of Thine own intelligence? Therefore the soul has communications as from a world outside of its direct sight. It seems to see, at times, more than is contained in the objects of its vision or its reason. It desires much more than it can ever have upon earth. And it hears unearthly voices; voices which are not the voices of its passion or its natural impulse, but which come from another sphere. Why should not God speak to the soul? He is hidden, no doubt, and must be hidden, during this time of our probation. But if He made us, He must love us, and must be solicitous about us; and since we are not as irrational beasts, unable to comprehend the language of the spirit, surely He must communicate with us! Not loudly; not so as to upset the arrangements He has made for time and space; but gently, sweetly, softly—to those who are regenerate—to those who acquire the habit of listening—to those who go apart from noise and distraction—to those who strenuously silence the clamour of their earthly appetites. There are great and strong winds overthrowing mountains and breaking the rocks in pieces; there are earthquakes; there are fires; these are the things by which men mostly are impressed. But it is when the whispering of a gentle air is heard, that the prophet covers his face with his cloak and prepares to listen to the voice of God.[1] "What is that," says St. Augustine, "which shines through my being, and beats upon my heart, yet bruises it not—and I am filled with dread and glow as with fire? I fear because I am

[1] 3 Kings xix. 12.

so unlike—I burn because also I am like. It is wisdom, true and substantial, that thus shines through me, piercing the mists of my ignorance—which yet close in again and cover me in darkness when I fall away from Thee!"[1]

There are precious moments when we seem brought face to face with the realities of our existence In silent moments, in solitude, before the Blessed Sacrament, in retreats, in sorrow—God seems sometimes to stand before us. Then we say: "My God, it is Thou! and I have forgotten Thee!" We hear distinctly as one hears a far-off bell upon a still and frosty night, the voice of One Who says: "Think of Me, for I am all that there is!" We seem to see that time is passing, passing, passing!—and all things passing with it. We have a curious power of looking forward to the point when time's stream has fallen into the abyss, and there is no more of it for us. We seem to feel what it is to die—to be wrenched from warm and living things, and stood shivering in the ghostly land where nothing will avail but spiritual things alone. We seem to sicken with a kind of terror as we feel the solid earth of friends, and life, and possessions quake and sink beneath us, as if we were about to fall sheer down into horrible emptiness. Then we know that nothing can hold us up but God—nothing can avail us but God—nothing can save us in the inevitable wreck but God—only God. Whose voice is it that tells us this?

[1] *Confess.*, xi. 9.

Whose voice comes so clear upon our heart? Do not say it is your efforts at meditation, or your prayer-book, or the preacher, or your nerves. It is God. For you belong to Him, and He is solicitous about you—and since you *can* hear Him speak, why should He not speak?

Nay, the very earth and sky and ocean round about have power to make you hear Him speak. If they lift you up to adore Him, if they fill you with a sense of His power, if they thrill you with joy that He is God—it is not they who speak. It is not the brightness of the earth, the changes of the sea, or the awfulness of the tempest which strike upon your heart. Millions of eyes and ears see and hear it all, and yet there is no comprehension, no impulse towards heavenly things. With you it is different—because your reason and your heart are God's instrument, which He has attuned, and on which He plays. Why do you not strive to hear more distinctly? What else is there on this earth worth listening to?

You make a great mistake if you think that the "voice of God" is only a figure of speech. There is inspiration, there is revelation, and there are the miraculous locutions which the saints are given to hear; with these we are not at present concerned. But besides all this, there is that low and tranquil, yet never-ceasing, speech of God to the heart of man; the speech of the God of nature; the speech of the God of grace and redemption. Even among the impulses which enter into our ordinary life, there is none that, on occasion, may be more powerful than the voice of God. You can see its power if you look into your own life. You have, at some time, turned earnestly from sin; or you have dedicated yourself to God with fervour. There is a psalm of David which describes what has happened, what does happen, and what may happen again in your soul, and the soul of every creature of God.[1] "The voice of God is on the waters: the God of majesty hath thundered; the Lord upon many waters." Your life and being is the chaos of waters that lies tossing in its tides and swellings, until it hears the compelling voice of its Creator. "The voice of the Lord is power; the voice of the Lord is magnificence." All your ends and your aspirations, all your strivings, all your attainings sink into insignificance when that voice is heard. Things break in pieces; things you have sown and grown; edifices you have built; accumulations you have heaped up of gain or of fame; they break in pieces like the "cedars of Lebanon" when the thunder of God's voice speaks, and the lightning that there is in it darts this way and that— "dividing the flame of fire," as the text says—and the desert shakes, the beasts flee in terror, and the floods come out. This we have felt, O my God! This, in moments of remorse, of resolution, of decision, of conversion, of dedication to the Master we had forgotten. Perhaps it was in early youth, when

[1] *Ps.* xxviii.

we were new to sin, but beginning through lightness to take the wrong path in life's journey. Perhaps our hearts, yet unspotted, heard that masterful voice. Or it may be that it came when sin had been beforehand, and when our soul was horrible with offences and negligences; we may perhaps remember the day, and never without thanking God for all His mercies. Tepidity, foolishness, the entanglements of passion, the paralysis born of vanity—all these, or any of them, have, perhaps, been shattered by the voice of the Lord. Strong voice of my God! I have known Thee, I have heard Thee! Let me remember, now that I am before Thee, O Lord, all the mercies of Thy solicitude, and of Thy inspirations! Let me feel how near Thou always art to one who has used his liberty to turn his back on Thee!

To hear the voice of God, the creature must do that which the psalmist calls "lifting up the soul". In the psalm[1] which begins with these words, "To Thee, O Lord, I have lifted up my soul," there are described the various ways in which God can, and does, visit the heart with His speech. The words *Ad Te levavi animam meam* are the first words of the introit on the first Sunday of Advent; the faint glimpse of the Light of the world comes through the dark expectation of the four mystic weeks, and the soul rouses itself to see it. So through the confusion of life comes the voice of God; and the heart must rouse itself to be sure of it. "Show, O

[1] *Ps.* xxiv.

Lord, Thy ways to me, and teach me Thy paths. Direct me in Thy truth and teach me. On Thee have I waited all the day long."[1] It is true; even in the days in which we did not think of God, we "expected" Him—we "waited for" Him. Not our conscious will, alas! or our attention; it was not these which looked longingly for God. But human nature is wiser than any human being. A human being may go astray, shut his ears to his God, and wreck himself. But his human nature can never make a mistake; and it is because human nature always points to God, and will continue to point to God for ever, that eternal punishment is possible. So that, all these years, ever since you began to live your life, your God-made nature has been "expecting" God; has with anxious solicitude made dumb signs that He is not far off; has let you feel that you must have Him, or be miserable; and has turned unceasingly, like a prisoner on a tower, to try to make out the sound of His approach. "On Thee have I waited all the day long!" You did not know it, but so it was. And now that you are conscious what He is to you, make with the utmost fervour of your spirit, those petitions which the Holy Spirit puts into your mouth. "O Lord, *show me* Thy ways!" Among all the ways that lie open to me as I live in this world, it is Thy ways, and Thine alone that I wish to follow. Other ways lead to destruction—Thy ways to life. I am very blind

---

[1] *Ps.* xxiv. 4, 5.

by nature, and by the wounds of original sin; it is for Thee to show me, in the mists of ignorance and foolishness, which is Thy way. "*Teach me* Thy paths!" I will have no master but Thee. Other teachers have tried to lead me; remember not, O Lord, the sins of my youth and my ignorances! The flesh has laid its precepts on me; the world has given me its directions; even the demon has dared to command me. Henceforth, teach me Thou, and Thou alone! "*Direct me* in Thy truth!" Let not Thy voice be the passing word of a call or a command, but do Thou *direct* me! When I begin to take my feeble steps, direct me! When I hesitate, let me hear Thy comfortable word of exhortation! When I stumble and fall, speak to me that I may rise and take courage once more. In all my depression, my doubts, my cowardice, my ignorance, do Thou, O my God, *direct* me! It is Thy voice that I am most concerned to hear of all the sounds that my nature can attend to. Let me understand this, O Thou Who didst make my spirit!

Points for Mental Prayer.

1. Contemplate thy soul, endowed with powers to hear the voice of God. He made thee so because He loved thee, and would speak to thee, not once, but continuously from thy birth to thy judgment. He longeth for thee to hear Him.

Acts. Lift thyself to Him by *Attention*. *Adore* Him

Who bends Himself down to thee. Most humbly *thank* Him that is so full of thy concerns.

2. Look at thy life; consider thy inattention, lightness, distraction, dissipation; the ignorance thou hast cherished, and the sin in which thou hast lived.

Acts. *Sorrow.* O my Lord, I am filled with sadness that I have lived so as not to hear Thee! *Regret.* Who will make up to me the time spoilt, the days thrown away, the occasions lost! *Resolution.* Henceforth, O Thou Who didst create me, I will avoid those things which defile me—I will put times of real recollection into every day—I will seek solitude—I will cut off all distractions as far as I may—I will strive more to live for Thee, and Thee alone!

3. Show me Thy paths!

Teach me true wisdom!

Guide me in every step, through life's hazards till Thy voice ceases and Thy face appears!

IV. GOD.

Let us approach Him Whose name overshadows this earth and the existence of every creature. God is above all comprehension. Yet it is excess of light rather than darkness which here baffles the intellectual sight.

In the eighth psalm, the singer exclaims: "O Lord, our Lord, how wonderful is Thy name in all the earth".[1] This psalm is inscribed *"pro torcularibus,"* that is, "for the wine-presses"; and it is not impossible that it was one of the songs to which we find such a touching reference in Jeremias (xlviii. 33): "The treaders of the grapes shall not sing the accustomed cheerful tune". It may have been one of these songs of the vintage. And it would appear to have been sung at night, for there is no mention of the sun. The singers lift their eyes to the heavens; they behold the moon and the stars, which God has made, and as the voices of the young men and maidens sound His praises, the heart cries out: "What is man that Thou art mindful of him? Thou hast made him a little less than the angels; Thou hast set him over the works of Thy hands—yet it is Thou alone who art wonderful—wonderful over all the earth!"

[1] *Ps.* viii.

The words which mortal lips must use to shadow forth the Majesty of God are deep and pregnant and august. They are man's grandest words. They come, like cool water from the depths of the earth, out of the hidden places of man's spirit. They are such words as living, intelligent, just, true and good. These words are pictures or conceptions derived from man's own nature. He has nowhere else to go for them. Yet he is not wrong in looking there for them, for he himself bears a participated similitude to God. "Living" means possessed of the power of self-motion. "Intelligent" denotes the highest kind of life we can conceive—the life of our own spirits, as seen and understood by our consciousness; that supreme kind of "self-motion" by which a power moves which can look before and look behind, which can double itself back upon itself. If we call Him "just" it is that our reason tells us what it is to be "just," and that it is impossible for the Supreme Being to be anything which contradicts that idea. He is true—nay, the very truth; because all things that are were primarily mirrored in His intelligence before they began to exist; and they exist only because they are faint copies of Him; and thus their "truth" means the being conformed to His mind. We call Him "good"; we know that things are "good" because He made them to express His own mind; and, therefore, if they are not marred somehow, or spoilt, or stunted, but are full, complete, finished, perfect of their kind, they so far stand for

Him. We know that the "goodness" of the heart of a man is derived from its pointing at and tending towards what man was made for; that is, God Himself; and therefore "good" is in Him as in its fount. O burning Sun of all perfection! I know Thee, yet I know Thee not! I look around and see all things noble and fair; and Thou art all these things and more. I am struck with the thousand beauties of this universe; and they are only a faint effulgence of Thy Being. I rise from reading of the wise, and the just, and the noble, and their record is only the pale moonlight, waxing and waning, of an imperial Sun unseen. I know Thee, yet I know Thee not! And in my awe and reverence for the veiled yet absolutely real Lord of all power and majesty, I use my eyes and reason to lead my heart to adore that which neither eye nor mind can adequately know.

For all these great words and thoughts are like wandering spirits which on earth are never pure and all their own, but are always mixed with lower clay, chained to halting comradeship, imprisoned in the thickness of a dungeon. Life is fettered; intelligence is limited; justice is mingled with unrighteous bias; truth is hidden in mists; goodness falls short by a thousand defects. We can manage sometimes for a brief instant to conceive them as absolute, unconfined, unconditioned—filling all space and time—or rather without the very idea of number, weight, distance or duration. Then we faintly feel the infinity of God! God is—all the perfection we can conceive, purified to absolute purity and measureless simplicity! Truly, O my God, Thou art a hidden God![1] Yet Thou dost draw no veil before Thy face; Thou sittest not in awful solitudes, repellent to the heart of Thy creatures. But rather Thou drawest them on by Thy beams, which reach like hands of gentleness into all the paths of this universe; and when they follow Thee, then the sweet glory of Thy presence begins to blind their unanointed eyes; yet they see Thee, though they see Thee not!

Next, the soul may consider her most intimate dependence on the Infinite God. We must not say that we, or our souls, or our intellectual light, are an actual part of God Himself. This would not only be wrong and sinful—because it would be Pantheism—but it would be absurd; for if God is the Infinite, He can have no parts; and, therefore, that limited, definite thing which we know ourselves and other people to be, could never be God. One could as well say that wisdom was made up of all the wise men. But still it is true that we are connected with God—something like the sunshine in the air is connected with the sun; or the far reverberation is connected with the burst of the lightning. When a thing comes about by the causation of another thing, however philosophers may refine, a real something passes into the thing caused.

[1] *Isa.* xlv. 15.

When the hammer strikes, or the light flashes, or the vapour explodes, then, in different ways, according to the nature of the material, the cause passes into the effect. When mind meets mind, and speech produces conviction, or determination results in obedience, there is a more real communication and permanent change. But what is it when first there is nothing, and then, by an act of causation, a being springs into existence? What "cause" is this? Can any words describe it? Can any plummet sound its depths? Can any solvent help in its analysis? For so God has "caused" my soul! By an act of His Infinity; by a transcendent exertion of His omnipotence; by a sovereign and masterful invocation from the depth of nothingness, God made my soul to BE! How much of God must there be in me? For existence is a thing which no secondary "cause" could have brought about. It is a Divine effect; only the Infinite could have produced it. Therefore, a wave from the Infinite has passed over my head; I have somehow been submerged beneath the Divine, and have risen up a living soul. What is more, that supreme influx has not passed away. My soul is thrilling with it now; it pulses to the confines of my being. And it will never ebb away, or die down. For I shall never cease to be; and so the potency of that creation will be in me for ever and for ever, mixed in my being, holding me on in that existence which it alone could give. Shall I refuse to call Him "Lord" and "Master," Whose hand thus supports my inmost being? What is there that I have not received from Him? What rights have I that are not His, first and before all?

And if my proud spirit insist that having given me the awful gift of rational free-will, He Himself has made it impossible for me to bow down even to a Creator unless that Creator were good and just, then let me learn that goodness and justice and the right to exact true submission of the heart, are all involved in the idea of creation. For the great result of creation is the creation of man's rational soul; and the essence of the soul is reason; and reason is modelled on the Divine reason. Therefore reason's rules (when reason is not blinded) are God's rules; and when I see that I must conform my will to what is good and just, I see in that self-same vision that I must bow down before my God!

But, whilst I speak of abstract qualities—of truth, and of justice, and of reason—I must never forget that my Lord and Master is a living Person. In the Godhead, indeed, there is the marvellous and incomprehensible fulness of a threefold personality; Father, Son, and Holy Ghost. But for the moment, it is enough to consider that God is personal. I know what personality is. I know that by it I myself am lifted out from among the things that exist and live but do not possess the Divine gift of intelligence; things that move but do not see; things which daily look forward but do not know the "how" and the "why"; things which dumbly feel but are never conscious of a living self. My personality means myself mirrored in myself; a breathing consciousness, apart, self-supported, independent and alone. But God is all this, and in a higher plane. How can we understand the purity of that stupendous act of infinite consciousness, by which His most pure intelligence burns from all eternity! It is not necessary that we should understand it; it is only needful to fall down and worship—and to understand that as two created persons upon this earth can communicate with one another, by virtue of their personality, so the Divine Being can communicate with every intelligent creature. Not by a mere communication of cause and effect, as when He created us; not by the passing from Him to our poor nature of gifts and graces, however great and salutary; but by personal knowledge, personal esteem (if I may use such a word here) and mutual communion. He knows me; that is, I, somehow or other, am in His Being, as the things I know are somehow in me; and as the thing I know somehow makes me different from what I was when I did not know it, just as the ripple transforms the surface of the tranquil lake, so God, in apprehending me, though we cannot say that He is altered or changed—far be it from us to conceive it!—yet He does hold or apprehend us, in the way that the Infinite can hold or apprehend the finite. We must leave philosophers and theologians to explain as they can God's way of knowing; it is enough for me to realise that my God knows me as I know my friend; and that as my friend lives a second life in my intelligence and my heart so I live in the infinite abyss of God's knowledge. And as He knows me, He "esteems" me. To esteem means to weigh, estimate, regard, value, with a conscious intellectual act. Clod cannot value clod; a brute cannot regard with intellectual appreciation its fellow brute. But mind can appreciate mind. This is personal intercommunion. And, as I am so made that I may thus even lift my eyes to my God, so my God (in His infinitely higher way) does cast upon me the regard of His condescension,— that is, the regard of His love. There is only one thing which can prevent the Creator from loving the creature; and that is sin. Even when there is sin, still there is some kind of love—nay, how much love!—for the thing which His hands have formed. But we are here speaking without regard to the disturbing presence of sin. And thus God and His creature are by the act of creation, placed in relation one to the other; not as an artificer to the thing he has made, but as two minds, knowing, loving, mutually expecting, reciprocally aspiring, fitted to give and to take, as only one intelligent nature can be related to another. O my soul! this is thy lot and fixed fate—to be the object of thy Creator's knowledge and love! To thee that infinite Intellect directs its fires—for thee that most mighty Will reaches out in inextinguishable love! Man can speak to man; man can touch his fellow-man's hand, and look into his face; man can feel to another man what mutual friendship is. We say it—yes, we dare to say it!—so is God to us! He has His ways of letting us know it; His speech and His touch are not as those of mortals; but if there is any truth and reality in that light of kindliness and that spring of love which are part of the very make of these hearts of ours, then they are equivalently in God, too; and He knows me and loves me—as my Friend and Father, would I say?—ah! how far more really, with what infinitely deeper truth!

Points for Mental Prayer.

1. Look towards thy God afar off—awful, inaccessible, incomprehensible, alone!

Acts. *Bow down* all thy being before Him Who alone is. *Wish* that all the universe may adore Him for ever and ever.

2. Withdraw thy gaze from the distance, and look into thy own soul; and see there the True, the Beautiful, the Just, the Good; it is He Whose beams light up thy soul; He is very near thee; thou mayst know Him.

Acts. *Greet Him* in thy soul, and *welcome* Him. Oh wonderful power which enables thee to know thy God! What efforts, what self-denial could be too great to keep the eyes of thy being pure that thou mightest never be blind to Him! Yet, how little thou hast known Him! How late thou hast loved Him!

3. Reflect that He is no mere word, or phantom, or abstraction; but a Person Who knows thee as none other knows thee—a Person Who loves thee because thou art His creature. All other friends may fail; the essential love of thy God can never fail; it is part of Himself.

Acts. *Choose* and *prefer* Him to every other being. *Long* that thy heart may be as fixed towards Him as His to thee. Say, O only, true, and immortal Friend! What have I on earth or in heaven but Thee? Take my heart—take my understanding—take my will! Speak to me often; touch me with Thy friendly touch; seize me in Thy mighty grasp, so warm, so true—that I may be Thine, and Thine alone, for all my life, and all eternity.

V. THE PERSONAL NAMES OF GOD.

It is more necessary to meditate on "Who" God is, than on "What" He is. For the most vital business we have here below is to comprehend as far as we can, and to live up to our personal relations with Almighty God. In one sense, there is no one but God and myself in all the universe. For whatever affects me on the part of men and things, it is all ordained by God, and all subject to modification from my own intelligence. That is, God directs everything that happens, and nothing that happens can harm me except so far as it is accepted by my own rational and free will.

The twenty-second psalm was written by David towards the end of his life, when he looked back and saw all that God had been to him. It begins: "The Lord ruleth me, and I shall want for nothing;" or rather, according to the Hebrew, "The Lord is my Shepherd". It is the Psalm of the Good Shepherd. A time was to come when this touching name was to be taken by God in a more complete and abounding sense—when the Incarnation had taken place, and Calvary was in view. But the words of this psalm speak of what God would have been to us even had He not taken flesh and dwelt amongst us;

and they are true of Him always and essentially. He setteth the soul in a place of pasture, as the Oriental shepherd searches for a spot where something grows, and leads his flock thither. There is the " water of refreshment "; there are the " paths of justice," that is, the right track among all the tracks of the desert. The " rod and the staff " of this Divine Shepherd are the comfort and trust of the soul. There is always food—" a table " against them that afflict or seek to harm us. There is the flow of the healing and strengthening " oil," symbol of Divine gifts. There is the " cup " or goodly chalice which inebriateth. And as the soul reflects on all the titles by which her God befriends her, she exclaims: " Ah! that I may ' dwell in the house of the Lord for ever and ever!' "

No thought is more comforting than that God is always, and must necessarily be, a Father to His creatures. Nothing that we do—even the commission of the blackest sin—can dissolve this tie between us and Him. He may be " angry " (in the sense in which anger can be ascribed to the Deity), and He may allow His eternal laws to work themselves out, and punish us. But He can never cast us off. The reason is that He created us. For nothing but His love can have been the reason of creation. Therefore, a rational creature, merely on account of its existence, must always be the object of God's love; or else it would cease to be. Man, as far as he is concerned, may, by his perversity, put himself in such a position that it would have been "better that he had never been born,"[1] because to miss heaven is worse than not having been born at all. But the dreadfulness of hell-fire does not exclude the mercy of God; and though the lost can never hope to enter heaven, God may temper even their damnation. For nothing can be more absolutely certain and demonstrable than that God *always* loves the creature. And if we dare to cling to this Divine certainty, even when we gaze with half-averted face on the doom of those who have passed the gate of death in obstinate perversity, how much more confidently can we reiterate it of those who, however desperate their situation, have still the chance of being saved! And how true and undoubted this comforting persuasion should be in regard to each of us, in our own case! For we have, at least, no desire to turn our back on our God. We are far from being obstinately impenitent. We may be tepid, and negligent, and imperfect; but we are not wanting in good-will and in a certain kind of love for God. Even if—which God forbid!—we were in mortal sin, we need not remain in it a moment longer than it takes to turn to God; and we have only to turn to Him to be sure that He loves us still. "For though I should walk in the midst of the shadow of death, I will fear no evil, for Thou art with me!"[2] Thou art with me! To say this, is to turn to God; and, therefore, no one who says

[1] *Matt.* xxvi. 24.   [2] *Ps.* xxii. 4.

this can doubt of God's protecting love. It is rather of sin that this inspired verse should be used than of any physical evil or personal danger. It is our sins which more than anything else tempt us to think God does not unceasingly love us. Our sins seem to shut Him out from us; and so they do, no doubt, in a very true sense. But it is often when there has been real repentance—that is, repentance of the will, unaccompanied perhaps by feeling—that the "shadow of death" still seems to hang over us, and that we do infinite harm to our spiritual life by disbelieving in the love of God; that is, by not making acts of belief in this love. Sinfulness is never made any less by not claiming God's love. The act which best draws upon us the Precious Blood to wash away our sins is that by which we say, humbly but undoubtingly: "Thou, O my God, art with me!"

The name of Father is not only the name which befits our Creator, but one which He has taught us to use. We are commanded to say "Our Father!" The ineffable dispensation of the Incarnation has given that word a deeper meaning. But, after all, the Incarnation itself is merely a consequence of our being God's children. He was not obliged, certainly, to become man. Yet from what we know of Him we are sure He would any how have saved us, and saved us abundantly. But since He has done it in the way He has, we cannot help having irresistible evidence that He means to act towards us as a

Father. It was because He loved us that He gave His Son. If He has done this, what is there He will not do? You say: "My sins! my sins! my ingratitude!" But He foresaw it all. Sin is no obstacle, provided it is detested. Only the will which remains obstinate in evil can keep us from the love of our Father. And, we must remember, He is a true Father. A father's duty and joy is to care for his child. He may not always caress, or give; neither does he always behave with severity. But he has his child's interests before his eyes, and he dispenses his loving communications or withholds them as he sees him to require. Can God be any different? Not unless He is deceiving us in making us call Him by the name of Father. Above all, He is ready to forgive. We may be sure of His forgiveness. True, we cannot be infallibly certain that we are in His grace. But we can be morally certain. For we have only to "turn to Him". An act of contrition, accompanied by a purpose of confession, is enough; and although an act of contrition requires a serious and attentive effort, yet, by God's grace, it is very, very far from serious difficulty or impossibility. "Oh my Father! how near Thou art to me! In the depth and on the height, in crowds and in solitude, amidst worldly noise, distraction, even sin, Thou art close beside me, so that when I enter into myself I need not to journey far to find Thee, but only to turn my thought and heart, and Thou art there!

If God is our Father, it is certain that we have a still greater right to call Him Friend. The word friend has a peculiar significance among men, because it is only too true that, on earth, such names as father, spouse, and brother, although names of near relationship, are not always names of love. But our heavenly Father is our most devoted Friend. Other friends may be real and true; but the bond between us is not that of creation. We cannot say of any friend but One that He made us to His own image and likeness, with the aim and intention of making it impossible for us to be finally happy except with Him. Other friends have not humbled themselves to infinite depths to place us on their level and to draw us to them. No other friend knows us as He does; they come and they go, and their interest is greater or less; but He lives in our very hearts and requires no man to give Him any information about us. We have friends who can do much for us; but they are mortal after all, and the hour comes when they will disappear and we shall know them no more. The hour comes when they will want friends themselves. The moment draws near when no friend will be of any use to us; for our eyes will grow dim, and our ears will be closed, and Death will draw around us the folds of his tent, and no voice or touch from the outer world will affect us any longer. Oh! for a friend who then can stand beside us! And there is One, and only One, Who can, and will be near us when all human help, even the ministrations of priests, shall fail before the advance of dissolution. He is faithful; He is strong. He is the Lord of the darkness as of the light, the master of Death, and the ruler of Eternity. Happy we, if we have not repulsed Him, but have clung to Him when the light was with us, that He may watch beside us when the darkness falls!

What, then, are all other things in comparison with God? What can hurt us if He is on our side? What can avail us if we have not Him? He keeps Himself very silent whilst the time lasts which He has created to run its course. It is a period of probation, and because He has made us with reason and free-will, some such period there must be, or merit would be impossible. Therefore He lets the sinner run his riot. The proud man tramples on his brother, the ambitious builds his fortunes up, the unjust carries things his own way, the avaricious gathers in the good things of the world; and the good, who shape their lives after Nazareth, have often the worst part. But God is not asleep; and all the time He is still the God Who wields the thunderbolts. The moment comes when He will sit as judge. He will summon every creature before Him; He will judge acts and thoughts; He will restore the order which has been broken through, quell the violent with His glance, destroy the Babel towers which men have so frantically tried to build, and avenge the persecuted, punish the wicked, reward the good. This is the Father Whom we are proud to serve—such a one, and no other. He is the One with whom rests the final power and the everlasting settlement.

As for me, I have forgotten my Father and Friend, and have gone after masters treacherous and false! How have I to reproach myself with the sins of my youth and my ignorances! I knew Thee not, O Lord! I was brought up in the precincts of Thy house, yet I did not think of Thee! The good spoke to me of Thy majesty; I listened and yet did not take it in! Thy holy name was heard on every side of my path, yet I lived without heeding Thee! Soon, perhaps, I utterly turned my back on Thee by mortal sin. But even if Thy mercy saved me from falling so low as that, how dark and cold was my heart in those days! I loved the world, I loved pleasures, I loved vanity and selfish pride and dangerous enjoyments; the world seemed bright, my spirits were high, the dark hours of trouble were unknown to me, and death seemed a long way off. Therefore I thought but very little of my God! Therefore I tried to live without the friendship of my Father! Therefore my time was lost, and the precious moments fled away, never to be found again. Remember not, O Lord, these youthful sins; ignorances I would fain call them —but who knows how much there was in them that was guilty? Yet remember them not, O my God! but let me now at least turn to Thee with my very heart —Thou Who didst make my heart, and make it for Thyself! Thy prophet prayed: "Give me understanding! Thy hands made me and fashioned me, give me understanding!"[1] How is it that I have not "understood" before? These things, these existences of the earth which are not Thee, have been ruining my life. By them I have been taken up so as to neglect Thee. By them I have been attracted so as to turn away from Thee. They have been my danger, my temptation, nearly my eternal ruin. I detest them all in so far as they interfere with the knowledge and the love of Thee, my Heavenly Father! I renounce them. I resolve to beware of them, to guard myself from them, to trample upon them. To Thee I turn, to Thee I pray for help! For I am weak, O my Father; and my ignorances and my impulses seem at times to be stronger than myself. Do Thou take me and protect me under the shadow of Thy wings. Thou findest me in a desert land; do Thou lead me, and teach me, and keep me as the apple of Thine eye; and as the eagle enticing her young to fly, do Thou spread Thy wings and carry me.[2] For in Thee alone I trust; to Thee alone I wish to give myself up; for Thee alone I wish to live!

POINTS FOR MENTAL PRAYER.

1. Contemplate the Almighty Lord of heaven and earth as thy Father; Who essentially loves thee, thinks for thee, provides for thee, watches over thee, and will not be turned from thee, even by

[1] *Ps.* cxviii. 73. [2] *Deut.* xxxii.

thy ingratitude. Open thy eyes to this amazing situation.

Acts. Prostrate thyself before Him, and *adore*. *Admire* His love for one so poor and lowly. *Accept* this love, with aspirations of the warmest gratitude.

2. Look as from a great height on all this world, all time, all existences. Thy Father and Friend has made this universe in order to draw thee to Himself. To Him it is as a grain of sand. But to thee—how often is it loss and danger, because thou dost foolishly turn to it instead of to Him? Yet all will perish, whilst He alone remaineth!

Acts. Adore the Divine "jealousy" of thy God. *Give Him,* a thousand times over, that which He asks thee for—thy heart! *Pour forth thy sorrow* that it has ever belonged to the creature. *Protest* that never again shall it be given to anything except to Him. *Pray earnestly* for that *purity of heart* which lifts human nature above the whole world.

3. All that is not God is fitly the object of our aversion, in so far as it interferes with our belonging wholly to Him. The creature distracts thee—sullies thy heart—fills thy time—spoils thy powers and faculties—ruins thy life.

Acts. Conceive a great *apprehension* of the danger thou art in of losing thy God through creatures. *Avert thyself* from them, especially as to certain matters (which may be summarily brought to mind). May I never more be unfaithful! O my God and

Father! may I never be separated from Thee! Be Thou with me always—with me in memory, in reflection; with me in my deepest and strongest will and choice; with me in my heart and imagination; with me in all my aims and purposes, my views, my work, my hopes; with me in prosperity, with me in trouble; with me in health and in sickness; with me in every moment of my life, with me at the hour of my death, with me for all eternity!

VI. REDEMPTION AND GRACE.

WE have now to pass on to a series of considerations which should bring us, in the most complete surrender, to the feet of our Lord and God. God has not been content with creating us to His image and likeness. He has endowed us with a gift which is so wonderful and so startling in its effects that theologians and the saints can never dwell upon it sufficiently. For Divine grace is not only an additional gift; it is a gift which is equivalent to a new and fresh creation. If God were to give a spiritual and immortal soul to a stone or a clod, the change would not be so complete as when He pours sanctifying grace upon the soul of man. The rivers of Paradise flowed to every quarter of the garden of Eden, bearing fertility to it and to the universe. But the great stream of Calvary brings a higher and a more stupendous life and abundance.

For the reason and origin of the gift of grace lies in the Beatific Vision of God. That vision means not merely the sight of God in the way that mortal faculties, however pure and unimpeded, may look upon Him. It means, as Holy Scripture tells us, the seeing God *face to face;* [1] it means that we shall

[1] *Cor.* xiii. 12.

see Him *as He is*.[1] The Holy Spirit has said over and over again that no man can see God; "no man hath seen Him," says St. Paul, "neither can see Him".[2] Yet mortal men are to gaze upon His face for ever. Upon His face! How can this be possible? It could not be, unless the spirit and faculty of the mortal creature were somehow raised, elevated and altered. "The light of Thy face hath been signed upon us,"[3] says the psalm. And again, "In Thy light we shall see light".[4] Increated light is required to see the Increated. That "light of glory" will be ours in the world to come, if our souls are saved. Meanwhile a most wonderful thing happens. We are given to possess on earth a gift of light and life, which is substantially the same as the light which shall flood us in the heavens! For "the grace of God is life everlasting".[5] The apostle is saying that the result of sinfulness is death, and liberation from sinfulness is holiness; it is this holiness which he calls the "charisma," or grace of God; and of this "charisma," he says that it *is* life everlasting. One would have expected him to say that its "result" was life everlasting. This would evidently be quite true. But St. Paul's vivid expression is more true; for grace not merely deserves the vision of God, but (the veil being rent in two by bodily dissolution) takes, or has, that vision, as the eye takes in the morning when sleep departs.

[1] 1 *John* iii. 2.   [2] 1 *Tim.* vi. 16.   [3] *Ps.* iv. 7.
[4] *Ib.*, xxxv 10   [5] *Rom.* vi. 23.

We must not say that grace is actually the Holy Spirit. But what St. Paul says is that it is "spread abroad" or diffused "in our hearts *by* the Holy Spirit Who is given to us".[1] That is, it comes directly from the presence of the Holy Ghost, and is thus a Divine quality which transfigures and dignifies our humble souls much more really than the sunshine transforms the material world. Let us detest the heresy, too common, alas! at the present time, which asserts grace to be entirely external—to be merely God's way of regarding us with favour. He "diffuses it" in our very hearts. And how beautifully has He allowed His prophets and apostles to speak of this glorious gift! It is called light; and naturally, as we have seen; for it is the light of our eternity. And one of its most powerful effects in our time of mortality is to make visible to us the things of God, which as yet are dim and distant. Grace, taken in its wide sense, for faith vivified by charity—for regeneration and sanctification—is that substantial possession of the things we hope for, that argument or demonstration of the things that appear not, of which the apostle speaks.[2] It is the "light" which is said by St. John to be the prerogative of those free from sin.[3] It is the sun of a higher and better world—a world of higher aims, of supernatural principles, of a Divine life. For it is also called life. Our Lord says that He came in order that we might have "life," and have it more abundantly.

[1] *Rom.* v. 5.   [2] *Heb.* xi. 1.   [3] 1 *John.*

Men had life before the Redeemer came—but not such life. (All life is the power of self-motion. The clay and the stone are inert; but the plant has its living motion, the beast has still higher manifestations of internal activity, and man has the highest of all. Local movement, sensation, intelligence—these are various kinds of "life". They suppose a root, or principle, of life, corresponding with the grade; and each principle and grade has its own proper series of acts. These series of active manifestations we generalise under the name of "life". To say that grace is "life" is, therefore, to say that it implies a principle of activity, a real state, and a corresponding series of proper acts. It is just as if on an exquisite marble statue were conferred a living soul.) The cold marble is penetrated through and through with something which shows itself in warmth, contractility, sensibility and intelligence; but which is itself more than all of these. (For grace is diffused through our spiritual souls, and there ensues within our souls a new heat, a new energy, a different kind of strength, a strange understanding, a supernatural will-power. In a word, there is set up within us what is called the "supernatural" life—with supernatural ends, supernatural perceptions, and supernatural acts, all springing from the supernatural principle which is Divine grace. O my heavenly Father! may I live this supernatural life, and no other!

If grace is "life" it is also beauty. "Thou art

all fair," [1] is the phrase which the Lord of heaven and earth applies to the mystical spouse—the soul of man adorned by grace. To one daughter of Adam is that word applied by eminence and by excellence —to her who knew not even the merely natural taint of our origin. But if Our Lady is " all fair " it is only because she is " full of grace ". So it is with all who are in grace; they are beautiful in the eyes of God and of His angels. Human and corporal beauty arises from some inexplicable proportion, harmony and colour, combined. Spiritual beauty is the same as excellence; and the more like to God is that excellence the more does it ravish and delight. How full of devotion are all those epithets, scattered through the Holy Scriptures, which express the beautifulness of the soul which is pure from creatures and beloved by God! When we meet with them, we should lift our hearts in aspiration that we may care for no other beauty except the loveliness of God's grace. Almost to the same effect, grace is called a robe or garment—as by our Lord Himself. [2] By the Prophet Isaias it is called the "robe of salvation". [3] In the book of Ecclesiasticus it is Wisdom herself who is clothed with this "robe of glory" [4]; yet the same Divine vesture is the garment of him "who fears God". [5] The Beautiful One in His robe [6] is our blessed Lord Himself with the unction of the Holy Spirit adorning His most sacred human

[1] *Cant.*   [2] *Matt.* xxii. 11.   [3] *Isa.* lxi. 10.
[4] *Eccles.* vi. 22.   [5] *Ib.*, xv. 5.   [6] *Isa.* lxiii. 1.

soul; and the white robes which St. John saw in the Apocalypse are not put on at the entrance to the heavenly kingdom, for if they are washed in the blood of the Lamb, it is only on earth that this can have been done. Wash me, O Lord, yet more—yet more! For I must either be in the filth and horror of sin, or else clean by the precious blood! Therefore do Thou make me safe, that when the King comes to the marriage He may find me with a wedding garment!

Another most suggestive and devotional description of grace is found in its making us "sons" or "children" of God. We have contemplated God as our Father by our creation. But grace is a new creation, for it is a new life. It is most justly called new, for the difference between the natural and the supernatural is greater than the difference between death and life. Grace gives us the right to the Beatific Vision. This is called by St. Paul "heirship" to God, or co-heirship with Christ,[1] who is by nature the Son of God. Therefore all these most loving titles by which our Heavenly Father bound Himself when He made us, He has taken upon Himself *in the supernatural order* by endowing us with grace. Read, therefore, over again the twenty-second psalm—the psalm of the Good Shepherd—and see how true it all is of redemption. Or there is another psalm—the fifteenth [2]—which one may use to express in prayer the Father-

---

[1] Rom. viii. 17.   [2] Ps. xv.

hood of God in redemption: "My God, I have put my trust in Thee! I have said to Thee, Thou art my God!" The reason given in this psalm for this magnificent trust is that God, Who wants nothing from man on earth, even from the holiest, is, on the other hand, ever ready and longing to enrich us with what the psalmist calls a complete "inheritance" of spiritual wealth. "The Lord is the portion of my inheritance and of my cup; it is Thou that wilt restore my inheritance to me!" What a pathetic significance there is in that word "restore"! Yes, it was ours once, and it was lost; Oh, infinite riches of Jesus Who hast brought it back! "The lines are fallen unto me in goodly places"; as if the fertile land were measured out to the joyful possessor; "my inheritance is goodly to me!" The rest of this psalm with its thanks, its joy, its hope, and its clear anticipation of the Beatific Vision, we must here pass over; but it may be used to supplement this meditation.

There is one more description of grace which must be noticed. St. Peter, in a phrase which has been noticed with amazement by theologians, calls those who are redeemed "partakers of the Divine nature".[1] The great and precious promises of God made through Christ, are, he says, intended to have this effect. He can only mean that by grace we do become in some way sharers of God's nature. The explanation seems to be this: No created nature

[1] *1 Peter* i. 4.

can by its natural resources, ever look on the face of God. To be able to "see God" is a prerogative of God alone. God could not create a nature which should include among the faculties or powers due to it such a power as we speak of. Yet God, in His infinite love, has given to angels and to men the power to see the bliss of His face unveiled. This gift, beyond and exceeding all natural endowments, is supernatural; and its essence lies in this—that it lifts the soul of the creature so high, or, we may say, intensifies its powers so indescribably, that it can look on God. And, therefore, St. Peter, in a phrase that we thank and bless him for, affirms that it makes us partakers in the very nature of God! How true it is, O my God, that Thou hast crowned me with glory and honour! Thou hast set me far above all the other works of Thy hands. What are all my powers when they are not employed on Thee! What is the earth, its attractions, its science and its occupations—what are they all in comparison with Thy face and that gift of grace which is to lead me to it!

No Christian, then, is worthy of that name who does not live in and by the supernatural life. The supernatural life means that life which springs from the redeeming grace which floods the soul of the redeemed man; that life which our Heavenly Father has given us for the special purpose of the Beatific eternal Vision; that life which, therefore, aims solely at this everlasting bliss; which is directed by our reason and will with a view to this alone; a life which consists of thoughts, words and acts motived by supernatural considerations; a life in which one judges things, weighs things, chooses things, and decides things by supernatural light, or in which at least one longs and prays for such light.

In a word, grace, considered in its source (which is God's redeeming love), its purpose, its own self, its effect upon all our powers, and its transformation of all we do, is a vast, wide, and august system, world, or kingdom, in which the Christian should find his principal life and business.

We may reflect, therefore, how we have undervalued grace; preferring worldly, temporal, even sinful, things—acting on merely natural impulse—with little thought of Christ's blood on our soul. We may lament, in particular, that we have undervalued prayer, which is, as it were, the spring which sets in motion the whole activity of grace; neglected it, thinking more of speech, or of work, which are of no value except through the elevation of the heart in prayer. "My heart was withered, because I forgot to eat my bread."[1] Oh withered hearts of many who seem to be spiritual persons! Withered lives, leafless trunks! They do not know where their life and nourishment lie! Let us accuse ourselves, moreover, of having failed to spiritualise the innumerable thoughts, words and acts, of which our life is made up; thus wasting the life that Jesus has

[1] *Ps* ci. 5.

died to make golden and meritorious. It is possible that we have undervalued the cloister, obedience, vows, silence; that we have even neglected the Divine dispensation of Christ which is His holy Church, and taken small pains to understand the stupendous supernatural advantages which we have in her teaching, her precepts, and her sacraments.

By thus disparaging the supernatural we have done harm not only to our own souls but to those of our brethren, or neighbours; by tepidity and carelessness; by criticising and judging; by worldly conversations; by contempt of small practices, and by general sloth.

Points for Mental Prayer.

1. Consider the new creation—the streams of your Saviour's Blood—the springing into existence of a life, beauty and dignity without parallel on earth. Consider the love of your Saviour for your soul on which His blood thus shines.

Acts. *Adoration.* Sing to the Lord a new canticle, for He hath done things marvellous indeed! *Wonder.* What is man that Thou art mindful of him? O my Jesus! is there anything Thou couldst have done for me and hast not done? *Thanksgiving.* What can I give Him? Even my heart, which is all I have to give, is of no value except by the transforming power of His own grace. Yet He wants my heart! But He wants my whole heart! Take it then, O my Sovereign Benefactor; from this moment onwards for ever it is Thine, and Thine alone!

2. Consider this kingdom out of sight—this kingdom of grace; its vastness, its gloriousness, its ministers, its delights. My soul has been placed in this kingdom, as in an Eden planted by the hand of God.

Acts. *Long for* this invisible kingdom, so near thee on every side. Long for the sweetness of the cup that inebriates—that is, the infusion upon your soul of the Holy Spirit. Exclaim: "The Lord is my portion; the kingdom of His grace is my true inheritance!"

3. Pray that the *kingdom* of God may *come.*

Adveniat regnum Tuum! May it come in myself, in this community, in all prelates and superiors, in each brother or sister, in the whole world, in sinners, in heretics, in all the work and progress of this universe as long as it lasts!

4. *Detest* your own ingratitude, in undervaluing so great a gift and dispensation of God; in neglecting means of grace; in intercepting grace from the souls of others.

VII. SIN.

It would be a great mistake to confine our meditations to God's love and God's most sweet gifts. We have also to consider ourselves—and above all to look earnestly at the terrible fact that man is apt to turn his back upon his God, to despise His love, and to trample upon His gifts. Sin is a terrible fact; because it is a fall from so high a place, a rebellion against so great a love. The most beautiful lands are those which are visited by the most awful storms.

The mere fact of mortal sin is very awful. Think of a soul in grace; let it be, for example, the soul of a child which has just attained the use of reason, and is now capable of deliberately offending God in a grave matter. That soul is God's dear creation; it is clothed in that beautiful robe of sanctifying grace, more precious than any angel's natural birthright. It is the heavenly Father's child. The Sacred Heart looks upon it with joy and thanksgiving, as the trophy of its Passion. Upon it is the complete armour of Faith—the helmet of salvation, the sword of the spirit, the shield, the shoes, the breastplate. On its hand, as a precious ring, shines Hope, a pledge of present love and future beatitude. On its breast the flames as of a priceless ruby mark where celestial Charity, queen of the theological virtues, sits on her throne of grace. There is a diadem on the brow; it is the crown of the Seven Gifts, by which it is to live and move in its life of supernatural endowment. The natural virtues of humanity—classed under the four heads of prudence, justice, fortitude, and temperance—adorn it with a brightness not their own, for they are elevated and transfigured by a higher glory. Thus, at the outset of life, the soul steps across the threshold of that world where death lies in wait. "Every precious stone is her covering."[1] Then the moment comes when, deliberately, with a full knowledge and in a serious matter, that soul turns her back upon her God! The prophets have left us pictures of that woeful day. "A day of darkness and of gloominess, a day of clouds and whirlwinds. . . . Before the face thereof a devouring fire, and behind it a burning flame; the land is like a garden of pleasure before it, and behind it a desolate wilderness."[2]

For what has happened? That innocent and beauteous soul, in its dignity, its happy security, and its immortal certainty, has chosen to stoop to the earth, to put itself below the brute beasts. It has looked around; it has understood; and it has deliberately given itself over to death. It has felt the unholy blast of passion; or the hot wave of angry vanity; or the stirrings of grasping desires; or, in some form or other, the imperious promptings

---

[1] *Ezech.* xxviii. 13. [2] *Joel* ii. 2.

of the lower self; and it has surrendered, as the bird surrenders to the serpent. Its God was before its eyes; but for what the earth and the flesh can give it, it has deliberately turned its back on its Creator and its eternal hope. And it has drawn the lightning on its head. For in the moment of mortal sin, the thunder-bolt has fallen; and there is a dead and blackened corpse. Its beauty is stripped from it; Divine grace has fled; the ruby of charity is gone; the armour of faith is rusted; the pledge of hope well-nigh extinct. The diadem of gifts has been torn away, leaving bleeding traces. The natural virtues are once more earth of the earth. And the glorious robe lies in blackened shreds! But look up to the heavens! Behold how the Sacred Heart has taken that catastrophe. Jesus can suffer grief no longer; but the grief *was* real; and it is *His* grief. That rebellious child is dead, and its Redeemer looks down from heaven in sorrow; as David, in the high chamber over the gate, wept for Absolom. "Oh Absolom, my son, my son, Absolom! who would grant me that I might die for thee!"[1] He would die for that soul over again were it needful.

Such is the fact of mortal sin. Let us turn to our own lives. This happened to me the day I first committed grievous sin—every day on which I forfeited grace by sin. This is the state, perhaps, in which I have lived for weeks, for months, for years!

[1] 2 *Kings* xviii. 88.

And in my case there has been so much to aggravate my sin. It is not as if I had been left to ignorance, like so many poor creatures, who hardly know, at first, what is sin and what is not. I have known my God from my childhood, have been of His household, have learnt to love His name, have tasted the sweets of His bounty. Probably He has shown me special graces of vocation; calling me to follow Him, inspiring me with the desire to give Him my whole heart. In spite of this, I turned my back upon Him! There was no great, or violent, temptation; I grew cold to Him by degrees, and then I left Him. I allowed passions to grow strong and bad habits to take hold of me, and I yielded to some miserable attraction. I became slothful, worldly, dissipated, neglectful of prayer, and I fell when the enemy tried me. And this not once, but, alas! how often! After confession, after Holy Communion, after sorrow, after good resolutions! Moreover, some of my sins have been very base; sins which I should be ashamed that my most intimate friend should come to know of; sins revealing the deep-seated and reckless love of self which even human respect makes me disguise, and disguise even from myself; sins which are a worship of my lower nature, and a rejection of all that is spiritual and eternal. Then again, so many of my sins have brought death not only to my own soul but to other souls; sins in which others have shared; sins which, through reckless carelessness, I have allowed others to see, to their own ruin; sins in which I may even have played the devil's part of a teacher of evil.

Sins of youth and of past years, although they must not be dwelt upon in detail, yet should be always present to the conscience, as hair-cloth and the prick of iron chains continually torment the flesh. "My iniquities are gone over my head, and as a heavy burden are become heavy on me."[1] And very justly; for although we can have our sins washed away, yet the fact always exists that we once were at enmity with our God.

Contrition is one side of Love; God's most holy fear first pierces our flesh;[2] but fear is not enough. Even for the forgiveness obtained by the priest's absolution we must have some beginning of the love of God. But, indeed, with persons who are trying to be even in the least degree spiritual, though fear is a steadying force, yet the easiest motive of contrition is that child-like attraction of the good and beneficent Father Who would desire to be ours for all eternity. Thus it was with the Prodigal Son. He was carried from home by passion, by petulance, by folly, just as we have been. Then he came to suffer for it all, and this moved him to return. But when he met his old father, and felt his tears and the warmth of his embrace, then it was that he was really sorry, with a sorrow not only sincere but intense, with that intensity which one's will feels when it is in unison with one's feel-

[1] *Ps.* xxxvii. 2.   [2] *Ps.* cxviii. 120.

ings. Not but what there may be true contrition with no "feeling" at all; but we call feeling here all that effect of Christian and Catholic training which has made God a part of our very nature and character. "O Lord, Thou art my hope from my youth; by Thee have I been confirmed from the womb; from my mother's womb Thou art my protector. . . . Thou hast taught me, O God, from my youth! Thou hast brought me back to life; Thou hast multiplied Thy magnificence" in sacraments and communications; "O my God, who is like to Thee?"[1] Happy the heart which is saturated with the early knowledge of God. For such hearts can understand what contrition is. And in order that, in a retreat, or at any other time, our sorrow may be intense and enduring, we cannot do better than turn and turn again to the consideration of what God is, what He is to us, and what He has revealed Himself to be by His ineffable Incarnation.

Let not even the most innocent pass over this meditation on mortal sin. No one is without sin. Each one is a nature so weak, so blind, and so wounded, that mortal sin is inevitable except by the grace of God. To live on and to lose sight of this, (even if the fall does not happen), is to make ourselves perilously near to a fall.

Let us, therefore, in order to saturate our whole being with the detestation of sin, go through a fourfold exercise.

[1] *Ps.* lxx. 5, 17, 19, 20, 21.

First, let us earnestly, once more, renew our contrition for all past sins, so far as we have been really sinners. Let us mourn for the spiritual murder we committed when we gave way to sin; for the lamentable and miserable defacement of the beautiful thing which God had made and regenerated; for the evil employment of our princely reason; for the irrational defilement of our free will; for the spurning of the gifts of God; for throwing away, like most true fools, our heavenly inheritance; above all, for having crucified then our loving Saviour, and turned our back on our Father in heaven.

Next, whether we have ever grievously offended God or not, let us humble ourselves for our nearness to sin; for that softness, that worldliness, that constant dissipation, that want of Christian courage, that love of things that tempt us and lead to evil thoughts and evil acts, and that acquiescence in unchecked habits—which have combined in our past life to make it a miracle of God's mercy that we are not among the worst of sinners. "Unless the Lord had been my Helper, my soul had almost dwelt in hell."[1] The seraphic St. Francis said that if the vilest of men had received as much kindness from God as he had, that man would have been more grateful than himself; "therefore," he said, "I seem to myself to be the greatest of sinners".[2] But how literally true it is of us, that

[1] *Ps.* xciii. 17.
[2] St. Bonaventure's *Life of St. Francis*, ch. vi.

unless God had shown us the mercy He actually has shown us in the past, we should have been at this moment in the state of deadly sin, and only awaiting the moment of death to fall into hell.

Thirdly, let us well understand that mortal sin is possible, any day and any hour. We are human; we stand in the midst of temptations; the demons are strong and cunning; and our will (with God's grace) is all that there is between us and the worst of deaths. Certain years of our life have yet, perhaps, to run. We shall have to face a thousand temptations, a thousand dangerous occasions. Who can assure us that we shall not fall? And what is more likely to make it certain that we shall fall than that unheeding confidence, or rather presumption, which keeps us so slack in God's service, and so careless of the means of grace? "The perils of hell have found me," cried the prophet, "O Lord, deliver my soul!" There is no other way than humility and confession of our weakness to keep us safe. "The Lord is the Keeper of little ones; I was humbled and He delivered me."[1]

And, fourthly, let us make the practice of contrition a constant and permanent feature of our spiritual life. The fiftieth psalm, the *Miserere*, which occurs so often in the offices of the Church and the use of religious houses, should be the type and expression of our daily sorrow for sin. That psalm is divided into three parts. From the begin-

[1] *Ps.* cxiv. 3, 5, 6.

ning to verse eight inclusively is confession and sorrow; and these eight verses contain a remarkable declaration of the weakness, the blindness, and the wounds of man's nature—a state which, like St. Paul afterwards, the psalmist calls "sin," because it leads to sin, and makes sin, in a certain sense, natural to man. This most essential and most humiliating truth,—that is, the dogma of original sin,—he declares (in verse eight) to have been revealed to him by God. The next five verses describe the holy and joyful regeneration of human nature by the blood of Jesus Christ, under the different figures of washing, blotting out, the creation of a new, clean and righteous heart, and the restoration of the Holy Spirit; this regeneration being accompanied by joy, gladness and strength. Then, from verse fifteen to the end, the regenerated child of God sings in fervent strains of the new life that will follow justification and sanctifying grace. David—for the psalm, it must be remembered, is his own historical act of contrition [1]—promises three things: first, that he will devote himself to the conversion of sinners; secondly, that he will abstain from blood and violence; and, thirdly, that he will honour God by all external worship, yet always with real internal contrition. (The two concluding verses were evidently added at a later period.) Thus, in the *Miserere* there is sorrow, and hope, and resolution. Let that deep and earnest cry for mercy

[1] 2 *Kings* xii.

be ours. Let us pray every day: "Have mercy on me, O God—have mercy on me in Thy great mercy! According to the multitude of Thy tender mercies, blot out mine iniquity!" "Wash me yet more—yet more!" "Thou hast forgiven me—but sin is in my very bones—wash me yet more!" "By Thy grace, my sin is before me; by Thy light I see that it is Thee I have offended, and not others—wash me yet more!" "The truth of Thy holy words has come home to me, and I see the wickedness of my life—wash me yet more—yet more!"

Acts of Contrition.

1. O my God, Who art afar off—awful in Thy majesty and Thy power, pardon me my sins!

2. O God, Who art so near me, yet so silent and so patient, pardon me for having forgotten Thee!

3. O Lord and heavenly Father, Who holdest me up, Who speakest to me so often, Who promisest me eternal bliss, grant me forgiveness for having slighted Thee!

4. O my Father and my only Friend, Who hast watched over me from my first existence, Who hast prevented me with blessings and calls, forgive me for the sins of my youth and my ignorance!

5. O Lord of all goodness, Sun of all perfection, Infinite Majesty, Eternal King, I detest from my heart every thought, word and act in which I have ever offended Thee!

6. O Saviour Who hast shed the last drop of Thy blood for me, I throw myself down at Thy feet and pray for pardon!

7. O Lord, mighty and jealous, may the dread of Thy judgments, the thought of the fire of hell, the idea of the horrors of an eternity without Thee, pierce my flesh with compunction for my folly, my pride and my self-love!

8. O Holy Spirit, Who lovest and carest for the immortal souls of all, I repent from my inmost being of the sins by which I have made others sin! May I spend my life henceforward in teaching my fellow men to know and love my God!

9. I accept, O Jesus, in satisfaction for my sins, and in order that I may never sin again, all the sufferings, crosses and afflictions, whether of mind or body, which it may please Thee to send me—in union with Thy cross and with the sorrows of Thy Sacred Heart.

10. To Thee, and to Thee only, O my Redeemer, do I turn—to Thee on Whom in the past I have so often turned my back. Inspire me, by the presence of Thy face, with a true resolution of amendment! May I be firm in my purposes, and resolute in self-restraint! Above all, may I never depart from Thy feet, and from true humility of heart! Give me the deepest trust in Thee, and the utmost fear of myself—for thus only, O my Master, can I be secure of never offending Thee again.

11. Most Holy Mary, refuge of sinners, I have

offended in ways without number Thy Son, Whom Thou lovest; yet because He came to save sinners, Thou art the Mother of sinners who wish to repent; receive me therefore, assist me, and obtain for me the grace of true and lasting contrition.

12. Most Holy Joseph, open the door of the holy house of Nazareth to one who would wish to throw himself at the feet of his Saviour! Intercede with Him for me that I may never more offend Him.

VIII. DEATH.

As we look earnestly, during a retreat or at any other time, into our mortal life and its course, there is a thought always dimly felt, if not constantly present to our mind, which affects and colours all our purposes and all our resolutions. It is the thought of Death. For death is the great interpreter of life; the great rule, the grand regulator of the complex existence that we lead. "I must die," is our reflection; "how will this or that look from the point of view of my death-bed?" This is the reflection of those who are wise in time. For it is only too notorious that numbers of men and women refuse to entertain the thought of death, and even drive it away, shuddering, or reckless. And of these is true what the Following of Christ says, that they only learn from death itself what their reason ought to have taught them when there was yet time, and that if they had to live their lives over again, they would live "very differently"—*multo aliter*.

"Very differently!" Can this be prophetic of my own death—that when it comes I shall wish I had lived "very differently"? It will be so, unless I prepare for death. St. Vincent de Paul from the time he was thirteen years of age, never lay down at night without preparing himself as if he were to die before morning. How far am I from that serious treatment of death which is implied in this practice of a saint!

For death to a Christian is a thought which is full of innumerable ideas. The mystery and the horror of death which prevailed in pagan times, and even among the Hebrews before the captivity, no longer exist. To a pagan, death was simple horror. It was the quenching of the cheerful flame of life; the loss of this sun, this earth, and all that can give enjoyment. There was a wide-spread feeling that it was not utter extinction; but if existence continued beyond the tomb, it was an existence unsubstantial and gloomy, as of ghosts and shadows. To the Hebrew, death was also very repugnant. They knew that death was the appointed punishment of sin. They also knew, with a knowledge which grows more distinct from Genesis to the book of Machabees, that a Redeemer was to destroy the power of sin. Therefore they laid down their mortal lives with trust in God. But the revelation of a future life was very vague, even beyond the days of David. The reason why the chosen people had so little definite knowledge of the life to come was probably this: The ideas of which the life to come is made up, such as the vision of God on the one hand and the pain of loss on the other, the absence of carnal pleasures and enjoyments, and the dogma of judgment by a God Who was at once most merciful and most just, were almost impossible to be taught to a people circumstanced like the early patriarchs or the Hebrews. Such ideas require the revelation of the Christ and of His grace to make them comprehensible. Look at the Mahometan idea of a future life, as seized upon by a race which does not acknowledge the Incarnation. Look at the Protestant views of futurity; *viz.*, that both heaven and hell will be slightly varied repetitions of the present life; Protestants having, as a rule, no idea of grace as elevating the soul to the capability of the vision, or of the rejection of grace making the soul worthy of the pain of loss. It is only the Catholic faith that presents futurity in its complete spirituality, yet with the assurance of a bodily resurrection.

To us, therefore, who believe, death has many sides. There is much to fear; much to long for; much to labour for; much to trust to God for. Death has its joyful side and its mournful side. Doubtless with the most of us, the mournful side predominates. and rightly so, It is not every one who can meet death with a *Te Deum*, like St. Aloysius and the Blessed John Fisher. Considering our sins, the uncertainty of our repentance, the dangers of the last moments, the terrible interests at stake, we have much reason to fear. Death was meant as a punishment for the world's sin. And, therefore, even Christian faith, even the light of Christ's resurrection shining on the open tomb, cannot appease the shudderings, the repugnances, the physical torture of the act and of the apprehension of death.

Let us then go forward, in thought, to the day of our death. It may, indeed, be much nearer than we think. This year, this month, to-morrow, this very night—we know not how soon it may be. For the day and the hour are fixed and certain. Suppose that it has come, and that we lie upon the bed whence we shall never rise. Probably our death will be sudden; sudden in its coming upon us, sudden in its consummation. Experience shows that most men do not expect Death, even when old age or infirmity might have let them understand that our Lord was knocking at the door. Moreover, many persons die long before they breathe their last breath. They may not fall into delirium or stupor; but their faculties collapse and their power of apprehension breaks down; and thenceforward, with the exception of brief moments when the influence of good habits may enable them to turn to God in contrition and resignation, they cease to live a rational or responsible life. Even when a man has noted Death's approach and has measured him and is waiting for the hand-to-hand grip that is coming, it comes suddenly at last. The tissues of existence have been gradually wearing thin; and some moment when the watcher of the day is changing places with the watcher of the night, or when the dawn of a new day has brought some relaxation of vigilance in those about, or when there is no one present but some tired attendant, the end comes. The priest is away, the dearest friends are absent, there is solitude, loneliness and helplessness—and the hand comes out from behind the curtain, and a heart ceases to beat for ever. But, indeed, death must be lonely even if the moment were certain, and if all God's ministers and all one's most helpful friends stood round the bed. For the approach of Death draws down round the dying a tent whose shadowy folds are more impassable than the thickest walls. Voices cease to be heard, hands cease to be felt, the faces of the most familiar vanish from the sight. Alas! the light is there as it has been, and the dying is surrounded by loving cares—the darkness is in himself, and he is being withdrawn into the tabernacle of Death. Only one Friend has the power and the right to be present within that dread solitude; happy those who have not turned their back upon Him! "In the midst of the shadow of Death, I will fear no evil, for Thou art with me!"[1] Do we ever think of that moment when we recite the Psalm of the Good Shepherd in the Matins of Sunday?

How much physical pain there may be in the act of dying, it is very difficult to say. But it is certain that most men experience a sense of abandonment, of apprehension, of suffocation. The kindest of friends naturally grow a little indifferent with one who is old, useless, and long in dying. Let us look forward to this part of our share in the desolation

[1] *Ps.* xxii. 4.

of the Cross. Our nature is sure to struggle and to resist, as the overworked heart gradually fails, and the failing breath is more and more choked. Let us think of this in time, in our health and our vigour. Everything will pass; and to this we shall come. O my God, and my Last End, "when my strength shall fail, do not Thou forsake me!"[1]

The mental trouble, the fears, the apprehension which accompany death, will be more painful than bodily suffering. The moment is come when time must cease, and eternity begin. The moment is come when we must appear before the awful face of God. At times, during our life, this thought of irrevocable fate—of the certainty of life's ending—has seized our imagination, and perhaps terrified us. But we have always been accustomed to look at that moment as if it were a long way off. Now it is unmistakably upon us. Like a poor hunted animal, we are caught by our fate, and escape is hopeless, and the thought which presses upon our fevered brow is that we are NOT PREPARED.

We cannot account for it. It seems so miserably foolish not to have had this hour in view—not to have made ourselves ready for it. Our life has been long (or long enough), our opportunities ample. Our childhood looks now a long way off; yet not so long but that we can remember well how we mis-spent it. Our youth was a period of preparation; but for what? For our mortal life; for that brief, fleeting, unsub-

[1] *Ps.* lxx. 9.

stantial career that is now closing for ever; for that period of grasping, gaining, suffering, losing, which is now all at an end; for that fortune, reputation, and enjoyment which has gone like a summer's day and left us, diseased and worn out, upon the bed from which we shall never rise any more. At times, during our life, we have thought of eternity. There have been moments when God's visitation, or the word of His minister, or His voice within our heart, has moved us to repentance, to amendment. But the effort was short lived—the resolutions did not last; and we fell back again into indifference, worldliness, and sin. Many times, perhaps, have we thought that now we would begin to live so as to be ready to die; and behold! *Death is here*, and we have not yet made even that beginning! How good God has been in giving us helps and warnings! Yet we are not in any sense near to Him, even yet. How contented we have been with the gratifications of the flesh, the pleasantness of this poor world, the laborious frivolity of what we have called our life! How little have the awful realities of the hidden world of grace, and of our Saviour's Blood affected our actions or our thoughts! We can see it all—now, from the bed of death. Why have we not done something? Why have we not been in..earnest? Why have we not been faithful in the holy practice of confession? Our confessions have been irregular; or at least careless, hasty, almost without contrition or good resolutions; and they have made us very little better. Why did we not pray?—pray daily, pray warmly, and so live in God's light and direction? Why have we been so tepid, or negligent in holy things, so scornful of good customs, so indifferent to the supernatural? Why have we not restrained our flesh, and fought against our evil passions? Why have we set ourselves in opposition, cherished our pride, refused the obedience of our heart? Why have we not followed our Lord Jesus Christ, instead of forsaking Him for the world and the promptings of nature?

Thus shall regrets pursue each other through our troubled fancy in that hour when we approach the awful portals of the grave. Regrets and—fears! Are my sins forgiven? Is there any unrepented guilt of my past years still dark upon my immortal soul? With all my confessions have I not mocked my God? Shall I be saved or—lost?

It would not be so terrible could we make sure even of that last hour which our merciful Father gives us before He summons us to judgment. But we cannot do exactly as we would. It is difficult to think. There is an over-mastering drowsiness upon us that would wrap us in quiet forgetfulness, but for the efforts of our alarmed soul. The brain, the nerves—the instruments of spiritual activity—are worn out, attenuated, almost useless. Yet the most awful crisis of our existence is now upon us, and we want all our powers at their best to meet it. What is far worse is, that we are bound in fetters of another kind, the result of a life of selfishness and sin. For we must never forget that, on the death-bed, it may be *impossible*, morally speaking, for a man to make an act of contrition. It is true that contrition is always, by God's grace, possible; but it may be so difficult that it becomes morally impossible. For although contrition is an act of the will, yet the will, as we well know, is enormously influenced and drawn by passion, habit and temptation. To resist temptation, and to rise superior to evil custom, will be, on the death-bed, peculiarly difficult. We read of men who, at that hour, notwithstanding their many apparent virtues and good qualities, have been seemingly *unable* to renounce or reject some sins in which pride, avarice or lust were concerned. And they have refused to repent, and turned to the wall and died in their sin! Their imagination, their pampered passions, and the inveteracy of evil habit had been too much for them, even in the presence of death. O Judge of all men! Give us Thy grace to purge our hearts, before this dread moment, of all that deadly poison which may paralyse our wills even when we would turn to Thee!

Let me, then, whilst now there is time, enter seriously into the thought of my wasted life. For has it not, up to this time, been in great part wasted? Have I not lived for foolishness, for that which passeth away, for that which cannot help me on my death-bed? Shall I not begin now at least—

and begin from this very moment? O Jesus! give me Thy strength to begin a new life, a life of prayer, of serious watching over my passions, of total and complete surrender to my God!

If I fear that any sin is unforgiven, let me examine earnestly into the circumstances; yet with obedience to my spiritual father, lest, perhaps, the devil tempt me to despair, or entangle me in unprofitable scruples.

My careless life has left the legacy of more than one strong passion. These passions are my danger, in my life and in my death. They are beforehand with my will and reason, and almost seem at times to force me to sin. But I will seriously labour to diminish their power; by strong resolutions; by resisting fervently and generously the very beginnings of temptation; by the Holy Eucharist; by prayer; and above all by the loving contemplation of my Saviour's humility, obedience, innocence and patience.

Next, I will endeavour to form strong habits of virtue. There is nothing (except the grace of God) which will be so advantageous to me at the hour of my death as *habits* of virtue; that is, humility, purity, contrition, resignation and love, which by God's help shall have become so much a part of my nature and character that they almost spontaneously break forth into acts. If I am thus prepared, my will, at the least touch of temptation, is then likely to recoil in horror and to resist with indignation;

at the slightest reminiscence of past sin, the act of sorrow will burst forth unbidden; at the sole thought of my God, the heart will lift itself up like a child to its mother's face. "In the day of my trouble I sought God, with my hands lifted up to Him in the night; and I was not deceived."[1] Happy are the hands that are accustomed in life to be lifted up as we shall long to lift them up in that day of trouble, that lonely night of death; happy the hands that are not weighted with heavy fetters—that are pure and free, and know where to find their Heavenly Father.

POINTS FOR MENTAL PRAYER.

1. Imagine that you are lying on your death-bed. Think of the inevitableness of that hour; of its pain, its abandonment, its fears, its temptations. Then accept it—and accept each of its circumstances; make a profound *act of conformity* of your will with that of your Heavenly Father, in regard to time, place, manner and surroundings. Make your own the words of Jesus: *Pater! in manus Tuas commendo spiritum meum!*—Father, into Thy hands I commend my spirit![2] They are the words of that thirtieth psalm which begins: "In thee, O Lord, have I hoped, let me never be confounded". How many saints—as St. Nicholas, St. John of the Cross, and St. Catherine of Siena—have died with

[1] *Ps.* lxxvi. 3. [2] *Luke* xxiii. 46. See *Ps.* xxx. 6.

those words on their lips! What better preparation for death than perfect resignation!

2. Picture to yourself the state of your mind in that hour; your regrets; your fears; your bewilderment and uncertainty. Then pray fervently to Jesus on the Cross first for *light*; " Open Thou my eyes! . . . Give me understanding, and I will keep Thy law with my whole heart!"[1] Next for *energy*; "My soul hath slumbered . . . strengthen Thou me"[2] to do now what I shall be so glad to have done then! And, thirdly, for *generosity*; that He would teach you to despise the world and all that it contains. "As the dream of them that awake, O Lord,"[3] so shall it be with too many at the entrance of eternity! "For what have I in heaven? and besides Thee what do I desire upon earth?"[4]

3. *Rejoice* in the thought of death. Rejoice that you are to go to God. This thought will carry you triumphantly through all fear and all dangers. "Thou art my portion for ever!"[5] Rejoice in the triumph of His precious blood, when the poor sinful creature, in spite of weakness and of sin, is about to be lifted up to the table of everlasting happiness. God comes in judgment "to save all the meek of the earth".[6] Where can I be more safe, more peaceful, and more happy than in the "hands of God"? Let me accustom myself to this thought during life.

[1] *Ps.* cxviii. 18, 84.   [2] *Ibid.* 28.   [3] *Ps.* lxxii. 20.
[4] *Ibid.* 25.   [5] *Ibid.* 26.   [6] *Ps.* lxxv. 10.

4. Pray for *perseverance*. Resolve that all the passages of daily prayer and of the Divine office which contain a prayer for perseverance shall be said henceforward with intention and fervour. *Sancta Maria, Mater Dei, ora pro nobis, nunc, et in horâ mortis nostræ! Amen.*

IX. JUDGMENT.

Let us consider that the seriousness of death and of life arises from the certainty of judgment. What has been said, therefore, of death, and of its accompanying fears and perils, is really a description of the shadow which the impending judgment casts over that dread hour. Hence, we have meditated on judgment in meditating on death. Yet there are some further considerations which may profitably be made.

First, let us reflect that every hour of life has to be answered for. The possession of reason makes us responsible beings. We cannot slip out of this. We may rebel, shut our eyes, drug our conscience with worldliness, refuse to think, or simply live as though we had no soul to save or lose. It is no matter. The day of reckoning must come. In proportion to our opportunities of knowing the right and the wrong, so will our judgment be. There is a day for all of us which Holy Scripture calls the "Day of the Lord".[1] Each man has his own day, long or short, chequered with various fortune, but sure to end when the fated hour strikes. Then comes the "Day of the Lord"—in which the conditions of

---
[1] *Isaias* xiii. 6, 9.

existence are wholly changed; nay, almost utterly reversed. No more labour, no more merit, no more liberty, no more illusion. Instead of these things there will be the inexorable truth, the indelible record, the irrevocable doom. Think of this, my soul, when life seems safe, when days seem bright, when the end seems far off. Think of this when tempted to recklessness, to the delights of sense, or the gratification of pride. Use this thought, above all, to order thy life with seriousness; to repent, to reform, to take up holy practices; to give up the world in all its forms, and to consecrate thyself wholly to thy God. Who can think of the day of Thy coming, O my Lord and my Maker—who can think of it, and not set himself to prepare for it? Grant me true wisdom! Grant me the gift of holy fear! Grant me the constant sense of Thy salutary presence!

To those who are studying perfection it should be a matter of serious concern that every hour of life, and every second, will leave an ineffaceable mark on the soul's immortality. Hell, purgatory, heaven—we are constructing them for ourselves as we live. As we make them, so they will be. Even if we escape the fire of hell, it were shameful and sad that these golden moments should be spent in gathering dross for that other fire; or lost in frivolities which will bring us no nearer to the bosom of God in the land where one degree of sight is bliss and ecstasy. Loss of precious time; misuse of crosses and sufferings; want of regularity in prayer; the tepidity which prevents our ridding ourselves of certain occasions of sin, or fighting in earnest against certain sinful habits—these things are eating up our time of preparation; and if we do not see to it we shall find ourselves at God's tribunal with empty hands, poor, and even imperilled.

No thought has such a steadying effect on life as the thought of the judgment that follows death. To one who, in the midst of his days, can go down to the gate of Hades and get face to face with judgment, there comes that spirit of deep and calm resolve which belongs to the sailor who knows what the small black cloud means so far off, and is aware that all his resources will be to the utmost strained to meet it. Nothing is so heavy on the spirit of man as to realise that, on one day soon, he must come face to face with the Absolute. We are too much like children; but even a child sometimes feels in its spirit the relentless on-coming of the huge mysterious ocean, even in the inch-by-inch advance of the waves that seem to play with him. "God is not mocked,"[1] says St. Paul. Is not my life a mocking of my God? an attempt which I know to be foolish, but which my wretched weakness leads me to renew again and again, to serve and to gratify myself, and yet to obtain the rewards of my Heavenly Father's kingdom?

There are two aspects of the judgment which may,

[1] *Gal.* vi. 7.

either of them, serve for meditation: the general judgment, and the particular; the judgment of all mankind, and my own judgment. It is of the general judgment that the Holy Scripture reveals the most; but all its features appear in every judgment that a child of Adam undergoes at the moment when the soul parts from the body.

The place of my judgment is the spot where I die. That will be my Josaphat. The trumpets of the universal judgment will not be needed for me; but, instead, there will be the Almighty power of God's hand, which will hold me there to hear my doom. My soul, myself, who never could be held to the presence of God during the dissipation of my mortality, will now be constrained to stand with painful attention before His face. "Understand this, ye who forget God!"[1]

God will come; God will be there. At the last day it will be Christ my Redeemer, Who once more will revisit this earth which His blood has sanctified. He will come with the clouds, the cross borne before Him, and the tens of thousands of the angelic host surrounding Him. Although Christ does not descend upon the earth at every death of a man or woman, yet on dying we shall find ourselves mysteriously in His presence; we shall know Him; we shall tremble before Him. I shall find myself on a sudden in the light, the purity, and the justice of my Saviour. The angels will throng

[1] *Ps.* xlix. 22.

around, ministering to Him as they minister for ever; but it will all pass in an instant; I shall see, and be seen, and be judged. God will see me; God will pierce me through with His light; God will sentence me. "The Lord doth interrogate the just and the unjust!"[1] Oh! awful interrogation of my God! What could I answer if He called me at this moment? Give me grace, O Jesus, in fear and trembling to work out my salvation![2]

Let me consider the Judge, and my own conscience as it will be in His sight.

It is fitting that God should judge me. He made me for Himself; His design has been that I should merit my happiness by His grace, which has ever been lavishly bestowed upon me.

He redeemed me; and redeemed me in such a way as to draw my heart to love Him and to form myself upon His most beautiful human life.

He hides Himself during my mortal career. He is silent and invisible, whether men serve Him or sin against Him. Even His visible incarnate presence, which He gave to the world for thirty-three years, has been withdrawn since He went up from Mount Olivet—though His story and His words remain like a luminous trail of light across the sky of human life.

But He cannot be silent or hidden for ever. Now, when the span of life is accomplished, and the mysterious rupture between spirit and flesh which

[1] *Ps.* x. 6.   [2] *Philip.* ii. 14.

men call death has taken place, He solemnly resumes His sway.

He comes now as the Master. In life, it seems often difficult to say who is the master. Money seems the master; unbelief seems the master; worldliness seems the master. Wicked rulers, impious conspiracies, the brute force of numbers, the reckless management of the mob, the unreasoning pressure of public opinion—these things too often have the world all their own way. And I, in my want of faith and my cowardice, have oftentimes given in to the pressure that I felt around me. But the day inevitably comes, for the whole race, for each single man and woman, and for me, when the true Master shows Himself. "Show Thy face, O Lord, and we shall be saved,"[1] was the cry of the Hebrews of old when their enemies were stronger than they. Happy those who can pray that the Sovereign Lord of heaven and earth would show His face! There are so many to whom that revelation will bring confusion and terror. Those who have forgotten Him; those who have broken His laws; those who have fought against His Church; those who have lived in the world and with the world;—all these will fear when in sovereign majesty He assumes the sceptre He seemed to have laid aside so completely.

Again, He comes as the Rectifier. All that is wrong in the earth must be put to rights. For

[1] *Ps.* lxxix. 4.

wrong cannot finally triumph; evil and injustice are not the normal condition of things. It is one of the strong proofs of God's existence and of man's immortality, that there lives in the breast of every human being the unextinguishable conviction, or aspiration, that evil cannot finally triumph. At the last day a strong hand will put men in their places and will restore the right order of things. And at the end of my life, however I may have erred, or followed my free-will, or bent things to my own pride and pleasure, I must give in to the power of God. If my heart has been given up to creatures, it will now be forcibly brought to see their emptiness and their foulness. If it has turned its back on its God, it will now find itself longing for Him, according to the nature which He gave it. If it has found peace in a life without prayer or self-denial, as so many do find peace, it will now be roughly awakened to a sense of trouble, of destitution, and of failure. For the laws of being, which are the laws of God, are inexorable. When things seem to go wrong in this our present life, when the good seems without support, and evil seems to drive her chariots through the human multitudes, spreading dismay—happy are those who recollect that earthly life is only a span of temporary trial. What is to last for ever must be the right and the orderly, and the triumph of God's kingdom. O Lord God, Who when Thou comest shalt put all things in order, fill my heart with the sense of Thy dread coming! May Thy judgment restrain me! May Thy judgment comfort me!

For I must not forget that when Thou comest the just have the right to lift up their heads; for their redemption is at hand.[1] Thou wilt come as the Rewarder. Then all those who have read aright the meaning of life will reap the fruits of their faith and patience. Then those who have followed the footsteps of Jesus Christ will deserve to look upon His gentle and smiling face. Then those who have, by Thy grace, restrained themselves, and chastened themselves, and purified themselves, and struggled for so many years to persevere in the uphill work of perfection, will be made secure and received into peace for evermore.

On the other hand, it will be the day of vengeance as well as the day of reward. For God must be an Avenger. True, it is only those hearts who have wilfully resisted Him to the last that will feel His indignation. But He must avenge Himself on these; not because He is subject to the stirrings of passion, or is affected by any throes of feeling, however righteous; but because the Good must be king and master, and all those who contradict Him must perish before His face.[2] If I, by God's mercy, am striving to avoid deadly sin, and to live in some sense according to His will, then the thought of His avenging judgment need not disturb or distress me. But it should always be with me—as the traveller in Alpine

---

[1] *Luke* xxi. 28   [2] *Ps.* ix. 4

regions sees close at hand the fatal precipice which awaits the false step. And if dangerous habits of carelessness, laziness, murmuring, or unkindness seem to be creeping upon me, in the name of the awful judgment let me beware!

Our Lord and Saviour wishes us to face the thought of judgment without undue terror or excitement. And therefore whilst He has revealed its terrors, He has not made it appear difficult to prepare for it. He has, as is usual with Him, pointed to one or two very common duties, and has promised that if we are faithful in these the judgment may be awaited with confidence.

"Judge not, and you shall not be judged."[1] To judge others means to dwell uncharitably on the faults and weaknesses of our neighbour—or, what is worse, to reveal them and comment upon them. It is one of the commonest of sins. It is found among all ranks and degrees, wherever there is intercourse and conversation. It is found within the walls of convents almost as much—though not perhaps to such a serious degree—as in the drawing-room and the cottage. To strive to repress unkind conversation and unkind feeling is to be in earnest in loving God with our whole heart. Therefore, it is to secure for ourselves safety in the day of judgment.

"As you do to others, so also will my Heavenly Father do to you."[2] This refers to kind actions.

---

[1] *Luke* vi. 87.   [2] *Matt*. xviii. 85.

In order, therefore, to make sure of safety at the judgment, we cannot do better than study to show kindness to one another. If rich and well-to-do people are kind, they are safe; but the kindness must be true kindness. It must be a kindness that is anxious for the immortal souls which our Heavenly Father chiefly longs for—which gives or procures instruction, sacraments and good example. It must be a kindness which not only bestows money, but also comforting words and wise intercourse; a kindness which not only gives what is superfluous to the giver, but is given at the cost of sacrifice and trouble. In a community, the brother or the sister who helps, advises, or cheers others, and who consistently strives to be unselfish, is making our Lord's judgment easy and merciful.

"If we judged ourselves, we should not be judged."[1] The habitual practice of confession, of examination of conscience, and of serious reflection, accompanied by constantly renewed resolution, is a most certain security against a severe judgment. What is the cause of worldliness, but the neglect of serious thought about the eternal truths? What leads a priest or religious sometimes to perdition, but the abandonment of meditation, caused perhaps by the stress of occupation? What checks tepidity, disaffection to superiors, and habits of venial sin—what checks these before they grow and harden into deadly transgression— except the practice of self-inspection? Every day,.

[1] *Cor.* xi. 31.

every night, let us prepare for the coming of our Lord by earnest, if not prolonged, reflection on our sins, imperfections, motives and prospects; and this, not primarily or chiefly for the purpose of correcting ourselves, but principally in order to lay our poverty and our unfaithfulness at the feet of Jesus Christ, that His mercy may pardon and His grace may heal us.

Points for Mental Prayer.

I. Contemplate the scene of the Last Judgment; our Lord Jesus Christ coming in the clouds, with His Cross, and the army of His angels; before Him all generations of human beings. *Adore* Him as Creator, as Master, as Rectifier, as Rewarder, as Avenger. *Welcome* Him to this earth, which belongs to Him. *Rejoice* at His coming, for the sake of His own great glory. *Long for* the "Day of the Lord".

II. Contemplate your own judgment; that swift, unerring, just and final judgment! Observe your own unpreparedness; possibly, unrepented sin; certainly, mistaken views, thoughtlessness, indifference to the interests of Jesus, and selfishness. Ask, *petition* for light—for earnestness—fidelity and loyalty to the cause of our Lord. *Elect* to be on the side of Jesus with your whole heart, in lowliness, obedience, sacrifice and suffering; in everything, all your life.

III. *Resolve* to advance the interests of the souls of others by thoughtfulness, kindness, and the absence of all kinds of uncharitableness in deed, in mind, and even in thought, as far as possible. *Elicit strong desires* to this effect, and, as it were, *consecrate* and *dedicate* yourself to this kind of life. *Dirige, Domine, in conspectu tuo viam meam.*[1] O Lord, direct, order and sustain this life of mine, which is only a path and a way to eternity, that in Thy sight it may be passed, as before Thy face it must be answered for!

[1] *Ps. v. 8.*

X. HELL.

EVERY thought which helps to impress upon our unstable hearts the stern and inevitable reality of existence is useful. Such a thought is that of the everlasting punishments of God Almighty. They flow from His sovereignty; they are not contradictory to His nature, or incompatible with His love. If the hour of death finds us turned away from our last end, then hell follows inevitably. When we awake to that fate, neither struggle nor prayer will any more avail. Our destiny is fixed. We are like a skiff caught in the smooth resistless water which is only a few yards from the cataract. We had our free-will, and sufficient—far more than sufficient—grace; we had our appointed time of probation. The time is finished, and the hour has struck; and as we have died, so we must live for evermore.

At present, it is not easy to put ourselves in the position of one whose fate is fixed. We are occupied, amused, distracted. All our failures in a life of virtue come from our being taken up with the present world and with our lot therein. To become steady we must be serious; and the inevitableness of the future—of death, judgment and (under certain conditions) hell—is well adapted to make us serious. Fill me, O my God, with Thy holy fear! Keep before me Thy judgments! Hold not from me the awful precipices that are in my path! Make me prepare for the hour when eternity will close over my head!

These thoughts are certainly calculated not only to make us serious, but also sad. Yet sadness may be needful for us. There is a sadness which keeps its eye covetously on creatures, longing to enjoy and be happy. There is a sadness which turns its back on God and on spiritual things, as if there were no enjoyment to be found there; and this does most certainly lead to sin. But there is also a sadness which is indeed felt in our lower nature, because our poor human weakness is sure to be unhappy if we daily keep it in restraint; but which is more than compensated for by the delight we experience in the friendship of God and the life of grace. The frequent thought of death and eternity must sadden our inferior nature. It is different, no doubt, with the saints; they have schooled even their natural weakness to be heedless of the things which wound it. But with most of us, the thought of the awful truths is painful, depressing, and distasteful. If, when such feelings come on, we can only manage to turn to God and cling to Him, then our sadness is unto salvation. The thought of hell is intended, indeed, to steady us and sober us; to frighten us, if you please, into self-restraint; but it is intended to do more than this: it is meant to turn us to Christ. The sadness which springs from our giving up creatures (or being forced to give them up) without taking hold of our Blessed Lord, is the only sadness which is fatal. Very early in life we have to learn this lesson. Easy circumstances, pleasant occupations, perhaps the feeling of youth itself, combine to make us enjoy life. At first, Christian self-restraint seems unendurable; nature mocks at it. Yet, with careful training, the heart is gradually turned away from vanity; there grows upon it the gradually sobering effect of supernatural views. Happy those who come under good influence of this kind; so that they are led, through the practice of recollection, to become by degrees more steady, less impulsive, more humble, more considerate, more mature.

Let us first, then, worship with lowly reverence that awful attitude of God—His anger. There is no such thing as "anger" in God. Anger, as we know it, is a feeling and a passion. God is a most pure Spirit, passionless and unchangeable. But when the finite creature sins mortally and so turns away from God, that turning away causes in the creature the same effects as if God were really changed and "angry". Anger in God denotes that awful state of opposition and of abandonment in which the soul is, and feels itself to be, when it is turned away from its last end. If a man plunge into some dark and chilly vault, he feels the cold and the horror; but the unchangeable sun is shining overhead, as bright and as warm as ever. It is not God Who is "angry," it is the sinner who places a barrier between himself and that Being Who alone is his happiness. The sinner, therefore, damns himself. A soul in mortal sin only requires the dissolution of its mortal frame to be, by that very fact, in hell. This is what is meant by the "anger" of God. All the visitations of God upon a creature may be mercies, with the exception of one—and that is when He permits us to die in mortal sin. Probably even this is, relatively, merciful; He foresees that it would be better for us to die at that moment than at any other. But when we pray to God, "Cast me not away in Thine anger,"[1] or "Rebuke me not in Thine anger,"[2] let us for the future make these aspirations a prayer against dying in mortal sin.

Neither hell nor death is a subject on which people like to dwell. The world often thinks and speaks foolishly and sentimentally about death, as if, for all sorts of men, it were the end of trouble and the beginning of rest. A Catholic can never talk like this. A Catholic who goes into a churchyard, and sees the green, quiet graves, and the grey church and the dark yew trees, will hope, indeed, and pray that those who lie there may be at peace. But if they died in mortal sin, then their graves may be peaceful, and their resting place solemn and hallowed—but they themselves are in hell-fire.

[1] *Jerem.* xxxii. 47. [2] *Ps.* vi. 2.

Let faith look down, through those graves, beyond that sleeping-place of human dust.

You have read of a terrible pestilence in a great and populous city, in which so many people died that there was no time to bury them one by one. But at night, after the darkness had closed in, the pest-cart came round, and the bodies of the dead were collected; and then, unshrouded and uncoffined, they were carried to a remote spot, and cast as quickly as possible into a wide and deep pit. And so it was done each night whilst the pestilence lasted. If a living man had been, by accident or carelessness, flung into that pit of horrors, perhaps the thought of such a thing might give us some image of hell. There he lies, corruption beneath him, over him, about him; no light, no help, no escape, no hope; worse than the dead. Such a pit is no fiction. Or rather it is a feeble fiction; a feeble representation to the imagination of a pit which awaits sinners; covered up, silent, mysterious; but real and not very far away. It seems to say, Mortal man, in a few years, or perhaps days, the question will be tried whether or no you are to come to me. The day will soon be here when your body will be left stiffening upon the bed of your death, and your immortal soul will hang for an instant between heaven and my abyss.

For hell is possible, and we must contemplate its reality.

A pit of fire! dark fire, creeping blindly round

and round, and penetrating with a tooth sharper than that of a venomous snake. Stinging fire! inextinguishable, gnawing as if it were alive. Clinging fire! wrapping its victim round, fitting itself to him like water, passing through him like continuous lightning-strokes. Horrible fire! a scourge to every sense; a union of every loathsome element, acting on man as though all earthly shudderings and shrinkings were intensified beyond the power of reckoning. Binding fire! with fingers like to vipers, strong as steel fetters, and blistering like red-hot iron, that clasp the arms, the limbs, the throat, and hold the victim fast to the dungeon floor. This is the fire.

And the fire is already tenanted by living creatures; creatures that are fiercer and stronger than anything upon this upper earth; more hideous and fearful than any apparition that ever terrified man into the loss of his reason. Living creatures that were once mighty angels, and are now strong, cruel, jealous, and horrible devils. These beings will be your masters there. If the fire leaves any fibre of your being without pain, these things will find it out. And all the finer and most inward powers and faculties of your immortal soul, where pain can be more acutely felt than in life we are capable of conceiving—all that noble spiritual nature, destined for eternal joy, will be delivered over to them to rack; and with a horrid readiness they will use their powers, howling themselves for pain, and stung to madness with the sight of redeemed souls with all their sacramental character clearly showing even in that everlasting darkness; for they are the appointed ministers of the "anger" of God.

But look into the abyss where lost men already lie, and you will see another sight of terror. It is a shadowy thing. It seems to be part of each lost being—and yet it is not so. It lies close to him; the fire cannot consume it; the strongest devil if he would could not drive it away. Mortal man, that is the worm of conscience. You carry it about with you even on earth. But on earth it is not troublesome—would it were more so! On earth it is quiet, gentle, seldom loud, seldom importunate, though at times its bite gives a foretaste of what it will be after death. On earth, conscience is as your guardian angel, sharing with your angel the work of causing you to love Jesus and to fear sin. But after the judgment it turns into the worm that never dies. Creeping close to the very vitals of the soul, there it fixes its teeth, and never quits its hold. There, amidst the fire, among the demons, it exercises its necessary ministry of vengeance. Its tooth is the memory of the past; the past, so short, so precious, so foolishly squandered, so irrevocable now! Have you lived for this? it will say; did God make you for this? Did the blood of Jesus redeem you that you might come here? Did you repeat your innocent prayers at your mother's knee only to find your way to hell? Did you make your first communion only to be damned? Did the pure flesh of Christ hallow this body of yours, which is now a loathsome carcase amidst these flames? You were a child of God, the heir of Heaven, the partaker of God's very nature—and yet you are here! Here, in this terrible pit of despair, where no hope can come near, where you must lie for ever! Can it be true that you will be away from Him for all eternity? You learned to love Him; nay, you loved Him once. You used to think of seeing His face one day. You will never see it. Your lot is darkness. For endless ages you will stretch out impotent desires to behold Him, to be near Him; and ever and ever sink back in fathomless despair amid these flames. After so much grace, so much love, so many delays, such sweetness of mercy, such patience of compassion, the hour has come, and you are lost! O fool! Why did you not heed your conscience when it was yet the daylight and you might have worked? Why did you let your passions drag you down? Why did you not repent and amend in time? Now all is lost! Your very friends—your parents, brothers, husband, wife, children—they are for you no more; the abyss is between you. You lie here for ever; no change, no turning, no respite, no relief, no death!

For ever! Monotonously, for ever! Without cessation the fire will burn and bind, the demons rage and tear, the worm gnaw with its insatiate tooth—on and on for ever! Up on the earth the years will roll by—the centuries will finish and begin—no change, no hope! The thunders of the last day will resound at length, and the pit will be sealed up; no change, no hope! The eternal years will begin to be—duration without motion, changeless, uniform—a noontide heat without a breath, a wilderness without a limit, a dead sea without a ripple—and never any change, never any hope! Still the untired ministers of your own death-sentence will hold you there, scourge you, mock you, while time seems turned to stone, being is failure, and immortality is death.

Points for Mental Prayer.

1. Form to yourself a picture, or vision of hell. Place before your eyes the pit, the fire, the demons, the worm that never dies; and the eternity. Imagine that you see yourself there, suffering, despairing. Make acts of *Adoration* of God as the awful Holiness Who necessarily averts His face from the unrepenting sinner; and of *contrition* for your own past sins, especially the more grievous.

Then *take refuge* in your Saviour's arms, Who alone can deliver you from the danger of eternal death. Save me, O Jesus! Save me in temptation! Save me in the hour of death! Pardon me, O Jesus! Thou art all mercy now—in Thee I trust! On Thee I cast my weakness and my sinfulness! In Thee alone do I hope—let me not be confounded for ever! Help me, O Jesus! Give me day by day and minute by minute Thy powerful efficacious grace, which alone will save me from hell!

2. Look again down into hell, and see *how* all the lost souls came there. Not by any necessity, by any fault of nature, or by any failure on God's part; but by pride, by impurity, by sloth, by unchecked passion. Look more closely, and you will see how these millstones that have sunk them in that sea of fire grew to be so great; how they began from want of self-restraint, from idleness, from dissipation, from carelessness about the sacraments, from ill-advised friendships or books, from selfishness, from temper. Then pray fervently for that spirit of complete and entire *conversion* to God which alone makes life safe. O my God, I give Thee my heart—my whole heart! I detest sin from the bottom of my soul! I wish no longer to have the slightest attachment to creatures! Grant me the spirit of detachment—of purity of heart! Strengthen me unto perfect self-restraint!

Think over what bad habit, or what affection to venial sin, seems to be dangerous in your present way of life. As such things too often lead to hell, *conceive a holy fear*, and resolve to break with them now for good, by God's help.

3. Dwell now more particularly on what is the essential character of everlasting suffering—the loss of Almighty God. This heart of yours—this immortal spirit, with all its magnificent endowments—must finally possess God, or be for ever miserable.

Not to have God will be hunger, sickness, darkness, fetters, tears, despair. Make acts of *vehement desire* never to lose God. "My tears," said holy David, "have been my bread day and night, whilst it is said to me daily: Where is thy God?"[1] O my Maker, let me never turn my back upon Thee! O my Father, may I never force Thee to abandon Thy child! O my only Friend, let not the day come when Thou too shalt stand afar off! O my last end, my crown, my joy, make me spend this short life so wisely and lovingly that I may possess Thee for all eternity!

[1] *Ps.* xli 4.

XI. CHRIST OUR LORD.

We have meditated on God and on ourselves—on God's designs for us and our essential need of God. The question now is—how can we so live our life as to be in conformity with our last end, and to belong entirely to God? Nearness to God, union with God—such have been the phrases used by the saints of all ages in order to express the purpose of mortal life. There is a union which the believer looks for after death, and not till then. But there is also a state of union which can exist even during this time of our mortality. For we are so made as to be able to approach God, to take hold of Him, to live in His presence, and to act under the impulse and influence of His spiritual contact. We are so made that this is possible. But at the same time such a life is not naturally easy. Under the conditions of our state here below, God does not overwhelm us. He does not grasp us with a hand of irresistible power. He does not shine like a sun upon our intelligence, or dazzle our will and our fancy. He is afar off, He is obscure, He withholds Himself, He is silent. To know Him and to grasp Him requires effort. To live in His atmosphere must be the work of our own faculties, aided by His grace.

Yet all the power, and the love, and the stupendous designs of our Father in heaven would be of no advantage to us unless somehow or other this work of our own intelligence and will could be made easy, and more or less certain. Union with God is a more or less conscious striving and working of our own faculties; and therefore the grand work of life comes to be this: The knowing God better, the serving Him more continuously, and the loving Him more fervently; and the greatest blessing God could bestow on His creatures, next to their creation and destiny, would be to facilitate their knowing Him and loving Him. This we might be sure He would do, even if it were true, as in strictness it is, that He is not bound to do so. The grand plan or design by which He has actually proved His desire to bring us nearer to Him could not, however, have been guessed or conceived by any created intellect. That plan was nothing less than the Incarnation.

Let us consider that to love God above all things is an attitude of man's soul which, as a rule and speaking generally, depends upon a great many circumstances. It requires some intimate knowledge of God; it requires that God should be in a certain sense seen by our minds; it requires that the feelings, the imagination, and even the senses, should be affected and touched; and it requires that the associations connected with our idea of God should be nearly connected with our own life, our wants, our joys, our sorrows, and our weaknesses. For no one can serve or love an abstraction. God could never be altogether an abstraction. We have, even by nature, sufficient knowledge of Him to be able to give Him names which signify how much He is to us, and what He has done and is prepared to do for us. Still, as we have seen, He is afar off, and silent. His extreme, or rather absolute, spirituality prevents us from having any mental picture of Him which has not to be qualified, and in a greater or less degree to be explained away. His infinity makes even our most spiritual conceptions of Him utterly inadequate. All His attributes are conceived by us with drawbacks of this kind. Thus, His very love, though we know it is real love, and (with whatever hidden glories) real in the same sense as our love for one another, can only be talked about, not seen or grasped; because love in God is not an emotion, but partakes of the immutability and the impassibleness of the Divine nature; and of a love of this kind, however firmly we may believe it to exist, we can have no complete conception.

It was to give to us Himself in such a state that He could, as it were, be brought home to our faculties, to our complex human nature, to our feelings, to our hearts, that God was made Man. In this meditation we will pass over the thought of redemption, considered as our salvation from sin and hell by the act of Christ's sacrifice. That is a thought which wonderfully helps the understanding to know better the majesty and the compassion of God. But as a devotional consideration this thought is found repeated, reinforced and illustrated in the spiritual results of the Incarnation and Passion. For if Christ "died for our sins, He also rose again for our justification";[1] that is, He did a great deal more than die for us—His human life and history, together with His perpetual word and His never-failing sacraments are an influence which unceasingly enables us to live the life of "justification," or of union with God. Ah! my Jesus! In what a profound sense are these words of Thy prophet verified, that there is "no nation which hath its gods so near as our God is near unto us."[2] And how many of us live a life which is so given up to sense and to exterior things that we are strangers to this region of Thy grace and love!

It is thus easy to understand why the Incarnation is the central event of all human history. It is not merely that without it we should have been excluded from everlasting bliss; but that it has enabled man to know and love God in a way which, to natural reason, would have seemed impossible. It has brought God near. It has revealed Him to man. It has placed God within the reach of human faculties. It has made it possible for man to worship Him in ways entirely new.

For, consider how the Incarnation reveals God. It shows God as interesting Himself in my soul and

[1] *Rom.* iv. 25. [2] *Deut.* iv. 7.

the souls of my fellow-men. Let us understand this. Natural reason, to say nothing of revelation, would always have told us that God did, and must, interest Himself in the souls He has created and destined for Himself. But God dwells in inaccessible light. The Incarnation brings Him before our eyes. It is so stupendous a thing that God should assume human nature, and that, consequently, there should be a Person Who is at once God and Man, that such an act not only proves God's interest in us, but fills our whole being with the appreciation of it. The Almighty Lord of the heavens and the earth is so solicitous about your soul and my soul that it is only His Divinity which holds Him from behaving to you and me like an earthly father, an earthly friend—from manifesting to us all the goodness which so truly exists in His supreme nature. But even His Divinity has not hindered Him! He has found means to be human without ceasing to be Divine —to be a man, without ceasing to be God. Some men might have doubted, perhaps, of the reality of His love for us; not of the effects of His love, but of the existence of any attribute corresponding to love in the wholly spiritual Godhead. Therefore He would assume a human nature, with a human soul, a human heart, and human emotions, in order that even our sluggish and incredulous natures might be overcome with the revelation of His true and real affection. With His human nature He can love us as we love one another. And He is not content with being made man, but He lives a human life, which is full of the exhibition of love in work and in word. All His acts and words being the acts and words of God, no one who thinks seriously can help being overwhelmed with the idea they give him of his God's affection. The Incarnation is, as it were, the human language which interprets the divine and eternal thought of God.

But if it reveals how our God is disposed towards His creatures, it also reveals what is the value He sets on them, and on their immortal souls. Why has this ineffable dispensation taken place, except for the sake of our souls' salvation? From one point of view, a soul, with all its immortal powers, is to God as a drop in the ocean, as a grain of the desert sand. Philosophers might have argued in this direction, and might perhaps have persuaded the unhappy human race that the little life and single fate of any one man, or indeed the destinies of all men, could be of no more account to God than the perishing of an insect. Science, or rather the men who pursue science, has insisted on this view in our own days. But the Incarnation has made it impossible to deceive mankind. If my God became a little Child, and walked among men, and urged them with His own mouth to save their souls, the soul must be stupendously precious in His sight. If He could assume human nature for the sake of His creatures, why should He not do everything? No miracle, no interference with natural law, no loving and persistent pressure on the moral and intellectual forces of this world below, can now be extravagant or uncalled for, seeing that God has begun by doing so much. The whole course of human life, as St. Paul so well understood, is governed by the law that "all things work together unto good,"[1] to those whom God so dearly loves. So that the Incarnation is, as it were, the Sinai of the universal human race. Its trumpet, its fires and its clouds proclaim to all generations the grand revelation which God wills the world to grasp and accept—that He loves every soul, cherishes every soul, and would save every soul.

It is an essential part of one's spiritual life, therefore, to be deeply impressed with the mystery of the "kindness and benignity of God our Saviour,"[2]— the taking of flesh by the Eternal Word. Place yourself in spirit in those ancient days before the coming of Christ. Think how the world expected Him; how the patriarchs looked forward to Him and the saints lifted their prayers to heaven that He might come and make no delay. For even then, although Bethlehem was not yet, the shadow of the Incarnation made it easier for men to know God and draw near to Him. Join in spirit with all the predictions of the psalms and the prophecies; with all their glowing descriptions of the Son of Man, in His most sacred flesh and in His most noble and royal soul. "Many shall see," said holy

[1] *Rom.* viii. 28.   [2] *Titus* ii. 11.

David, speaking of the days of mercy and truth to come, "Many shall see, and shall fear, and they shall hope in the Lord."[1] Ah yes! shall hope so much more devoutly and passionately when they shall have that august vision before their eyes! Contemplative souls shall sing in all ages that "new canticle"[2] which has been taught to human nature by the Incarnation. (A devotional and meditative recitation of this thirty-ninth Psalm, *Expectans expectavi Dominum*, will form an admirable lifting up of the heart in the direction of the present meditation.) Turn next to the forty-fourth Psalm—so often recited in the Breviary Office, on the feasts of our Lord, and of His Blessed Mother. The Incarnation is that "good word,"[3]—that blessed and joyful announcement, with which the Holy Spirit had inspired the singer. "Thou art beautiful above the sons of men; grace is poured abroad in Thy lips; therefore hath God blessed Thee for ever." Might, comeliness, beauty, truth, meekness—these are the qualities which he sees in the Saviour to come, and which we do well to acknowledge and confess every day of our lives, in reciting this Psalm. Under Thee shall people fall—Thy arrows shall pierce hearts! For no heart can hold out against God made man. If you wish to join in spirit with another grand seer of the ancient times, go to the eleventh chapter of Isaias. There you read of the Root of Jesse, and the single perfect Flower which

---

[1] *Ps.* xxxix. 4.   [2] *Ib.*   [3] *Ps.* xliv. 1, 2.

shall spring up from that Root. Then he describes the magnificent human soul of Him Who is so beautifully typified in the one unique Flower of this earth. "And the Spirit of the Lord shall rest upon Him"—he goes on to intone to the listening people those seven stupendous names of Divine grace then first revealed to human ears—(seven names which exhaust the amplitude of the Holy Spirit's outpouring upon the nature of man)—"the Spirit of Wisdom and of Understanding; the Spirit of Counsel and of Fortitude; the Spirit of Knowledge and of Piety; and he shall be filled with the Spirit of the fear of the Lord".[1] The whole chapter may be read as a prayer. It describes Jesus, with all His gifts and glory, passing through the land to pour out His fulness on us and on all mankind. He is to be the lover of the poor and the meek; justice and truth are to gird Him; men, who heretofore had lived as beasts that fought with one another, are now to learn the lesson of brotherly love; the earth is to be filled with the knowledge of the Lord as the covering waters of the sea—an image and prophecy of that Church which is the fruit of the Incarnation.

POINTS FOR MENTAL PRAYER.

1. Endeavour first to excite in your heart that holy and *ardent desire* to see and know God, without which you will not appreciate the Incarnation.

[1] *Isaias* xi. 1, 2

My God! Afar off, in Thy supreme and inaccessible majesty, I adore Thee! Blessed be Thou in Thy exceeding great glory! To Thee I stretch forth my hands—for Thee I sigh. What am I, and what is my life without Thee, O my Father in heaven? Grant me to know Thee; grant me to have Thee near to my poor human faculties; to occupy myself with Thee, to find it not too hard to keep Thee in my thought and heart! My nature, though made by Thee and for Thee, is of itself a veil which hides Thee from me: give me Thy help to pierce this veil, and in the very effort to see Thee better! My sloth and indifference to spiritual things have made a darkness round me; I detest them now, and beg of Thee to make me henceforth fervent and devout! My numerous sins, habits of sin, and imperfections silently acquiesced in, have made me neglect for too large a portion of my life to turn to Thee and to seek to know Thee! Pardon me, O Thou most patient of friends, and convert my heart to Thy saving presence! Show Thy face, and I shall be saved! Reveal Thyself to my understanding, to my will, to my memory, to my imagination; impress Thy presence on my very senses, that all my being may have Thee near!

2. Next, *thank* your Saviour that He has answered this prayer of your heart, and of the hearts of all mankind. *Welcome Him* to the earth. O my Jesus! Thou art come! My God has come from the realms of awful light, to make me know Him! My God

has looked at me with the eyes of a little child, touched me with His hand, spoken to me in sweet tones of mercy, carried His cross and died that I might understand Him better; that I might understand His love, and the value of my soul!

3. How have I corresponded with His loving advances? Alas! I have to reproach myself that my Saviour has been almost *out of my life!* Out of my thoughts—out of my memory—out of my occupations—out of my time—out of my pleasures—out of my sorrows! My Lord and my God, I am sorry, and ask forgiveness. Come now into my being, and possess all my powers! May I study Thee, dwell on Thee, aim at Thee! May I live at Bethlehem, at Nazareth, in the Garden, in Calvary! May'st Thou be ever before my eyes and in my hands all through my life, and at my death! Amen.

XII. LOOKING UPON JESUS.

There are other considerations connected with the Incarnation with which we have now to deal.

God became man in order to draw men to God—or to bring God nearer to men's faculties.

The God-man attracts the human heart, first of all by the mere fact of being human. That my God should be as myself—with soul and body, mind and heart, feelings and sensations (without sin), should certainly draw my interest. Then, He is not only Man, but a Man with a definite and well-marked career, a Name, a place of birth, a Mother; a history made up of marvellous facts, touching stories, beneficent deeds, Divine sayings, and mysterious sufferings. There is not one point in all this history on which I cannot fasten my contemplation; not one which does not speak to me of the love and the designs of my God. Instead of gazing up into the blank heavens to try, in vain, to find out what He is like, I have only to think of the little Child, the Boy of Nazareth, the Preacher on the Mount, the Sufferer of Calvary. Had He simply been made Man, and rested on the earth in some august seclusion, ministered to by angels and the universe, even then the bare fact would have afforded my mind and heart something on which to fasten their worship—something better suited to stir them than the pure spirituality of the Divinity. But, instead of that, Jesus has deigned to tread the stony and dusty paths of humanity. He has sought men out and lived among them, poor, travel-worn, and carrying humanity's burden. He has taken no privilege, but allowed fortune (as it is called), circumstances, the chances of life, and the forces of elemental nature, to jostle and buffet Him as they do the least of His creatures. He has joined Himself to men on the way—the way which human feet have to tread; and it is our own fault if we do not recognise Him. It is this ineffable intimacy with mankind, and most efficacious interference in human concerns, of which the Psalmist speaks in the eighteenth Psalm. By the Incarnation, a new sun has appeared in the heavens, to cheer and fertilise the earth.[1] "As a bridegroom coming out of his bride-chamber" (of the inaccessible divinity)—"He hath rejoiced as a giant to run the way" (of human life).—"His going out is from the end of heaven, and His circuit even to the end thereof"—(for there is no point in the whole cycle of human joys and sorrows which His life has not touched and sanctified)—"and there is no one that can hide himself from His heat." No one; for although many men regard but little the Incarnate God, yet all history has been affected by it, and all humanity; and every man and woman of

[1] *Ps.* xviii.

the generations both before and after Bethlehem, has been wiser, happier, and nearer to God through the office of the Word made flesh. Well may we exclaim, in the concluding words of this Psalm, "The meditations of my heart shall be always in Thy sight, O Lord, my helper and my Redeemer!"[1]

How much more easy does the Incarnation make the grand human duty of worship! In the thirty-fifth psalm the inspired singer begins by blaming the sinner who lives on without the fear of God before his eyes. He goes on to describe how near God is to men; and this description of the nearness of God is evidently prophetic of the Incarnation. From the sixth verse onwards the four grand attributes which usually in this Psalm denote the Incarnation— "mercy, truth, justice, and judgment"—are the theme of the Psalmist. God's mercy is "in the heavens," that is, visible in the firmament; His truth is "in the clouds," which is a variation of the same phrase; so that God's "mercy and truth" are part of the earth's atmosphere and light. Next, it is said that God's "justice" is around man like the "mountains," and that His judgments are as visible as the seas and oceans; they form part of human existence. These attributes refer to the union of the humanity with the Divinity; and this grand dispensation brings God before our very senses. Then, as the sacred text goes on, the very "wings" of God seem to be over us, we share in the plenty and the

[1] *Ps.* v. 15

inebriation of His presence, and in new springs of life and light.

To worship God is man's essential act; for this he was created. Worship is a mental and intellectual act; the will and the mind must produce it, or it does not exist. But intense, continuous and hearty worship of God depends greatly upon the heart and feelings. Thus, in order to worship God, how much am I assisted by Bethlehem, by Nazareth, by Calvary! How easy it is to seek out the manger, and to fall down on my knees and adore the Babe Who lieth there! And as I adore, I know that I am adoring the Infinite God. How natural, in moments of prayer, to place before my eyes the obedient Jesus, the Jesus of poverty and hardship, the Jesus of the poor family of Nazareth—and how sweet to reflect that as I turn to His image, I turn to my God and my all! If I find it difficult to fix my mind upon heavenly thoughts and to keep my attention to spiritual things, how effectually am I helped therein by some piercing words of my Saviour, or by some beautiful act of His compassionate heart! Is it not true that my mainstay, my very rock in a desert land, is the sacred humanity—which gives me thoughts, aspirations and good resolutions? If I would express sorrow for my sins, I place His passion before my eyes. If I would thank Him for His graces and benefits, I fall down at His feet like the healed leper, or the grateful Apostle. And there is one most wonderful help to intense worship which is supplied by the Incarnation, and which could never have been foretold. What wisest man or most prescient angel could ever have foreseen that it would have been possible to worship the Infinite God by *compassion?* There is no deeper spring of loving service than compassion; for although it is in itself rather a feeling than spiritual adoration, yet it has a power which no other feeling has of disposing the heart to attachment and tenderness. Pity is a feeling which seems to stir up and liquefy all the numerous component parts of our nature; so that a devotion which before was cold, dry and unemotional, becomes, through pity, warm, melting and enthusiastic. And we are allowed to pity the God-man! When we meditate on the sorrows and the sufferings of Jesus, and offer Him our compassion, we are really adoring the God of heaven. When we follow Him in the *via dolorosa*, or hold His crucifix in our hands and weep over it, our tears are acts of worship of the Almighty; and in proportion to the ease with which they flow is the ease with which the Incarnation enables us to use our beings in the adoration of Him Who made us. "O surely His salvation is near! . . ."[1] Mercy and truth have met each other; justice and peace have kissed." O eternal Lord, Who dost stoop so low to draw me near and to lift me up; why must I be for ever immersed in my indifference and my trifling, and thus neglect so precious a salvation?

[1] *Ps.* lxxxiv. 10.

Why do I live so wholly without Thy sacred Humanity? Why is not my prayer more lovingly concerned with Thee—my recollection more strenuously taken up with Thee?

There are persons whose disposition it is to consider that the essence of the spiritual life is rather "improvement" (or "progress") than love and worship. Doubtless, true spirituality implies progress. But it is a deep mistake to suppose that the best progress is made by efforts to acquire virtues and to root out vices. Such efforts must be made; but there is another and a better way (which, at the same time, does not dispense us from making efforts). That other way is the contemplative union of our intelligence, will, and heart with the Sacred Humanity of Jesus Christ. For that Sacred Humanity has a most powerful, and almost miraculous, efficacy of transformation. Laden with our weakness and imperfection, we gaze upon Jesus, and they begin to melt away and disappear. An hour, or half an hour, of devout contemplation of His obedience, His patience, His humility, His love of suffering, will change our poor natures for the better more effectively than many days of striving to practise these virtues, were such practice unaccompanied by the contemplation here described. This seems indeed only what might have been expected, if we consider:—

First, that the Sacred Humanity was intended to heal our bruises and to bind up our wounds. Our Lord came to give us Heaven, but also to give us grace; and grace, as we see from the enumeration of the gifts of the Spirit,[1] means not merely sanctifying grace strictly so called, but the healing of the intellect, which is wounded by ignorance,—of the will, which is weak and perverse,—of the reason, which is subject to blindness,—of the heart, which is attracted by folly and vanity,—of the affections, which are drawn to creatures,—of our courage, which is apt to fail in arduous things,—and of our imagination, which is subject to human respect and is with difficulty impressed with the fear of God. The good Samaritan, pouring oil and wine into the wounds of the unfortunate wayfarer, is the figure of our Lord healing fallen and despoiled humanity. How are we to share in this healing? In many ways; but whether it be by Sacrament, or by infused grace, or in whatever way the gift may come, it must always imply the use of our powers and faculties in looking on Jesus and loving Him. In the Sacraments, He does much more than our dispositions go. But even with the Sacraments, and even with the most mighty Eucharist, we must always in some way turn to Him; and the more interior and complete is our turning to Him the more He heals us. Indeed, the correlative of the Sacramental dispensation is the living in the presence of the Sacred Humanity; so that all our prayers may be, as it were, a preparation for Sacraments; a stretching out of hands and lifting up of voice like those of old who cried from afar, "Jesus!

[1] *Isaiah* xi.

Master! have mercy on me!" in order that there may come to us that touch of the hand and that healing word which is to save us.

But, in the second place, our Lord expressly wishes us to "come to Him," in order to be relieved of our burdens and to be refreshed. What burdens are these? Not merely mortal sin, though that burden is a terrible one; not sufferings, because the Cross is just the thing which He wishes to lay upon us. These burdens are our pride, self-love, impatience, laziness, dissipation and cowardice. Whilst oppressed with these, we cannot but groan and faint; relieved of these, we are eased and refreshed, because we are contented and at peace. It is to deliver us from these that He says, "Come to Me!" How are we to come? By frequent contemplation of His human and Divine life, with all its points and circumstances; by employing our minds and hearts on Him; by continually uniting ourselves to Him.

And, thirdly, there is in the contemplation of the Sacred Humanity a certain power of transforming our *hearts* into the likeness of itself, by a certain sympathy which it creates in us. The abysses of our Lord's most perfect virtues and endowments reveal themselves by degrees to one who gazes in prayer upon their depths. Just as the long continuance of a grand musical note makes all sonorous things around vibrate in unison, so the unfathomable annihilation, humanity and obedience of Christ touch the chords in our own beings which correspond; and we find ourselves lowly, submissive, self-forgetting. Just as one gazing in silence and solitude on the strong unbroken flow of a full river feels his being occupied and filled with a sensation which seems to devour or push out all other sensations, so when the thought rests in prayer on the powerful, perennial, unbroken, mysterious flow of the fulness of the Sacred Heart—Its devotion to God, Its firm choice of suffering, and Its utter and absolute spiritual life— even our imperfect natures seem for the moment to be lifting themselves up in union with that Heart, and each hour of such union makes us more and more resemble Him. Thus the saints found, in prayer before the Sacred Humanity, their book, their lesson, their mirror, their transformation. The same things shall we find if we approach Him with affection, with devotion, and with persevering service. For a mere glance at our Lord will not suffice; neither will a passing fit of devout feeling before the Crucifix or the Blessed Sacrament on Christmas night or during the sacred hour before Good Friday. We must persevere; we must study how to approach Him and how to occupy ourselves with Him; we must have our regular time of mental prayer, and be faithful to it. Such contemplation of the Sacred Humanity is far from being passive idleness or lazy sentiment. Preparation, attention, the excitation of the will, the humble exposition of our miseries, the making of devout petitions, the deploring of our past sinfulness and negligence, the energetic union of our heart with the Sacred Heart of Jesus in all its desires and designs—these things demand effort, and no slight effort. Such effort we are bound to make; and if our loving Saviour, after we have toiled awhile, lifts us up and speeds us more easily on our course, that is His goodness; we may hope for it, but we cannot expect it as a right. Nevertheless, as Moses and David and St. Paul have said, there is no one who is so loyal or "faithful"[1] as our Lord and God; and He will never fail those who do that which His word is always urging them to do, that is, "seek" Him.[2]

POINTS FOR MENTAL PRAYER.

1. Run over in your mind the principal features of the Incarnation; how God willed it from eternity, the world longed for it, most holy Mary was created for it; how Jesus was born in the stable of Bethlehem, lived in the cottage of Nazareth, sought men's souls in Judea and Galilee, suffered on Calvary, and rose again the third day triumphant in order to be the living source of the world's spiritual life. Reflect how all this Divine Counsel was intended to work upon your soul; to sanctify you; to leave its impress upon your childhood, your youth, your maturity, your vocation, your employment, your success, your failure, your happiness and your sorrows. Towards this tender Saviour, then, make

[1] *Deut.* xxxii. 4. *Ps.* cxliv. 13.
[2] 1 *Cor.* x. 13. 1 *Thess.* v. 24.

acts of *longing* such as the prophets and saints of old made in those times before He came. "O that Thou wouldst bend the heavens and come down!"[1] O Jesus! Seek my poor soul! Find me out! Discover Thyself to me! Be born in my heart—live in my bosom—speak to me—heal me—gather me in the darkness to the foot of Thy cross!

Make acts of *dedication*. Thou sayest, O my Saviour, "Come to Me". Behold, I wish to leave everything that hinders me in order to hasten to Thee! Thou sayest, "Learn of Me". I desire to learn, in all points and at every moment of my life, all that Thy holy life and death do teach! I long for Thy yoke! I long for Thy touch! I long for Thy saving word. Let my life, in all its details, take its form, shape, and colour from Thy Sacred Heart.

2. Exercise yourself upon your *burdens*. My God and Saviour! I lay at Thy feet my pride and vanity! O burning Fire, consume them utterly, and give me Thy lowliness!

I beseech Thee to look upon my self-love—and in the vehemence of Thy self-sacrifice for sinful man to annihilate in my heart all that feeds my miserable selfishness!

I pray Thee to take from me my impatience and heat of temper—and to pour upon my being the balm of Thy own meekness and humility!

I confess to Thee my sloth, indifference and cowardice, and I would cast them from me if I could,

[1] *Isaias* lxiv. 1.

and await a touch from Thy hand that should brace and strengthen me to do and to endure like Thy martyrs and confessors! O Lord, heal my soul, for I have sinned against Thee![1]

[1] Ps. x. 5.

XIII. THE HIDDEN LIFE OF OUR LORD.

In this meditation we have to find out, and to make our own, the grand principle of all spiritual activity and life—nothing less than the "Secret of Jesus". It is a secret which even good men and women too frequently fail to grasp; which is too often missed even by religious who have worn a holy habit and done holy things for many years. "I confess to Thee, O Father," cried out the Saviour of mankind, "because Thou hast hidden these things from the wise and prudent, and hast revealed them to little ones!"[1]

We are apt to think that great results for God's glory are achieved by God's saints in spite of their poverty, detachment and humility. The real truth is that these are precisely the weapons that win the battle—the material of the building, the root and branches which create and carry the fruit. What are "results" in the kingdom of God? The conversion of hearts, and their sanctification. What is it that can effect such results? Is it material force? No, certainly. For even if God's servants could command material resources, they could no more reach a human heart by means of these than

[1] *Matt.* xi. 25

the sword or the bullet could affect the course of a planet. Is it moral force? That is, words, example, personal influence? The heart of man is doubtless subject in this way to the power of other men. But consider how uncertain such influence must always be; how hap-hazard must be its application; how temporary its effect; how limited all the efforts of any man; how independent is the human spirit, and how fickle; and, lastly, how death inexorably destroys all that has been effected, and the work must be begun afresh with every generation. Alas! what philosopher, or reformer, what genius or discoverer, has ever possessed the heart or moulded the complete life of even a score of men in any generation? Yet the kingdom of God means the conquest of man's whole heart—mind, will and powers—and that in every generation.

We know very well that the virtues of our Blessed Saviour's life are the virtues that will best of all sanctify our own souls. But what we have to be persuaded of—thoroughly and warmly persuaded of —is, that they are also the generating forces of His kingdom. There is not one of us who is not zealous, in his sphere, for the promotion of the reign of Christ. Most of us have a line of work, of influence. We shall never work on sound principles until we understand that the humility and obedience of Jesus are the most mighty forces that exist, and (what is more) the only forces, practically speaking, that count.

Let us consider, then, the Hidden Life of Jesus.

We must remember that He had a stupendous work to do—to convert the world, and all generations of the world, to His love and service. He had precluded Himself from doing this by an exercise of His Almighty power—by an all-conquering flood of Divine grace. Had He acted so there would have been no need of an Incarnation. We assume that the world was to be brought to God and grace distributed, by the merit and efficacy of the acts of a human heart. How, then, did that Sacred Heart act? Jesus Christ might have had illimitable riches, influence, and material power. He might have been the greatest of the world's orators, philosophers, or poets. But He chose to have neither the material nor the intellectual; or rather—His right hand did really hold all the force and thunder of the universe, and His soul, even in its human endowments, was, when compared with the most sublime of possible intelligences, as the sun to the palest of the stars: but He would use none of it; He lived as though He had it not. And how did He live instead?

The holy narrative tells us that for thirty out of the thirty-three years of his earthly life, He was *hidden*. He chose to waste—as presumptuous critics would tell you—so many years of that time in the feebleness and uselessness of infancy. What reformer or regenerator, having the power to arrange things otherwise, would have condemned himself to the silent and humbling condition of an infant?

Even when He began to leave behind Him the things of a child, He still, and with greater intention and persistency, kept Himself hidden. What does the Evangelist tell us of the eighteen years that elapsed between His coming to the age of twelve and His beginning His public ministry at the age of thirty? Little more than this—" He went down to Nazareth and was subject to them".[1]

Observe these words. He goes "down,"—He did not seek to live in Rome, the capital of the world, whence He might have influenced the whole of civilised mankind; He would not even stay in Jerusalem—a provincial capital, where He would at least have had a chance of influencing the heads and the teachers of the Jewish race. He went "down"— away from society, education, books, news, and refinement.

He went into Subjection; that is, He chose, without any compulsion, to live in obedience, under the direction of those who, holy and wise as they were, were only human, whereas He was both God and Man. What good could it do to the world that He should ask Mary's leave, or take the directions of Joseph?

He "went down" and took up manual Labour; hard and real work of the most material sort. It is not only that His hands did this, Whose hands formed the heavens, the earth, and the sea;[2] but surely, of all kinds of labour, mere manual labour,

[1] *Luke* ii. 51   [2] *Ps.* xciv. 5.

when not necessary, is the least useful for the world!

He " went down " into Poverty. Can anything in this world be done without money? Is not a state of real, hard, grinding poverty a state which even a Saint would hardly look upon as one in which work could be done for God? Have not even religious founders hesitated to make poverty too absolute? The Sacred Heart of Jesus did not require the discipline of poverty. In It there was no attachment to the things of earth; It was detached, pure, and absolutely spiritual. We might have expected in our Lord's chosen home, modesty, moderation, sobriety: all this for good example's sake. But, instead of that, poverty—real want, insufficient food, comfortless lodging—was what He chose. Many a time, as a child, was there nothing for Him to eat! Many a time He had to suffer shame when asking for the wages of toil! Many a time was His toil, and the toil of Joseph and of Mary, long and severe. Hard was their bed, short their sleep, rough their living; and with all this they had to endure the contempt or the pity which exterior bad luck always brings with it.

As these conditions were deliberately chosen and taken up by Him Who was wisdom itself, with the purpose (which He had in view in all that He did) of winning souls to His kingdom, we, on our parts, have nothing to do but to try to understand and imitate Him.

Thus, first of all (if we wish to be like Him and to do anything for Him), we cannot do better than take up Solitude; aiming at being alone, not caring to know the great or to be in their company, not wishing to be talked of; and this although important interests are committed to us. Next, we must aim at Subjection; we must rejoice in a state of obedience, not for the wise direction or the safety which obedience brings (though this is a great advantage), but for the sake of the obedience itself. And if we do not live in a state where obedience is our duty, we are not safe until we find obedience of some kind. Further, we should take up Poverty. If we are really poor, we should love and cherish our state. If we are only relatively poor, we should take every occasion of feeling our poverty and accepting it lovingly. As far as permitted, we should cast away our possessions; how far this may be actually allowable we shall know by advice and by living such a life as to merit the interior light of the Holy Spirit. And, lastly, we must aim at a life of humble toil and hardship. At least, whatever share of this comes in our way should be welcomed. For it is one of the conditions of sanctification and of success.

These four things—Solitude, Obedience, Poverty and Labour—are what we may call the pillars of the holy House of Nazareth.

These conditions, however, are not, in themselves, the essence of the Hidden Life, or the full secret of

Jesus. They are rather, as we have said, "conditions"; conditions which help to concentrate the soul upon its interior, and to make the act of its union with God more intense and more continuous.

For the Hidden Life itself consists in that which is the only end, the only act, the only state, for which the soul was created; that is to say, the loving worship of its God. This is essential perfection —the more or less continuous and intense exercise of the act of charity. This it is which sanctifies, and which also leads to success. This act is what occupied the Sacred Heart of Jesus all these years. If we would imitate Him, we must do four things: First, we must give our attention to interior union with God; instead of being wholly taken up with the exterior. Secondly, we must attend to regular prayer, as a business. Thirdly, we must give ourselves to systematic spirituality—studying to understand the relations of our immortal souls with God, and with creatures. Fourthly, we must practise keeping ourselves at all times in the presence of God.

Our Lord and Saviour, then, chose the four conditions we have named above, not for their own sakes, but for the better carrying on the act of His Sacred Heart—an act which in Him was absolutely continuous and more intense than any human language can express.

But it is these "conditions" which, after all, are the greatest revelation and the profoundest instruction as far as we are concerned. For we are more prepared to hear that sanctification and results depend upon our constant prayer and union with God, than to learn that it is only under these conditions that such interior union is anything like complete or perfect. This is the Secret of Jesus. For practice we may draw the following corollaries on the subject of the Hidden Life.

1. The Hidden Life means, not idleness, passive quietness, or empty silence, but very great activity of spirit. It means the most strenuous endeavour, by means of solitude, obedience, poverty and labour, to make the heart's union with its Creator as intense and as continuous as possible. And it implies the adoption, for this purpose, of the means referred to above.

2. The Hidden Life thus implies a great simplicity of view—the view that if we love God above all things, it is for Him to take care both of ourselves and of His other interests.

3. Hence, it means the absence of ambition. Place, position, power and money are the dread of one who understands the Hidden Life. Against the spirit which seeks these things we pray in the Psalm "Turn away my eyes that they look not on vanity,"[1] —for all is vanity, except to be at home in the familiarity of God. The Saints never wearied of protesting to God that He alone was sufficient for them—He was their portion, their inheritance, their staff, their glory and their riches.

[1] *Ps*. cxviii. 87.

4. In the same way, the Hidden Life cuts down vain-glory, jealousy and anxiety about results. The imitator of Jesus sees that, except through that loving union with God which draws down grace, nothing can be effected either in one's own soul or in the world. Thus the apparent success of one's own eloquence, persuasiveness or skill, is often only apparent, not real—quite short-lived and unimportant; whereas the success which flows from the action of the hidden spiritual heart of a true servant by God is as certain and solid as the promises of God—though we, perhaps, may never see it come to pass. Neither can jealousy live long in a heart which is convinced that personal prominence is infallibly a drawback to success—unless accompanied by the spirit which dreads and detests personal prominence. And as for results, when one knows that an immediate success is often a disguised failure, and that, on the other hand, the prayer, or the suffering, or the prayerful activity of the truly hidden heart is as infallibly certain of result, somewhere in God's wide kingdom, as the circles on the water after the fall of the stone, one heeds but little what short-sighted persons christen failure or success.

5. The understanding of the Hidden Life leads not only to a well-ordered and severe life in greater things, but to a constant watchfulness over ourselves in small things and the avoidance of small relaxations—at least, without a really good motive. For

we understand that fervour and generosity unite the heart to God, whereas tepidity and laxity divide us from Him.

6. The Hidden Life inclines the servant of God to be, if possible, actually hidden. To be really and physically out of men's sight is evidently neither necessary nor at all times possible. But the Saints and those enlightened by the secret of Jesus, have always loved to be, as far as they could, really unknown; to be condemned, to be in subjection, and to have no external influence or authority.

7. The Hidden Life means that prayer has a predominating place in our lives. Thus, regularity and fidelity to times of prayer, the study of prayer, the practice of recollection, the love of spiritual reading and of visits to the church and the Blessed Sacrament—these things flow from the understanding that only one occupation is really essential and powerful in results—that is, the loving union of the heart with its Maker. And they lead by degrees to a prayer which is more or less continuous, as in the Saints.

8. Hence external occupation, and even important, anxious and absorbing business, is not incompatible with the Hidden Life. It may be God's will that one has to be thus occupied; the essential thing is, not to trust to what is done by hand or tongue or brain, but only to the spiritual activity—the busy elevation of the heart, intensified by silence and hardship—which may well go on in the most active

of lives. At least, if these things do not go on, that active man has begun active life too soon, and had better go back to learn his elements; for all his brilliancy and power will otherwise turn to smoke, as far as God's kingdom is concerned. Neither should any one thrust himself into doing more than his duty—that is, into taking up what there is no sign of God's will for him to take up. Intensify duty, but do not of your own motion add to external occupation. Sedulously cultivate indifference to the kind, amount and continuance of external work. Often check yourself in work, pausing to rectify motives, to purify intentions, and to repent of vanity, self-satisfaction and jealousy. This should chiefly be done in the times of quiet prayer. To prayer itself be scrupulously faithful. And often long after such a solitude as may enable you to live in humility, to know God better, to repent of your sins and to immolate yourself for the advancement of His kingdom.

Points for Mental Prayer.

1. Place before the eyes of your soul the holy Home of Nazareth. Behold Mary and Joseph, devout, silent, laborious; and behold Jesus—hidden, poor, subject, working, neglected, unknown. Make an act of *adoration*. I adore Thee, O sweet Jesus, my God! It is to draw me to love Thee that Thou hast taken upon Thee the lowliness of human nature, and the poor surroundings in which I see

Thee now! Be Thou adored, praised and thanked for ever and ever. An act of *admiration.* What other friend would have done so much for me? What mind would ever have devised so wonderful a dispensation? What power could have effected so stupendous an operation? The eternal God in this Child of poor parents under the roof of a humble cottage! An act of *compassion.* Accept, O my Divine Lord, the love of my heart in alleviation of Thy labours and hardships! Would that I could have helped Thee in Thy toil, shielded Thee from the heat, stood between Thee and the scorn of men, saved Thy Sacred Heart from some of its bitter sufferings!

2. Contemplate, one by one, the characteristics of His life at Nazareth. Observe the Simplicity of His view—*God alone.* O my Saviour, give me grace to aim at God alone! Hitherto I have aimed at many things—at the satisfaction of my vanity, of my flesh, of my ambition, of those about me! Hitherto my best actions have been tainted and spoilt by earthly, human, carnal and degrading motives! All this I now turn away from. Do Thou pierce my heart and penetrate it with the one grand purpose of my creation—the will to live for my God! Then observe His Holy Indifference. The Everlasting Word handles the tool of the workmen, and shapes mean material into humble articles of use! Give me, O light of my life, the grace to take up what is low as heartily as what is dignified, and what is

flattering as simply as what is humbling, and to see Thee beneath it all, and Thee alone! Lastly, His continuous and intense Elevation of the Heart. Oh! foolish and mistaken heart of mine! I fatigue my brain, my fancy, my tongue, my limbs,—and all the time, one thing is really necessary—to worship, to love, to offer up, to accept, to beg forgiveness! My Jesus, give me Thy Spirit!

3. O Jesus of Nazareth, obscure, silent and suffering, I *detest* all that is contrary to that Spirit of Thine. I detest unnecessary talk, which empties my spirit! I detest that coveting, that clinging, that having and holding, which binds me down to the earth! I detest the vanity of esteem and of success! I long and pray that my life may be hidden with Thee in God!

XIV. THE PUBLIC LIFE OF OUR LORD.

THE preceding meditation will have given us the key, or the secret, of the public life and the exterior apostolate of Our Blessed Lord and Saviour. The reason why it was so short in comparison with His Hidden Life, and why His whole career on the earth was so brief, is not always clear, even to spiritual persons. Human prudence would have suggested, not only that every hour should have been made the most of for preaching and organising, but that a life such as that of the Incarnate Son of God should have been prolonged to the utmost, so that two and three generations should have had the privilege of sitting at His feet and of hearing Him speak, Who spoke as never man spoke. But "My thoughts are not your thoughts, nor your ways My ways, saith the Lord".[1] These words are never so true and significant as when applied to the labours of the workmen in the Lord's vineyard. For exterior work —the work of preaching and persuading, of building and administering—is in very truth of the least possible use, as work. It effects nothing of itself; whatever it does effect is by the intensity of interior acts. It is doubtless true that there must be certain

[1] *Isaias* lv. 8.

ministrations for various reasons. There is a visible Church; men must gather together, pray together and partake of Sacraments together. There must be in the world that humble and childlike spirit which hears the word of God in the utterances of man and sees in a poor weak mortal the Heavenly Father Himself. There must be the warmth of inter-communion and the powerful influence of good example. For such reasons as these there must be external labour. But let us understand its value, and whence that value arises.

Jesus passes through the towns and the ways of Judea and of Galilee; He preaches, He calls disciples, He works miracles—and the whole country is stirred up before Him. The sacred narrative places this before us for our instruction and consolation; and what are the lessons that we can gather therefrom?

1. Let us observe, first, that Jesus, before He went out to preach, had thoroughly learned the Hidden Life. The Hidden Life, as we need not say, was in truth His own Sacred Heart. But although He needed neither instruction nor practice, yet He would live all those years, studying Obedience, interrogating Poverty, listening to Obscurity and Suffering. There, according to the prophecy of Habacuc, "there was His strength hid".[1] "O Lord, Thy work," exclaims that holy prophet in words which are often chanted at penitential seasons

[1] *Habacuc* iii. 4.

—" Thy work"—Thy grand work of the redemption of men—" bring it to life in the midst of the years!" He came down to do this—He came, God, the Holy One, from the burning " South" of His heavenly kingdom—He came with all His glory, covering the heavens and filling the earth; but "there"—in Thy Incarnation, at Bethlehem, at Nazareth—"there was Thy strength hid". And how great was the work which Jesus had to do, and which that Hidden Life effected! Death fled before His face. He stood and measured the earth; He melted the nations; the hills of the world were bowed down before Him; the tents of Ethiopia and of Madian, types of the vices of the flesh, were swept away; the floods passed by, the deep lifted up its hands, the sun and moon stood still.[1] This has been Christ's work in the world; the work of the Hidden One of Nazareth.

But we refuse to learn this lesson. We come out into the streets and among men, before we have put our armour on. We speak before we have learned to be silent; we would command before we have known what it is to obey; we mount upon pinnacles and into high places before we have felt in our souls the wise and salutary fear of all that flatters vanity and self-love. Moreover, we fill our life too full. Work is taken up—for God's sake, as we vaguely persuade ourselves—but really for excitement, for change, in mere overflow of spirits, or in reprehen-

[1] *Habacuc* iii. 11.

sible good-nature. We take up so much, or we so unsparingly throw ourselves into it, that prayer and recollection are impossible, or very difficult. And as human motives have so much to do with taking up our work, so vanity and self-love keep us to it—or, on the other hand, cause us to relax in it, or to leave it for something else. As long as we succeed—that is, seem to succeed—we are in good spirits, active, energetic; but the moment we meet with failure we grow discouraged, unhappy, despondent, and we probably cease to labour. Yet, behold our King! "All the day long," as He tells us by one who sung of Him in spirit, "all the day long"—during all His life, in all His apostolic career—" I stretched out My hands to a people that contradicted."[1] His efforts were met by resistance and by contempt, and there seemed to be utter failure. Yet never did these blessed Hands cease to be stretched out wide, inviting all, blessing all! May my hands be like to the Hands of Jesus! May my labour be supernatural like His! . May my toils and pain for the sake of immortal souls, wherever my lot is cast, never cease, as His never ceased, but be carried on to the end for His sake, and for His sake alone!

2. The second lesson that we learn from His public life is that all external work should be work of obedience. Although His most sacred human soul was profusely and absolutely enlightened by

[1] *Rom.* x. 21.

the gifts of the Holy Ghost, yet He would not be directed even by the wisdom, the counsel, or the prudence which filled it. What He took up, if the phrase may be used, was what His Heavenly Father laid upon Him to do. He calls it, "My Father's business". He looks up to heaven as He prays for His beloved ones and exclaims, "Yea, O Father, for so it was pleasing in Thy sight".[1] He went to His passion—the climax and the crown of His external work—because so it was ordained from eternity. The Prophets sung His obedience,[2] and the Apostles celebrated it.[3] Poor weak men and women, on the contrary, seek for employments, and even for dignity and responsibility. A man, who is not without enlightenment in spiritual matters, will complacently put himself in the way of an appointment, even if he does not suggest it himself, or perhaps scheme for it. The dignity of the priesthood is too often looked for with feverish impatience, which breaks out into words if one seems to be kept back. The Saints, imitating Jesus, dreaded the awful responsibility of the priestly office. Superiorship, which they feared like an occasion of sin, has no terrors for the empty heart which its Saviour's spirit has not filled. In the field of the Apostleship, and in the various careers of the active life, with men and with women, there is preference, choice, contention and self-will; and holy indifference, that touchstone of what is pleasing to God, that pledge of real success, is not

[1] *Matt.* xi. 26.   [2] *Isaias* liii. 7.   [3] *Philippians* ii. 8.

found even in the cloister. And, in the world, how few there are who strive to recognise in the work which they have to do—in the gaining of their bread and the maintenance of their families—the ordinance, will and loving providence of their Heavenly Father! Work or employment is endured; what it brings in is grasped with satisfaction; but in itself it is not lovingly accepted; and when it is hard or uncongenial there are too often murmurings and sinful impatience. O Jesus! teach us to take our work and labour from Thy hand!

3. A third lesson, and one of the most important, that we learn from the Life of Jesus, is the lesson of the intermittence of external work. In the midst of His preaching our Blessed Lord is recorded to have said to His Apostles, "Come apart and rest awhile".[1] It is certain that both He and they spent many hours apart from men, either on the solitudes of the mountains or in lonely places by the lake or near the gates of cities. His public life, after thirty years' seclusion, was preceded by forty days of silent meditation in the desert. His passion was begun by that most awful act of solitary communication with God upon the Mount of Olives. It was finished by three hours' silent agony and intense activity of the Sacred Heart amid the darkness of Calvary. Shall not we try to work in this spirit? First, we must offer up our work. Next, we must check ourselves in it from time to time, in order to purify motives, to reject vanity, to

[1] *Mark* vi. 18.

stifle temper and jealousy, to beat off those humiliating passions which, like the small winged creatures of some climates, would sting us into a fever if they could touch us. Then we must sanctify each step of our work by constant elevations of the heart to God; taking advantage of the hours that strike, of the scene that changes, of the progress that we make to place everything again and again at the feet of our Father in Heaven. Neither should we omit to offer Him our sorrow for what we do amiss, and to pray for pardon for the numerous sins and imperfections which gather inevitably on all the work we do. Most important is the duty of regular prayer, that is, of our daily mental prayer, morning and evening. It is this which most closely corresponds with that "retirement" and that holy "rest" of which we find in our Lord's life the venerated example. One who, for his work, neglects his mental prayer, condemns his work to sterility, his intelligence to darkness, and his heart to the loss of the spiritual sense. Obedience may, for one occasion, or for two, oblige us to defer or omit mental prayer; but no duty, and no superior, can oblige us to omit it for a considerable time, or can justify us in doing so. If we have the privilege of saying the Divine Office, the sanctification of work is thereby made the more easy. How fervent is the prayer of the choir—or even of the priest's quiet hour in the church, or in his chamber! How refreshing to the spirit is that rest which is sanctified by sweet words of psalms, consoling examples of Saints, and precious aspirations to God! How mistaken is the busy man who hurries over the "work of God"![1] Regular retreats are another means of imitating the "retirement" of Jesus. A retreat stirs up fervour, wipes away sin and sinful habits, brings light to the spirit, and lifts up one's whole life to the plane of the supernatural. Once a year, at least, the active worker should retire with Jesus into solitude, in order to drink in His spirit. "This is My rest," said the Lord in the prophecy of Isaias; "this is My refreshing."[2] There were men in those days who would not listen. "The priest and the prophet have been ignorant"—too ignorant!—"they have not known Him that seeth"—not known where to find Jesus, where to form their hearts on His. No wonder that His work in the world is badly done, and that sinners are not converted, when the ministers of Jesus are thus "ignorant of judgment".

4. Fourthly, we are taught, by the contemplation of the active life of Jesus, not to be afraid of failure, disappointment and natural disgust. Nay, more; we learn from it that "the Cross" is the pledge and the earnest of success; insomuch that all work in which the Cross is not felt is so far doomed to barrenness. One of the greatest temptations of those who work for God is to relish and cherish the good spirits which accompany meritorious labour, and to enjoy

---

[1] "Opus Dei"—St. Benedict's name for the Office, *Reg. cap.*
[2] *Isaias* xxviii. 12.

the elation of apparent success. On the other hand, uphill work, ingratitude, indifference to God's grace and constant relapse on the part of those for whom we are concerned—these things, which are naturally depressing, not unfrequently weaken our efforts and diminish our trust in God. That is, they disturb our interior, and thus prove to us how strong is our self-love still. It is true that the natural elation which comes from successful accomplishment, and the joy of labour itself, are not sinful, but only natural. But they lead us away from purity of intention—that is, unless we are on our guard. And they mean another thing also, which is not so much noticed by spiritual persons; they denote the absence of the Cross, and therefore (so far) the absence of any certainty that our work will be really productive and successful. The sermon which is easily written and really eloquent—which moves the listeners, excites visible approbation, and sends the preacher out of the pulpit with the agreeable feeling that people are only deterred by delicacy from congratulating him—such a sermon, it may be feared, will pass away like an empty sound. But if the preacher have struggled with distaste and disinclination, striven against pain and heaviness or worked under the stress of some cruel anxiety—then he may humbly hope that God has chosen that sermon to do His own work. So if he have failed in its delivery, or come short of what he could have expected—the natural pang thence resulting, if humbly and lovingly accepted, may be trusted to do far more than any persuasive words of human eloquence. And this, in its degree, is true of all labour for the Kingdom of God—whether that of superiors, of pastors, of missionaries, of teachers, of masters, of parents, or of writers. For our Lord Jesus Christ worked under the oppression of disgust, under the clear apprehension of the ingratitude of men, in the face of bitter disappointment, and under the constant weight of the Cross either actual or vividly foreseen; there can be no other earnest of successful work for God's Kingdom. In the Psalm *Salvum me fac Deus*[1] which describes so touchingly the constant interior sufferings of Christ, the final verses speak of the saving of Sion, the rebuilding of the cities of Juda, and the triumphant occupation by God's children of their everlasting inheritance. Those who have been with the Son of Man in His tribulation, who have been near Him when the waters went over His head, and the tempest submerged Him—they it will be whose work, with Him, will be found to have built up the heavenly Sion. O my Divine Master, give me Thy light to understand this! Show me how in my work for Thee I ought to dread pleasantness, facility and elation! Give me the strength to pray for the bitter but saving taste of Thy Cross in all that Thou dost permit me to do!

POINTS FOR MENTAL PRAYER.

1. Place before your eyes your loving Jesus in His

[1] *Ps.* lxviii.

earthly labour. Behold Him exercising the humble occupations which He vouchsafed to take on Himself in the holy house. Behold Him toiling along the ways of Galilee, preaching from Peter's boat, instructing sinners, comforting the mourners, healing the sick, rebuking the Pharisees. *Adore* your God, who deigns to do all this for your soul's sake, and to draw you nearer to Him. *Offer* Him your fervent thanks. Fix yourself in the *affectionate contemplation* of it all, desiring to learn all He has to teach you, exclaiming, O Jesus, teach me!

2. Contemplate His *Purity of Intention*. O my Lord and Master, cause me to love Thy will, to aim at Thy glory, to seek in all things Thy interests! His *constancy*. Jesus, my Lord, make me courageous in carrying on Thy work; strengthen me against depression; make me indifferent to merely visible results! His *love of the Cross*. Give me, O Christ Jesus, the light of Thy Holy Spirit to understand the value of the Cross! Lay it upon me, O Lord, but give me at the same time grace to carry it with Thee!

3. *Lament* at His feet for the *defects* in your external work. First, your *sloth*. Whilst souls are perishing, O my Divine Master, I have slumbered and rested! Whilst Thou hast spent Thyself, I have been easy and indifferent! Forgive my sluggishness! Forgive my love of ease! Forgive my self-seeking! Your *vanity*. I confess to Thee, O my hidden Redeemer, that I have cherished proud

thoughts, uttered many words of vanity, shown myself again and again to be full of foolish complacency. At Thy feet I lay the burden of my vain imaginations, that Thy shadow may consume them for ever! The *absence of the supernatural* in your labour. I have worked for the world, for human respect, for fear, for affection—but how little for Thee! I have worked, but I have not prayed! I have shortened my minutes in Thy light, and neglected to seek Thy spirit in retirement! Enlighten my culpable blindness, O Thou Light of the soul! Teach me Thy secret! Pardon my absorption, my forgetfulness, my living so much without Thee! Look on Thy servants, O Lord, and on Thy work, and direct them! May the light of the example of the Lord our God be upon us! Vouchsafe, O Jesus, to direct by Thy own Divine rules all the work of our hands! [1]

[1] *Ps.* lxxxix. 16.

XV. THE SUFFERINGS OF CHRIST.

No aspect of our Blessed Lord's life is made so much of by the Saints as His sufferings; and at the same time nothing is so neglected, or indeed contemned, by unbelievers and by worldly Christians. "All the Saints," says St. Alphonsus, "cherished a tender devotion towards Jesus Christ in His Passion; this is the only means by which they sanctified themselves."[1] "He who desires," says St. Bonaventure, "to go on advancing from virtue to virtue, from grace to grace, should meditate continually on the Passion of Jesus."[2] Indeed, the sufferings of the God-Man are the most mysterious part of the mystery of the Incarnation. He could have redeemed us without them. Even His Divine wish to satisfy for us to the utmost rigour of justice would have been fulfilled by the shedding of a single tear, the sacrifice of one only drop of His blood;—either of these acts would have sufficed to atone to the full for the sins of ten thousand worlds. On the other hand, it were blasphemy to say that God rejoices in human suffering, as such; to hold,

[1] *Reflections on the Passion* p. 15 (Centenary edition).
[2] See the whole of the First Part of the *Stimulus Divini Amoris*.

as heretics have done, that God imputed human sin to Him, and delighted in the agonies which that sin brought upon Him. Why, then, did He choose to suffer? and to suffer so terribly that, as His interior suffering and sadness was greater than any other earthly anguish could be, so His bodily suffering was more intense than mortal man has ever endured?

The reason, as we learn from the Saints, is that suffering gives a certain kind of intensity to acts of the will, which nothing else can give. It is this which recommended it especially to a Heart desirous of proving to men the reality and the depth of its love.

"The first cause of the Passion," says St. Thomas of Aquin, "was that He wished it to be known how much God loved man."[1] It is not difficult to understand the connection. An act of the will, or, as we say, of the heart, may be strong and intense; but unless it is done under stress of pain, it is wanting in a certain species of intensity. You may test this in your own experience. There is a moment when, let us say, you kneel before the altar of God, happy, contented, peaceful, and full of joy; your heart lifts itself up to God in sweet and earnest prayer, and your whole being experiences the feeling that to love God and to belong to Him is indeed the only delight that existence could offer. Then, let us suppose, you are suddenly pierced by some sharp

[1] *De Passione*, sect. 6.

THE SUFFERINGS OF CHRIST.

arrow of suffering; by some loss, grief, scorn, or physical pain, which in an instant diffuses the fire of throbbing anguish through your mental and physical being. Observe what happens. Up to that moment you were unconscious of self. Things ran so smoothly, so peacefully, so pleasantly, that you seemed to have merged your weak nature in God and God's love; and, as far as it went, your adhesion to God was genuine. *Now* there instantly starts up into sight, your *self*—with all its susceptibility and selfishness; your self, which comes and stands importunate beside you, protesting, crying, wailing, resisting. Thereupon, one of two things happen: either your adhesion to God is broken, your recollection scattered, and your loving activity stopped dead, by your attention to that hurt and smarting self; or else you refuse to be turned from God even by the excess of pain, you seize the pain itself and offer it, turning it into fuel to feed the flame of your heart, and so you intensify indefinitely the act of your union and your love. One of these two effects pain always has. It spoils many people. There are numbers of pious hearts who have been turned away from God by suffering. Self and its claims to attention have been too strong; and then piety has given way to self-pity, to murmuring, to resistance, to bitterness. It is thus with many who have to undergo punishment; with many of the young, unless their punishment is judiciously managed, and they are induced to accept it. Punishment and pain in general, far too frequently embitter the heart, turn it from its last end, and harden it in perversity. But if a man under suffering have the light and the grace to accept it, in submission, in resignation, and with a closer movement to the bosom of our Heavenly Father, then, never, never has his love of that Father in heaven been more thorough, more effective, and more intense!

It need not be added, that this mysterious element of suffering, with which Jesus willed to raise to a whiter heat the acts of His Sacred Heart, is also marvellously adapted to draw to Him the hearts of all men. There is a well-known phrase of St. Bonaventure—*Vulnera corda saxea vulnerantia, mentes congelatas inflammantia*—" Wounds of Jesus, that pierce hard hearts and melt the frozen breast!" It is not only that His sufferings proclaim His love, but that the sight of suffering causes pity and compassion; and when once the heart is touched by pity, all the emotions of nature are stirred to their depths and take part in making love and union easy. "Quæsivit nos infirmitate Sua," says St. Augustine. He would win us by His weakness. Thus, meditation on the Passion has been the grand occupation of all holy souls. Thus, again, the simple hearts of God's people, wherever the Catholic spirit has been saved from the world's taint, have ever shown themselves sensible to the words of any preacher who preached Christ crucified. "And I, if I be lifted up, will draw all things to Myself."[1]

[1] *John* xii. 82.

Oh! what arrows of fire hast Thou cast at our hearts from that throne of Thine—Thy holy Cross! Oh! how many souls hast Thou drawn to Thee there, and rescued from the jaws of hell!

We cannot, then, make too much of the stupendous fact that Christ suffered—and suffered all His life— in every variety of pain and anguish beyond what it was possible for mere mortal men to suffer. Suffering in the exercise of her divine and austere mission, was waiting for Him when He set His foot upon the earth. She stood beside the crib at Bethlehem, and accompanied Him in the wanderings of His infancy. She dwelt within the walls of the holy house, cherished by Jesus, Mary, and Joseph. When He went forth upon His Father's business, she trod the ways of Judea and Galilee by His side, and led Him by the hand to toil, to contempt, to ingratitude, to cold, and hunger, and watching. She caused Him to feel the sorrows of His Mother. She let Him taste the bitterness of being disowned by the high and by the lowly, rejected by His own people, distrusted by the little children. She wrung from Him, in the garden, that cry of anguish prophesied long before: "Save me, O God, for the waters have broken in even upon my soul!"[1] She beckoned Him to the pretorium, and to the mockery and horror of the crowning with thorns. She laid the Cross upon His bleeding shoulders, and went before Him on the road to Calvary. Then she stood

[1] *Ps.* lxviii. 1.

still on the mountain of myrrh and the hill of frankincense, where bitterness was to be supreme and sacrifice was to go up to the heavens; she stood still, and pointed to the Cross and the nails; and He said, "Behold, I come!" And when the Cross had been lifted up, suffering, for yet three hours, lingered in the silence of the darkness; for yet three hours—and then her mission was at an end; and, as when a dark cloud breaks and the rains stream upon the earth, suffering since that day has fallen on men and women in every age and over all the world, and every drop has been full of the fragrance of the Cross.

The Passion of our Lord and Saviour, therefore, is intended, first of all, to unite our hearts to His in that easy and sweet worship which is founded upon Compassion. It is intended, as we have said, to melt our hearts and to set our affections flowing. Thus, as unitive worship is the great purpose of our existence, and as the Cross of Jesus supplies us with such an easy way to worship and union, that Cross should never be far away from the interior occupation of all who live in order to love God. Mental prayer should often take the Passion for its subject; we should follow with loving care each step of Him Who bore our sorrows, from the Supper even to Calvary. Especially should this be the object of our contemplations during the season of Lent. But there are souls who, at all times, feel greater devotion in thinking on the sufferings of

Christ than in any other kind of prayer. Let them follow that attraction. No other will draw them nearer to Christ. What we think over in the morning should not be forgotten during the whole day. To turn to God frequently during the day is what we should all aim at—in order that by degrees the heart may dwell almost continually in God's presence, by adoration, oblation, petition, and satisfaction. Nothing assists the heart in this so much as the thought of Christ suffering. O my God, Who didst die for the love of me, let me die for the love of Thee! My crucified Saviour, do with me what Thou wilt! Jesus, scourged, mocked, spit upon, give me Thy love!

Above all, the great and fundamental disposition of continual sorrow for sin is wonderfully promoted by the constant remembrance of the Passion. *Te ergo, quæsumus, Tuis famulis subveni, quos pretioso sanguine redemisti!* "We beseech Thee, therefore, help Thy servants, whom Thou hast redeemed by Thy precious blood!" How sweetly does this invocation lift the heart to the Source of all hope—to the most sure and fitful trust in the love of our Heavenly Father! How can He not come to our assistance against sin when He has redeemed us with His precious blood! And how can my heart tolerate sin any longer when sin has bowed my Saviour's head in the agony, Sin has torn His flesh at the scourging, Sin has pierced Him with the thorns, Sin has nailed Him to the Cross! The repetition of acts suggested by such considerations is a powerful help to union with God.

(3) The saying or hearing of Mass should be made profitable by devotion to the Passion. Let us never forget that the Holy Eucharist has been given us in order to commemorate the Passion; and that the Mass is not only a memorial of His Death, but is a true and real renewal of His most loving sacrifice of Himself on the Cross. How, then, can we better assist at Mass than by recalling the circumstances of His Death? He who is present at the most Holy Sacrifice is present at Calvary; he joins with Jesus in what is done; his prayers ascend to Heaven in company with the prayer of Jesus; and the power of the Precious Blood streams over him, unto sanctification, forgiveness of sins, and every kind of gift of the Holy Ghost. Much more true is this of the priest who is the Minister of the Mass. Often, then, in hearing Mass, let us have the details of the Passion before our thought, to assist our devotion. This is very profitable. It is useful also, and very full of devout help, to portion out the Canonical Hours, so as to make each of them a memorial of some scene of our Lord's sufferings; and to apply the pregnant words of psalm and canticle to this most moving of all subjects of human thought.

There is nothing that happens in which the heart will not be directed, profited, and lifted up by connecting it with the Passion. Especially will this be found true in the commonest of all the events of a life on earth—hardship, trouble, and sorrow. When these things come upon us, there is no solid comfort or support unless we leave self and creatures, and turn to God. To resist, to fret, to bewail ourselves, to give way to impatience, to seek consolation in sin or imperfection, to indulge in murmuring or in dissipation of spirit—these things palliate trouble; but they leave it rooted in the soul. Only one thing plucks it out, and that is to turn with it to Christ. My Lord and my Master, we may say to Him, Thou didst suffer—and suffer far more than this. To Thee, suffering was familiar; Thou didst choose it for Thy lot and Thy inheritance—and I, I dread it and refuse it! By Thy loving acceptance of pain, give me the courage to accept all that I have to suffer! By Thy meekness, extinguish the natural disturbance of my breast against those who injure me! By Thy lifting up of Thy Heart, teach me how to make use of physical pain! By Thy silence, help me to repress murmurs and complainings. By Thine ardent love of Thy heavenly Father, enable me to understand how affection may intensify my love of my God! Acts like this, made perhaps with the crucifix in hand, will calm the resistance and the outcry of nature, and will diffuse a holy peace and a brave resignation throughout our faculties, as if Jesus laid His hand upon us, and caused virtue to go out from Him, and healed our imperfections with the balsam of His own sovereign being.

We must understand, also, that suffering is intended to sanctify us; that is, to remove imperfections from our spiritual work: and this in three ways. First of all, suffering makes us *act more purely* for God, and less for self-gratification. For when devotion is sweet and pleasant, there is always danger of seeking ourselves in our devotion. But when the will must act in the teeth of the bitter and biting wind of pain and sorrow, then the heart lifts itself to God for God's only sake. This is more particularly true of involuntary sufferings. When we kneel down to our prayer, laden with the heavy weight of trouble, or throbbing with pain, our prayer, if we persevere in it, is likely to be pure. Not that it is wrong to seek consolation; but we must seek it in God, and not elsewhere; we must seek it by clinging to our cross, not by struggling against it. Such moments of oblation and resignation have a most powerful influence in detaching the heart from all that is earthly—from bodily satisfactions, from small vanity, from the love of success and the dread of failure. Oh what a sure sign it is that God wishes us to be perfect, and to attain to great union with Him, when He sends us sufferings! "Lord," said a dweller in the desert, "Lord, Thou hast forsaken me! Thou hast not visited me with suffering!"

Next let us remember that suffering is a means of *expiation*, and thus of fitting our own souls and those of others for immediate admittance to heaven. "Oh happy penance," said St. John of the Cross, "which has merited me so great a glory!" But numbers of those who suffer make no use of their opportunities. It is not enough to suffer; we have to accept and unite ourselves with Christ. Suffering, merely endured, has no merit. The mere vibration of the nerves or the smart of the spirit is of no value whatever. There must be the act of the heart. But how sweet an exercise it is when we feel the scourge, the thorns and the nails of Jesus Christ, to unite our hearts with His and to say: O my Saviour, the act of Thy heart, intensified by suffering, destroyed sin, chained the demon, saved the world, and opened the fountains of grace; use my few sufferings for the same grand work of expiation! They have no merit or efficacy of their own; but as long as I live in Thee and Thou in me, my sufferings do Thy work (however feebly), and minister to the expiation of my own sins and those of other men.

Thirdly, suffering sanctifies us by the power of *mortification*. The efficacy of mortification arises from its setting up in the soul a habit of self-restraint, which is one of our most valuable weapons in the spiritual life, when such self-restraint rests on supernatural motives. Now suffering, lovingly accepted, is essentially an exercise of the will, restraining the lower nature from pusillanimity and complaint, and turning it to God. Hence suffering tends to fix the soul fast in virtue and in union with Christ. This is that "blessed violence" of which our Lord and His

Saints speak; no stoical hardness, but a humble striving and refraining, following the example of Jesus. "What can be hard to bear," says St. Bernard, "when you gather up the bitternesses of your Saviour?"[1]

Points for Mental Prayer.

1. Place before your thought the Agony of our Lord in the Garden. Observe His Divine Face pressed to the earth, pale, with the red drops upon His brow. Behold in Him a model and pattern of prayer in Suffering. *Adore Him* in His sacred humanity, at this moment so truly human, with human trouble (such as makes up so large a part of human life), settled like a black cloud upon His soul. It was for you that He took upon Himself this burthen; you cannot understand one-thousandth part of its heaviness. *Compassionate Him;* and the more because so few think of Him in this His agony, or try to requite His love. *Make aspirations:* O Sacred Heart, that lifted Thyself up in acts of pure prayer under the stress of Thy agony, touch my cold heart with a spark of Thy fire, that I may learn to pray in the hour of sorrow and pain!

2. Or place before your thought the scene of the Scourging. Behold Him bound—lashed, bleeding. Try to understand that fiery agony, as you gaze on His quivering flesh, and hear His breath come quick

[1] *De Diversis*, 22.

and short. Then turn upon yourself. O my Jesus, it is I who scourge Thee! My sins are the whips! O hateful love of pleasure, which turns me from Thee, keeps my heart without piety, degrades me, plunges me even into mortal sin! Take it from me, O dear Lord Jesus, by the burning fire of Thy scourging! Or at least draw me near to Thy pillar, to Thy streaming blood, that I may be strong to suffer all things for Thy sake, rather than offend thee in one iota!

3. Or, consider the Crowning with Thorns. Behold your Saviour as a mock King, meek and silent, with that cruel circle on His brow. Behold, by a yet more inward look, how that Sacred Heart bows itself to all the ignominy, and embraces all the pain—not tolerating, but rather rejoicing in it. O virtue of the Sacred Heart, come out and transform this heart of mine! Penetrate my intellect and will, and burn up my pride and my selfishness! Burn up my wilfulness—my bitterness of judgment—my independence of spirit—my self-esteem! Burn up my unkindness—my petty vanities, which separate me from Thy sweet Spirit! And in the hour when smarting thorns come to pierce my sensitive nature, give me strength to welcome them, and to grow by slow degrees more and more like Thee!

XVI. THE HOLY SPIRIT.

The spiritual life, being in so many ways at variance with what nature and inclination would suggest, is not unfrequently hard, barren, and irksome to all of us. At such times, we are tempted to rebel, to repine, and to contemn all that we are taught to practise. The terms of spirituality, with its processes and its states, seem to be unreal; the hidden life, foolish; mortification, puerile and useless; and the world of grace, a realm of phantoms and shadows. At these moments the heart fails unless it has a friend whose hand and encouragement can be felt. And it is absolutely necessary for all who would not throw up spiritual endeavour, and turn back to nature, to imperfection, and to sin, to know where to find such a friend. That friend is, as need not be again said, God Himself. But He has vouchsafed us a most notable series of revelations as to His loving care of us, which we must now, by His help, consider.

We must first, then, be most firmly impressed with the great truth, that spirituality is not the following out of a programme, or the living up to a system; it is the service of a Father. The Father whom we serve is also God Almighty, the King of

Heaven and earth, and the Judge of the living and the dead. But none of His august titles can make Him any the less our Father. It is the practical forgetfulness of God's fatherly love which keeps so many blameless Christians at a distance from Him. *Pater amat vos*.[1] "The Father loveth you." We are no longer servants, but children. But many of us are quite content to be servants—outside the house, strangers to God's designs, unaffected by the demeanour of His affection. Duty, the saving of one's soul, the will of God, the glory of God—these are most holy motives; and when adequately entered into they express everything; but they are too often a mere disguise or cloak for coldness and want of filial piety.

It is revealed to us that God hath sent the Spirit of His Son into our hearts; and it is that Spirit which cries, "Abba, Father";[2] that is, which so invests us with the Sonship of Jesus and impregnates us with His dispositions that we turn to God with the child's cry of "Father" on our lips. How this Holy Spirit dwells in us and what endowments He brings with Him—sanctifying grace, Divine charity, living faith and hope, and the seven gifts—we have already considered. We are now to try to understand what He does in us and for us; to see how He is, most really and truly, not a dead quality or a metaphorical phrase, but a living and moving Power, a true and active Friend. "You shall know that I am the

[1] *John* xvi. 27.   [2] *Gal.* iv. 6

Lord . . . when I have put my Spirit in you; and you shall live, and I shall make you rest upon your own lands; and you shall know that I the Lord have spoken."[1] No man, O Lord, can live in peace in the promised land of Thy redeeming grace unless he well understands that Thy Spirit is with him!

On the night before His Passion our Blessed Lord gave His Apostles the great revelation about the Paraclete. This Comforter Whom Christ was to send, and Who was to take the place of Christ, was the Spirit of Jesus, the Spirit of truth—the Holy Ghost. Let us observe what a revelation is contained in His being sent, in order that He might take the place of Jesus. "I will ask the Father, and He will give you *another* Paraclete."[2] The office of the Holy Ghost, when Jesus should have gone, was that He should be to the disciples what Jesus had been before He went away. Our Lord Himself had been a "paraclete"; His spirit was to be "another" paraclete. The word is a sweet and comforting word. It means teacher, prompter, encourager, consoler, and best friend. And this was what our Blessed Saviour was to those who were with Him on earth. He taught them to believe, to pray, to endure. He filled them with courage to face the world. He inspired them with noble aspirations. He received them back to His love when they repented, and comforted them when their hearts were failing. He kept them near Him,

[1] *Ezechiel* xxxvii. 13, 14.   [2] *John* xiv. 16.

within the sound of His voice, within the influence of His merciful eye, drawing them closer and closer to Him with the love of a father and the tender solicitude of a mother. For Him they had left all things. They had no home but His company, no friend to compare with Himself, no master, no leader, no beloved hero but Him. At the moment when they began to understand that they were to lose His bodily presence—when their hearts were filled, not with sadness only, but with consternation, He takes occasion to let them know, in words solemnly repeated twice and thrice, that although He must depart, yet Another would be sent to take His place. Now, the Holy Spirit had been sent even from the beginning. He had "moved" over the waters; He had put order in the heavens; He had sanctified the Saints; He had spoken by the Prophets. Therefore this "sending" was to be of a different kind. Doubtless, the sending of the Holy Ghost here spoken of was fulfilled mainly on the Day of Pentecost, when the Church and the Pastorate received their gifts and powers. But it is clearly true in a much wider sense. Our Lord introduces His whole discourse on this occasion by the following sentences: "If you shall ask Me anything in My Name, that I will do. If you love Me, keep My Commandments; and I will ask the Father, and He will give you another Paraclete, that He may abide with you for ever."[1] Prayer

[1] *John* xiv. 14-16.

and the keeping of the commandments—that is, intercourse with God, and the doing of the Divine Will—these were the subject of the exhortation of Jesus after the Supper. The hearts of the disciples were saying, How shall we ask, how shall we pray when Thou hast departed? How shall we walk in Thy commandments when we shall have Thee no longer with us? Therefore, without a break, He goes on to tell them of the "other" Paraclete who is to abide with them—that is, with those whom they represented—*for ever.* It was to souls who had depended upon the word and the prompting of Jesus that the Spirit was promised. It was to those who had been accustomed to familiar intercourse with Jesus. It was in order to cheer their hearts and keep up their courage, to enable them to pray as confidently as before; to help them to follow their Master after He had been lifted up to His throne in the heavens. The prayer of Christ, after the Last Supper, and the promise of Christ, were in behalf of His whole flock; a flock left behind in this world of trial, but united in one body by their faith and their love.

This Spirit of Jesus was, in very truth, Jesus Himself. Our Lord is One Person, and the Holy Ghost is another. But all the external operations of the Blessed Trinity, as it need not be said, are the operation of the Three Persons. When an external work is attributed to one person rather than to another, it is because such a work seems to belong by some special congruity to that person. And the external attributions of the Divine Persons serve to enable the mind to map out with greater adequacy the infinite spaces of the power of God, furnishing us with ideas, analogies and words to express to our own intelligence the multiplied operation of the simple and absolute Deity. Therefore, although the work of the Paraclete Who was to be sent was attributed to the Holy Spirit, that Holy Spirit is God, and Jesus is God; and so it was to be Jesus Himself Who should still be with His faithful band. But observe the difference in His mode of being present; a difference indicated in the two phrases by which, first of all, He is said to be about to "depart," and then that the "Spirit" is to be "sent" by His Father and Himself. The Sacred Humanity was to be no longer upon earth. The new presence was to be spiritual. Yet, for all that, spiritual though it was, it was to be a Presence which should teach, prompt, inspire, and console, as truly as Jesus of Nazareth had done all these things for His loved ones when He and they trod the streets of Jerusalem, the ways of Palestine, and the shores of the Sea of Galilee. O promise of Jesus! O divine word of comfort spoken to Thy children before Thou didst enter upon Thy bitter Passion! How has worldliness obscured Thy meaning of love! How has indifference held us back from understanding the splendid inheritance left by Thee, for the benefit of our souls! Thou art gone! But, in our pilgrimage, there is still Thy Spirit—

Thy true presence—to speak to us, to give us light and teaching, to guide us and to comfort us.

No longer, indeed, need we sigh for the visible Presence of our Master and Redeemer. He has gone so far as to say that it was "expedient" for us that He should go—precisely because on His departure the Spirit was to be given. It was not that His visible presence was of slight value; but that the presence of His Spirit would be more valuable still. Yes, Jesus was everything to His disciples—Teacher, Father, Friend. But the Spirit was to be all this, and, in a certain sense, much more. For Jesus on earth chose to be subject to earthly conditions. He was not in every place, but in one narrow corner of the world. His Divine Voice did not reach beyond the limits of the crowd which flocked to hear Him. When His chosen band gathered around Him by the way-side, under a friendly roof, or on the mountain, the thousands and the millions of the earth's sinners and toilers were still in darkness outside the circle of His Divine light. But His Spirit knows no limitations. There is no tract of the earth's surface where It is not close at hand. There is no age or sex that It is not ready to take up. There is no place whence an invocation cannot reach it, no moment when it cannot give all its Divine efficacy to every single human soul. It needs no words, no corporeal touch, no gesture or movement in material space. For when Jesus went up to the heavens in bodily shape, the bright cloud had no sooner shut Him out from mortal sight than He returned as it were to the earth, as the dark wave which climbs the rock returns in the spread of its white foam upon the sea whence it rose. "I will not leave you orphans," He said; "I will come to you."[1] And most efficaciously has He come!

We must next consider more closely how this "sending" and "giving" of the Spirit of Jesus is something more than that general action of God on men which always goes on in the spiritual world. God's most Holy Spirit must work upon the souls of His creation, both in the natural and the supernatural order—because He is the Creator, and therefore the Father of all. But the sending of the Spirit of Jesus implies something more. It signifies a special "grace of the Redeemer". Just as the companionship of Jesus with His Apostles and disciples was more than man could ever have expected, much less merited, so this companionship of the other Paraclete is more than the ordinary presence and action of God. What it means we have revealed to us in marvellous detail in the eleventh chapter of the Prophet Isaias. In that chapter the Prophet describes the human soul of our Lord. He tells us how the Holy Ghost dwelt in that Soul, and filled it with His gifts. Those gifts are described in seven names. There might have been seventy names—or seventy thousand —and yet that fulness of grace would not have been

[1] *John* xiv. 18.

adequately expressed. Earthly names are unequal to the task. But the number seven, as elsewhere, seems here to signify a full and complete order or class of things; and the names, as we have them, being expressly revealed by the Holy Spirit Himself, are absolutely the best names which human language can furnish for the description of what is intended. The names of the seven gifts which filled the soul of Jesus are, Wisdom, Understanding, Counsel, Fortitude, Knowledge, Godliness, and the Fear of the Lord.[1] The peculiar characteristic of a "Gift," as distinguished from the habits of the infused virtues of Faith, Hope and Charity, is that it brings the soul into communication with the Holy Spirit— as a listener with a speaker, a learner with a teacher, a disciple with a leader, a friend with a friend. Hence the effect of the "resting" of the Spirit of the Lord upon the human soul of our Redeemer was to make Him act as if some supreme but hidden influence were at work within Him. This is described in the verses which follow in the same chapter—He was not to judge by the eye, or by the ear, but "justice" and "faith" were to be His girdle (which signifies, His preparation for active work), and a strange supernatural influence was to go forth from Him, making beasts of prey lay down their ferocity and timid things forget their fear. Thus, the gifts substitute for a soul's merely natural activity an activity which has its spring and origin

[1] *Isaias* xi. 2.

in the Holy Ghost; not because the Holy Spirit paralyses the powers of the soul and acts in their stead, but because, retaining all their own vital energy and variety of action, they conform themselves to the sweet influence of His direction, and are reinforced with the mighty force of His resistless strength.

That this passage describes the gifts that are given to every soul in grace is certain. These gifts were the "fulness" of Christ; "and of His fulness we all receive".[1] This is the "unction of the Holy One" described by St. John.[2] The epistles are full of words which express the intimate companionship of the Holy Ghost with those with whom He takes up His abode. Not only is He said to "dwell" within us as in His "temple,"[3] to "rest" upon us (as He was said to rest on Jesus), but He is "given" to us as a sign, character, pledge and consecration.[4] We are said to "partake"[5] of Him, as each spot of the earth shares in the rays of the sun. More than that, we are so held and possessed by Him that we "live" by Him, "walk" by Him, are "led" by Him, and are "moved" or "driven" by Him.[6] By Him we "perceive" what in nature we could not have any perception of.[7] He "helps" us. He "asks" or pleads for us.[8] Certain lovely virtues in us are called His

---

[1] *John* i. 16.
[2] *Rom.* viii. 9; 1 *Cor.* iii. 16.
[3] *Heb.* vi. 4.
[4] 1 *Cor.* ii. 14; *Jude* v. 19.
[5] 1 *John* ii. 20.
[6] 2 *Cor.* i. 22; v. 5.
[7] *Rom.* viii. 14; *Gal.* v. 16.
[8] *Rom.* viii. 16.

"fruits".[1] And the Apostle, carrying out to its utmost the idea that He lives within us, implores us not to "extinguish"[2] the Spirit, as though He were a flame within our soul; and not to "contristate"[3] Him as though He were the most loving and the most sensitive of friends. How strange are these words of the Apostles to my worldly heart! How little I have hitherto lived with Him Who so familiarly lives with me!

POINTS FOR MENTAL PRAYER.

1. Salute the Holy Spirit dwelling within you by sanctifying Grace, by the Theological virtues, and by the Seven Gifts. O Holy Spirit of God, I adore Thee as my Creator; the Creator not of my body only, nor of my soul even, but of my supernatural being, by which I live to life everlasting. *Praised and blessed* be the incomparable communication of Thy sovereign Goodness which destroys my sinfulness and draws me to Thy bosom as Thy friend! Be Thou *welcome*, O Spirit of Jesus, to a heart which has spent many years in indifference to Thy presence, in neglect of Thy inspirations; but which now turns to Thee with all its strength and offers itself to Thee as Thy throne, Thy footstool, Thy habitation, Thy temple!

2. Consider this Holy Spirit as taking the place of Jesus Christ. Spirit of my Saviour! *Call me*

[1] *Gal.* v. 22.   [2] 1 *Thess.* v. 19.   [3] *Eph.* v. 30.

and *draw me,* as He called and drew men! *Teach me,* as He taught the ignorant and the sinful! *Heal me,* as He healed the bodies and the souls of the afflicted! *Strengthen me,* as Jesus strengthened Peter. *Comfort me,* as He comforted Mary Magdalen! *Guide me, hold me up,* as He held up him that was sinking in the troubled waters! *Save me,* O Holy Spirit, as my Saviour hath charged Thee to do!

3. Resolve upon conversion. Hitherto, O Divine Spirit, holy Paraclete, hitherto I have been a guide to myself! Hitherto I have judged things with eyes of the flesh, and weighed things in the scales of my natural reason. And this, whilst Thou wert with me, O Wisdom, O Light of Hearts! No longer will I neglect Thee! No longer shall my unspiritual nature leave Thee unattended to, uncared for! Touch my heart with Thy fire, and rouse me with Thy power, that I may henceforth live and walk by Thee, and Thee alone!

XVII. HOW TO LIVE BY THE SPIRIT.

Those who believe in the indwelling of the Holy Ghost are bound to use every means to live by Him Who has given Himself to them. We live by Him, and we must make it manifest that we live by Him. "If we live by the Spirit, let us also walk by the Spirit."[1] In other words, just as a man's life and career are the result of his character, endowments and acquirements, so the result of this presence within us of the Spirit of Jesus must be a supernatural activity corresponding with the Divine principle which thus animates us. "Thou shalt send forth Thy Spirit," says the Psalmist, "and they shall be created."[2] Create me, O Spirit of God! Leave me not to my nature! Leave me not to the earth, to sense, to the flesh, to human judgment and opinion; but give me other faculties and higher powers, that I may live in the region of the spiritual and the supernatural!

The chief effects of the presence of the Holy Spirit in our soul and heart should be Fear, Divine Love, and Peace. It would seem, perhaps, as if we should add Understanding to these three. But although the principal office of the Holy Ghost, according to the words of our Lord, is to teach, yet

[1] *Gal.* v. 25.   [2] *Ps.* ciii. 30.

the kind of teaching here meant is not teaching in the ordinary sense of the word. Intellectual illumination, in the strict acceptation of the term, is only rarely given by the Holy Spirit directly. It was given to the Apostles because they were the Apostles. It is given to many Apostolic men, as the world goes on—to great doctors and saintly pastors. But "teaching" as it regards the greater number of souls, results rather in the firm and luminous grasp of conclusions, than in the gift of proving such conclusions. It means the gift of being right, of loving what is right, and of enjoying what is right. It means wisdom rather than understanding. We pray to the Holy Ghost to "illuminate our intellect"—but it does not mean that we ask for learning, but for enlightenment as a means to piety.

The first manifestation of the indwelling spirit is Holy Fear. In the Scriptures, Fear is called sometimes the "beginning of wisdom,"[1] and sometimes wisdom itself.[2] In the first chapter of Ecclesiasticus, in which the outpouring of the Holy Spirit is most beautifully described under the name of Wisdom, Fear is first said to be the beginning of Wisdom,[3] and presently the "fulness of Wisdom".[4] It may be called both. For when we say that the result of the presence of the Holy Ghost is Fear, we refer to a very deep and most important effect which that

---

[1] *Ecclus.* ix. 10.
[2] *Ecclus.* i. 16.
[3] *Job* xxviii. 28.
[4] *Ib.* 20.

presence has upon our relations with Almighty God. Perhaps there has been a moment in our lives when we remember passing to a state of *consciousness of God*. Our previous state may have been ignorance, or indifference, or sin, or tepidity, or all of these at once. But the hour came when we began to feel God —to fear, reverence, apprehend God—to be anxious about Him; to be anxious about ourselves, our destiny, our career, our whole life from its beginning to its end. Then we began to understand the awfulness of God's majesty and the inevitableness of His power. Then we began to see how our beginning and our end were in His hands. We seemed to get glimpses of eternity. We stood in the presence of Death. We felt the tremendous anxiety of the Judgment. With these thoughts there came a consciousness of sin. We began to mourn for the commissions and omissions of our youth and our ignorance. We seemed to be standing on the brink of a precipice, with destruction threatening us. All this had the effect of making us turn to God—of urging, of driving us to God, as our only hope, our one and only Friend. It was a great grace. But probably that grace may have remained with us still. We have, at this moment, an habitual attention and reverence for God; we live in the sight of our last end; we meditate on the four last things; we dread the defilement of sin, enter into the seriousness of life, and are on the alert as to its spiritual dangers. We feel we must belong to God and save our immortal soul, cost what it may. O happy state of conversion!

O admirable working of the Holy Spirit! For it is He who has filled us with this filial and salutary fear. It is a state and condition entirely opposed to anything which could result from mere human reason, or from the promptings of sense, of self-love, of worldly wisdom or of human prudence. The worldling possesses it not. His fears, his apprehensions, look in quite another direction. He is blind to judgment, to the certainty of death, to the majesty of God. He seems to be deficient in some power or faculty, which the follower of Christ is endowed with. And this is true. The follower of Christ lives by the Holy Spirit. O blessed Comforter, give me grace to remember Thee!

The second effect of the presence of the Spirit in the spirit of man is Divine Love. When it is called the "second," it is not to be understood that these three effects are not simultaneous. Wherever the Holy Ghost is, there they are, as a habit of the soul, and there they ought to be as its life and activity. Divine love manifests itself in the tender, affectionate disposition of the heart towards God as a Father and Friend. Just as the worldling loves other human beings—relations, benefactors, congenial spirits, or perhaps loves no one but himself—so the spiritual man cares for God. He does not always feel towards God with the intensity of sensibility which is met with in earthly love and liking. But his will and reason adhere to his Heavenly Father. And by dint of thought and reflection, by dwelling in meditation on what God is, by living in His presence, by arousing and exciting all his being to praise Him, the time comes when the "whole" heart is given to Him. Thus we see in devout persons a tenderness and affectionateness to Almighty God which keeps them in an attitude of constant concern about His interests, as well as in constant certainty that He loves them. They love, also, for His sake, that stupendous manifestation of Himself in the Incarnation. They love the sacred humanity in all its mysteries, from Bethlehem to the Cross. They are fondly filial to His Blessed Mother, who is so bound up with all that He Himself is and does. The Holy Angels and the Saints are dear to them, as immortal spirits who are the conquest of the Precious Blood. Every trace of God on earth is precious to them. They would die for that Church which He has acquired by His blood. They glory in the Blessed Sacrament and in the whole of that sevenfold dispensation where the Precious Blood flows. There is no man, or woman, or child, but is the object of their deep and warm interest and sympathy, as being the beloved child of God, destined for the Beatific Vision. Contrast this spirit with that of the worldly person! What are his sentiments about the Church, the Saints, the Holy Eucharist, the Sacraments, the souls of Christ's little ones? What are his feelings to God Himself? From the bottom of your heart give thanks to that Paraclete Who has lifted you to this heavenly love of heavenly things!

Of Peace, which is the third effect of the indwelling of the Spirit, little need be said here. To understand what is meant, let us remember that the endeavour to live by the Spirit naturally and inevitably entails a continuous conflict. Our life is a "warfare"—because fear and love, as set in motion by the Spirit, are at variance with a score of other propensities and inclinations of our nature. The Peace, therefore, which is here meant is that deep, fundamental, and substantial tranquillity which subsists in the soul, in spite of innumerable conflicts on the surface. This is a gift of the indwelling Spirit. Thus, when we are in anxiety as to what course to take, or what means to employ, in order to draw nearer to Christ, such anxiety will not (if the Spirit acts in us) deprive us of Peace. In questions of vocation, for example, there is a sweet abandonment to God's will felt through all the trouble and the uncertainty of the process of decision. Temptations, again, could never drive the truly spiritual man to desperation or sting him into recklessness. Our dealings with others, even when our self-love is ruffled, or our rights invaded, or our good name injured, will never move our hearts from the attitude of charity. Nor will any kind of violent, heavy, or oppressive occupation separate us from God. His Peace, as the Apostle says, "surpasseth all understanding"[1]—that is, no one who engages in the conflict of life with merely human motives can conceive what it is to be at Peace even when you

[1] *Philip.* iv. 7.

are fighting. This is the Peace that we pray for, that we wish to others, that is expressed so constantly in the forms of the Church; it is the special Peace of the Incarnation, brought to the earth by the Prince of Peace, and breathed over all the world by His Spirit. Keep me faithful, O Divine Spirit, to Thy presence, that I may never lose the tranquillity of Thy operation! Anchor my soul deep down in the everlasting foundations firmly fixed by Thy power and Thy goodness, that no trial may move me, but that my fear and my love may grow for evermore in the supernatural tranquillity of Thy majesty!

For purposes of self-examination, then, and in order to arouse ourselves to co-operate with the Holy Spirit of God thus given to us, we may ask ourselves:—

1. Have we a keen feeling for the supernatural? Do we view things from the point of view of Faith? Do we value the Mass, the Sacraments? Are we in the habit of putting our eternal interests first? Are we anxious for the salvation of others? Or, on the other hand, are we indifferent in matters of piety; careless in spiritual duties; inclined even to show contempt for small religious observances; and fond of the world and its applause?

2. Are we sensitive in regard to sin? Does the thought of mortal sin in ourselves or others fill us with horror? Are we easy under our habitual venial sins? Do we anxiously avoid unnecessary

occasions of danger? Have we the good habit of making frequent, nay continual, acts of contrition?

3. Professing as we do to love God above all things, do we habitually find Him in the ordinary concerns of life? Do we see Him in superiors? in our religious brethren or sisters? in our neighbours? in those with whom we work? Or, on the other hand, are we in the habit of dealing with all these from merely human or natural motives, scarcely taking pains to purify our intention, or to restrain our temper, our vanity, or our jealousy?

4. Do we undervalue the supernatural life in general, and allow ourselves to fall in with those who talk of "common-sense" and "practical views"? Are we convinced that we may progress in nearness to God and in purity of heart? That such progress can only be made by attention to our interior life? That, in a degree, even perfection is within our reach, provided we study to detach ourselves from creatures, and watch, with much prayer, the motions of the Holy Spirit within us? Are we ashamed of the "folly of the Cross," that is, of that external loyalty to our Lord Jesus Christ which leads His servants to profess a spiritual life, and to make much of everything which is in the slightest degree connected with the Cross?

Moreover, we must remember that this Holy Spirit, being a true Paraclete, that is, our true adviser and comforter, may, and will, give us illumination in those innumerable matters of the interior life on which our progress depends. It is unnecessary to say that there is a certain danger in allowing ourselves to be directed by what we take to be the inspirations of the Holy Spirit. That danger, however, is very small, provided that we remember four things: Obedience must *always* overrule what seems to be an inspiration; we must always be open with our director; an inspiration which interferes with the due carrying out of our state of life cannot be from the Holy Spirit; and, lastly, whatever is unusual, extraordinary, or out of the usual way, especially in things external, must always be suspected. Keeping these rules in view, we may humbly expect guidance in such points as the following:—

1. The government of the tongue, and the moderation of doubtfully useful conversation. Most people lose much time by talking; and yet it is certain that charity and duty require us to talk. The Holy Spirit will certainly guide us on this head. Neither books, nor rules, nor superiors can do it adequately, from the nature of the case.

2. The use of Mortifications. Practices of penance, and especially external ones, must never be adopted except by advice and obedience. What is meant here is that we require light to know how much mental pressure we ought to put upon ourselves at every moment of the day, in the matter of self-restraint. There are some who are nervously anxious to be mortifying themselves every minute, and who fear they commit an infidelity in resisting this impulse.

There are others who are far too lax. Who shall direct the hesitating heart into the golden mean? Who shall keep us equally from foolish fidgetiness and from sloth? Only the promptings of the Spirit of Jesus.

3. The question of Friendships is one on which books and superiors can only give general rules. Yet it is one which intimately concerns the practice of perfection.

4. When obedience does not speak clearly, it is difficult to know when to accept an office or employment, and when to refuse it. It is hard to tell whether such and such a task will only overload and distract, or whether our own good and that of our neighbours requires us to take it up.

5. We are often uncertain whether we ought to suffer certain inconveniences, or to speak and obtain their removal; whether we ought or ought not to make a complaint against another; to apply for a change; to make an appeal.

6. Intellectual occupation, where it is not settled by rule and obedience, is another difficulty with those who would live an interior life. Must we study this and read that? Must we, for example, avoid newspapers altogether, or to what extent? Must we keep our thoughts pure from all contact with heresy, worldliness, and impurity—or must we confide in God's help, and, for good motives, make ourselves acquainted with subjects which will defile and disturb our imagination and our intellect?

In all these questions there is a right solution and a wrong one. To answer them by one's merely natural light is impossible. Neither is external guidance possible—for we should require a director to be as constantly with us as our guardian angel. There cannot be a doubt that the interior Christian will, if he duly listens, hear a voice of guidance which will prevent him from going far wrong. And we must not forget that this is a serious matter; for, as St. Paul says, "the wisdom of the flesh is death; but the wisdom of the Spirit is life and peace".[1] "As," to quote the words of Father Baltassar Alvarez, "the abundance and perfection of vital and animal spirits strengthens the limbs and gives perfection to the functions of life and sense; and, on the contrary, the want of such vitality is injurious; so the frequency and efficacy of the divine impulses make perfect the operations of the spiritual life, and carry the soul on to sanctity, whilst the rareness and feebleness of such impulses leave it weak and languid."[2]

All men who are in sanctifying grace have the gifts of the Holy Spirit. But, as many who are thus endowed do not "live by the Spirit," let us conclude by mentioning three things which may account for this.

1. The first is the habit of venial sin. There are certain habitual sins which, though by no means

---

[1] *Rom.* viii. 6.
[2] *De Discretione Spirituum*, lib. v. part. 4, cap. 1. no. 10.

grave, yet spread such a torpor and coldness over the soul that the Holy Spirit cannot act with His full power. Such are sins of vanity, sensuality, dislike, disobediences, worldly interest, and bad temper. If we would live by the Spirit, we must fight against habits of this kind.

2. Habitually low views of spirituality account in some measure for the want of the light of the Holy Spirit. There are some who never fully surrender themselves to a spiritual life; never own with full conviction that God and God alone must be their light and strength. To enter into spiritual views; to take the spiritual side in all things; to be determined to aim at complete detachment, genuine mortification, and nothing less than Christian perfection—these dispositions will effectively level all barriers between the soul and its Divine sanctifier.

3. A life of worldliness, or of undue occupation, is an obstacle to the working of the Holy Ghost. A soul which is filled with the petty interests of frivolous people is deaf to the whisperings of the Holy Spirit. Even serious and genuine work may have the same effect, unless it is carried on in a detached spirit, and unless there are regular times for prayer and meditation. The cultivation of a retired, interior, and silent life, enables the Spirit of God to speak to the heart.

POINTS FOR MENTAL PRAYER.

1. After again *adoring* the Holy Spirit of God,

dwelling with His gifts in your weak and purblind soul, *surrender* your soul to Him. *Confess* its *poverty* and *helplessness*, and beg of Him to *supply for them* with His mighty gifts. *Offer* Him your own *powers* —your will, your memory, your understanding, your imagination, your senses—and pray Him to possess, direct, and rule them. Take me, O Paraclete sent by Jesus!—form me—penetrate me—move me—perfect me!

2. *Thank* Him with joy, for what He brings to you. Spirit of my Jesus, I thank Thee for holy fear! O blessed endowment of spiritual sense and understanding, which keeps me in sight of my God, and of all those things which are connected with His love for me! I thank Thee for Divine love—which makes me feel my God so near! I thank Thee for that gift of supreme peace, which enables me to turn all earthly trouble into fuel for greater love!

3. *Detest* the obstacles which have hitherto prevented the Holy Ghost from operating in you. Why am I not ashamed, O holy Paraclete, of my habits of sin? Why am I not determined, with Thy grace, to rid myself of them? Give me determination! Give me *generosity*, that I may break these fetters, and may free the hands of Thy mercy! Take from me all low and unworthy ideas of the spiritual life! Infuse into my intelligence the science of the Saints! Make me understand that it is Thy seven gifts which alone can fructify unto life everlasting! Take from

me the love of the world! Detach my heart from all that occupies me! Breathe around me that atmosphere of recollection, silence, and prayer, in which Thou, my God, speakest; for when Thou speakest to me, all is clear, and easy, and delightful!

XVIII. THE RELIGIOUS PROMISE.

In the life of a religious there is nothing more important, more truly serious, than the promise he has made to God in taking up the obligations of the religious state. St. Mary Magdalen of Pazzi used to say that it was the "greatest grace, after baptism, that God could bestow". If a religious fails in his religious obligations, he fails utterly; if he is faithful to them, he is God's faithful servant.

Let us consider that the religious state is a means to an end, not an end in itself. It is a means adopted in order to love God with the whole heart. There are those who have been, in a sense, driven into religion by the thought of their obligation to love God with all their strength, mind and heart; and by the conviction that, being such as they were, they could not fulfil this terrible obligation in the world. There are others who, without feeling so deeply or so acutely as this, have entered religion because they longed to love God more intensely and more continuously. "Blessed are they that dwell in Thy house, O God; they shall praise Thee for ever and ever!"[1]

Everything that tends to keep the heart from

[1] *Ps.* lxxxiii. 5.

creatures, and to diminish the power of temptation, is a means to love God more perfectly. But the religious state has the advantage of being more than an isolated attempt, or an unconnected series of attempts, in this direction; it is what is called a *state*. That is to say, it sets up a stable condition of things, such as is adapted, of itself, to keep off all that would interfere with God's love. Thus it is a *state* of *perfection;* for it is a state which, by its very existence, necessitates to a great extent the absence of temptation and makes detachment permanent—these two conditions being conditions which, as a rule, ensure the perfect love of God. A soul not bound by religious vows may be personally more perfect than a religious, if it loves God more; but the religious is in a more perfect "state". Happy is he if he lives up to it! He dwells in a "house" with a roof over his head against the elements, and strong walls against hostile attack; but the house itself with all its bolts and barriers will not make him holy unless he loves it.

Reflect, then, that God's love has drawn thee into this holy state; where, as St. Bernard says, we fall more rarely, we rise more quickly, we live with greater restraint, and we arrive at detachment more rapidly.[1] Nothing but His love has drawn thee. In childhood, thou wert as others; perhaps more indifferent, more intemperate, more sensual. Or if,

---

[1] "Cadit rarius, surgit velocius, vivit parcius, purgatur citius."

by God's grace, thou didst awake early to His call, yet it was He Who called, and no other. It was He Who whispered in thine ear when thy head was bent down in recollection before the altar where thou hadst first received thy Saviour. It was He Who led thee to directors, who made thy way plain before thee. It was He Who breathed generosity into thy young heart, urging thee to mortification and detachment. Or, perhaps, it was otherwise with thee—and it was He Who lifted thee from the slough of thy sins, to conversion and to the knowledge of thy Redeemer. However it was, it was not for any merits of thine that He drew thee to Himself. Nothing can account for it except His love. "I have loved thee with an everlasting love; therefore I drew thee, having pity on thee."[1] Can any thought be better adapted than this to make thee feel that thou hast a Father in Heaven?

Reflect, again, that what He inspired thee with, and what was in thy thoughts when thou didst utter thy vows, was nothing less than a total and absolute sacrifice of thyself to His love and service. It is called "total and absolute," because what is given up by the vows of poverty, chastity and obedience, goes very far indeed to cover everything which *could* be given up. True, it is impossible to make vows which shall literally include every possession and every liberty. But, substantially, we do make a total renunciation; and, what is more, we wish and

[1] *Jeremias* xxxi. 3.

intend, as far as human weakness permits and the grace of the Holy Spirit enables us, to give up to God's love really and truly everything. The vow of Poverty covers every item of worldly property which we have or shall ever have. The vow of Chastity not only detaches us from a life which would have been sure to make us, to a greater or less degree, neglect "the things of the Lord," but it places a double restraint upon us, in a thousand matters which the infirmity of human nature makes exceedingly dangerous to our sovereign love of God. And the vow of Obedience affects the very well-spring of our self-love, with all its innumerable streams and channels. Thus, we have made a sacrifice of freedom, power, affection, proprietorship, ease, and enjoyment. "With holocausts" God has declared He "will not be delighted"[1]—that is, with the burnt-offerings of the ceremonial law; but there is a kind of holocaust on which He will look with Divine approval. He will not despise "a contrite and humbled heart". This is the offering of the religious—a heart which is "broken" by the renunciation of pleasure, and "humbled" by parting with that which is dearest to man,—the sense of being one's own master.

It is not difficult to understand how a life of this kind tends to intensify the act of charity. First of all, it is a life of sharp pangs of endurance; and, as we have seen (Discourse XV.), all pain, lovingly ac-

[1] *Ps.* l. 18.

cepted, intensifies our love of God and our adhesion to Him. How mistaken, therefore, art thou, O religious man, if thou dreadest, or triest to avoid, the rough things of thy religious life! For it is just these things which thou camest to religion to find. To be a religious, and to spend one's days in avoiding all that is irksome to the flesh or annoying to the spirit, is to be foolish and inconsistent to the last degree. Far better not to have left the world. The same may be said of him who seeks to weaken religious discipline, or to escape from rule and routine; for rule and discipline, enclosure, silence, and separation from the world, are the necessary consequences of the vows; they are the vows reduced to practice. Now, the object of the vows, as we have seen, is to put up barriers between ourselves and the first shock of temptation. Whoever, therefore, withdraws himself from regularity, withdraws himself from the beneficent influence of his vows, and to that extent weakens the bulwarks which he himself erected with his own hand in order to be more constantly near to his God. "Redde Altissimo vota tua!" Pay thy vows, O religious! Remember thy vows! Mock not thy God! Thou hast promised; and even in thy tepidity thou wouldst not wish to unsay thy promise. Shake off thy tepidity, then, and understand that the life of him who schemes to escape rule is the life of one who is in the way to be unfaithful to his vows.

Ah! when thou didst make those holy promises how filled with horror would thy soul have been hadst thou foreseen thy indifference and thy sloth that was to come! For thou madest that promise in thy fervent youth; nay, perhaps thou hadst virtually made it from thy childhood, and it had led thee on, like the pillar of the Lord, to the land of milk and honey, the land of the religious life. Thou didst make that promise in the fear of God, filled with the awe of thy Creator, impressed by the inevitableness of His power, and by the majesty of His immensity. Thou didst make it with the thought of thy deathbed before thee, and of what thou wouldst wish thy life to have been when thou camest to be stretched thereon. Thou didst make it in the fervent love of God above all things, with the feeling of His beauty and the conviction that He was thy only good, thy last end, and thy all. Thou didst make it in the joyousness of Divine grace, in the impulse of the Holy Spirit, in the magnanimity of His sovereign gifts, looking forward to the future as one looks forward to a pleasant journey. Thou didst make it in the hatred of sin, the loathing of its filthiness, the dread of its contamination; feeling that nothing could be sweeter or more delightful than to live pure and innocent all thy days. Thou didst make it in the ardour of the desire of perfection; in the fervour of the emulation of the Saints. Thou didst make it with the anticipation of thy heavenly country, where for endless ages the base and trivial things thou didst trample upon would be repaid thee with inconceivable bliss.

At first, perhaps, these impulses continued and grew stronger. The sweetness of Divine love led thee on—the fervour of a beginner made burdens light and the rough way smooth. But by degrees unfaithfulness crept upon thee. When the impulse of fervour was wanting, thy efforts grew slack. Having trusted, perhaps, more to thyself than to the grace of thy Heavenly Father, thou didst fall— fall in little things, perhaps in greater. Thou didst begin to keep things back from thy sacrifice. Thou didst allow thyself to scrutinise, and hesitate, and even refuse. The holy strictness of the rule began to displease thee. Thou didst not accept, as heretofore, the common life, the common food, the lodging, the work; thou didst fail in loving all persons equally for Christ's sake; thou didst try to cheat thy Saviour in those things which are intended to make the religious like unto Him Who bore the Cross. Perhaps thy vows, at that time, were little before thy mind. For from renewing them with a warm heart every day, thou didst hardly remember to recall them at weekly or even monthly intervals. More than once thy conscience has surprised thee in dislike of thy vows. There were temptations to regret having made them; temptations which were not rejected, but allowed to lie in the heart and poison its life. Dangerous thoughts, of instability —even of apostasy—were not by any means strange to thee in thy hours of sadness or of sloth. Thou didst come to neglect the observances and "little things" of thy community life. Thou didst grow to be slow, unpunctual, lax, and self-seeking; to love distractions and outside work or recreation; to disturb thy brethren by singularity, by the seeking of exemptions, the contempt of observances, the criticism of superiors, and general discontent with the religious life.

Whither does all this lead? Canst thou doubt it? It leads to the abandonment of the religious life; and, therefore—since it seems that God intends thee to save thy soul by the religious life—to thy eternal ruin. Even if this thought should shock thee, and thou shouldst refuse to allow thy apostasy to be inferred from thy laxity, there is another consideration. Such a life as is here described leads to the abandonment of the desire of perfection. Nay, it *is* the abandonment of that desire and purpose. No one can be relaxed, unmortified, and lazy, and at the same time desire to love God with such a whole heart as thou didst once long to do, and as every religious ought to long to do. But this is a miserable and lamentable condition to be in. Those who are in the world, though they be not fervent, yet as long as they keep from mortal sin, fail in fervour chiefly through their lawful occupations, their want of thought, their deficiency in spiritual instruction, and their low standard of supernatural aims. But it cannot be so with the religious. He has leisure for thought; he has been drawn into the sanctuary of God; and he has taken upon himself obligations grounded precisely on his appreciation of the supernatural. He has understood that nothing on earth is equal in value to one step of greater nearness to Christ. He has not only understood this, but has, to some extent, lived and acted up to it; so that if he abandons the desire of perfection, he abandons it through sloth, selfishness, and deliberate choice. To do this, and to continue to wear the habit and tread the cloister, is to be a cheat and a liar. No true and genuine heart could long endure to be in such a condition. There must be conversion, or there will be desertion. O my Lord and Saviour! Thou Who didst inspire me to pronounce my vows before Thy altar, give me light and the force of Thy powerful grace, that I may see what choice to make! that I may understand how contemptible and pitiable a thing is a religious who makes no effort to live up to the life of religion!

Every religious, then, is bound to aspire to perfection. Nor need this thought disturb any anxious heart. What he is bound to aspire to is not perfection in any absolute or transcendental sense; but such perfection as is naturally attainable by those who employ the means placed at their disposal by the religious life. That life, by its vowed renunciations, and by its consequent practical course—its prayer, its humility, its subordination of act and will, and its holy occupations—is quite certain to establish in the heart a progressive state, which may, without exaggeration, be called perfection; that is, a remarkably close union with God, through Jesus Christ. This, the religious is bound to desire; for, such a desire is implied in the acceptance of religious obligations; because, if a religious really accepts the obligations of his state, he either does so with the object of making himself perfect—as just explained—or he accepts them out of mere superstition, as a Stoic might have done, or even an Indian fakir. In order, therefore, to be sure that thou dost aim at perfection, thou needest to do no more than live with exactness thy religious life.

But it is to be feared that many religious fail to make the most of that holy life to which they have had the grace to be called. There is, in their habitual way of living, a want of intention, a want of appreciation—in other words, a want of solicitude, about their love of their Father in heaven. The vows and the practices of religion are helpful and salutary—but only to those who put some energy into their use. They are divinely adapted to intensify the acts of the heart towards God, but only if the religious thinks of it. They are most valuable in making our life one continuous lifting up of the soul towards its Creator—O happy condition!—but only if each hour is consciously used, and each act and hardship separately infused with spiritual intention. The religious who lives his life mechanically is losing his time, and squandering precious moments, which might merit for him the highest and the innermost heavens.

My Father! open my eyes, that I may see light! Grant me, that from the morning, when I am summoned to prayer, till the evening, when I lay down my head in prayer to rest, I may use to the full every moment of prayer, every word of reading, every slightest rule, every order of my superior, every encounter with my brethren, every step in the cloister, every touch of the outward world, every vicissitude of my spirit and my flesh, every visitation of the cross—to draw me to the lifting up of my heart, and to greater nearness to Thee!

Points for Mental Prayer.

1. Place thyself in the presence of Jesus calling thee to follow Him. *Recognise Who* it was that called thee—Who calleth thee still. My loving Saviour! No one called me but Thou alone! My vocation was not from persons, or from circumstances, or from my own good-will; but only from Thy love! I adore Thee as my God! I thank Thee as my only friend! *Desire to correspond* with your Saviour's call. I come, O my Master, I come! O blessed Voice! O happy call! O gracious invitation! I choose Thee, my loving Saviour, before all other things that have power over my heart—Thee, and Thee alone!

2. *Raise up thy hands*, with the holy fetters of Thy religious promise hanging upon them, and *rejoice* that thou dost bear their weight. O bonds

of love! O chains of joyful freedom! O fetters that unite me to my Saviour! I love you—I embrace you—I cherish you! If I did not already carry you on my body, I would hold out my hands to have you! I would seek you—I would welcome you! Never will I regret that I have found you! O Lord Jesus, as Thou didst gently place these bonds upon my wayward hands, so keep me faithful to them, and loyal to Thee; till at my last breath Thou dost lift them off and receive my spirit!

3. *Lament* and *beg pardon* for thine unfaithfulness. I have been disloyal, O my God, in the past! Forgive my unsteadiness of heart! my sloth and my laxity! Forgive my regrets! I confess with tears the foolish petulance which I have too often shown in my words and acts, the impatience with which I have borne Thy yoke! I confess my frequent disedification of others, who have heard and seen me! I confess my want of interest in my religious life—my neglect of observance—my depreciation of holy practices—my evil influence on the community! In all these ways I have not been Thy true servant or Thy loyal child; but I have rather been against Thee, and against the interests of Thy Sacred Heart! By the sorrows of that Heart forgive me and correct me!

XIX. OBEDIENCE.

We must enter deeply, during Retreat, into the mystery of Obedience; for on Obedience depends our religious spirit; and on our religious spirit depends life everlasting. Obedience, in the well-known phrase of St. Bonaventure, is in itself religious perfection. "Religious perfection consists totally in the renunciation of our own will."[1]

Obedience may be taken to mean a course of action, or it may be taken to mean the interior impulse with which one acts. It may describe the going round of the hands of the clock on the dial, or it may designate the mainspring hidden out of sight. We have to bring it home to our mind and heart in both acceptations; and we will begin with the latter.

For in a life of obedience it is the spirit of obedience which is all-important. A religious may obey through mere habit, by routine, for the sake of a quiet life, or through mere slavishness of disposition: such a one leads an outwardly obedient life; but he is not obedient. Much less is that religious obedient who obeys to the eye, but rebels inwardly.

The root or spring of true obedience must be sought

---

[1] *Tota religionis perfectio in abdicatione propriæ voluntatis.* Speculum Disciplinæ, c. 4.

in Humility. Now, humility is that attitude of absolute truth in the presence of God by which we acknowledge Him as the perpetually flowing source of all that we are and have; and keep persistently before our eyes that in ourselves and of ourselves we are and have nothing. For how does a man stand in respect to God? Consider a human being in his place in the world. He has, first of all, certain surroundings, which he calls friends, followers, servants, possessions, influence, credit. But these are in no way dependent on his will. They are like the tidal water on which the bark rides at anchor, which at the appointed hour will ebb away and leave it stranded in the mud. They depend on God, and God alone. If you object and say that the creation of these surroundings is to a great extent of a man's own doing, a moment's reflection will show that this is only a confusion of thought. For how does a man make his surroundings? By pure fortune in very many cases; that is, by God's act and permission. When his own act is in any way concerned in the matter, that act is the act of a power or a faculty which only exists as a living and energising thing by the inflow of God's will and energy. If God withdrew—if the radiation of God's power were interrupted—human faculty would wither like a blighted leaf. Therefore, our powers, our faculties, our talents, and the energy and insight with which we employ them, are to be ascribed to God much more radically than to ourselves—as the writing is to be ascribed rather to the master who holds the child's hand than to the child itself. The same may be said of our life, and our very being—until we reach the very centre of our existence; and there we find that, although we most truly exist, and our existence is utterly apart from that of God, yet He is so concerned in the commencement and continuance of our existence that it depends on Him moment by moment, as the glitter of the diamond depends on the presence of the light. It is in this sense that we truly say we *are* nothing and *have* nothing, except what God gives.

And here we will not dwell upon sin. Sin is our own,—that is, the deviation, the error, the turning away, the guilt, which are involved in what is called sin, are the result of the failure of our hearts to conform to what is right. Our falls, our wounds, our filthiness, are from ourselves and of ourselves. They are all that we have justly to boast of!

The true insight which the child of our Heavenly Father has into his dependence on Him is so far from bringing trouble or distress, that it is the source of all peace and all confidence. For when we have gone down to the depths of our nothing—we must not remain there, but we must rise again. Not to rise again would be to despair. Such despair sometimes does assail the servant of God; those whom it assails are very frequently those who have, by whatever means, been brought to see their sinfulness, their weakness, their utter powerlessness to do good, and who have not gone farther. Oh how crushing to the spirit it is to review one's life—one's beginnings, one's failures, one's unfaithfulness, one's weakness, one's instability, one's innumerable sins! No wonder despair lurks near, its pestilent breath poisoning the very air. Only those who have the secret can be safe.

The secret, after all, is no secret. "I can do all things in Him Who strengtheneth me!"[1] My being, my powers, my endowments, my graces, my merits—I have a right to claim them all—provided only that I refer them all to my Creator and my Saviour! They are His first—but He gives them to me, to be truly my own. Oh! blessed dependence on God! How sweet it is to empty oneself of all good and all merit, in order to lay all at His feet! How full of peace is the thought that all we have is all His! For if it is all His, and He loves us as He does, then we must be very rich; or if we are not rich, it is the fault of ourselves only; and the fault consists in our not claiming, hoping for, making sure of, the munificent bounty of our King. Let me not undervalue my virtues, my progress, my grace; only let me, with loving persistence, keep saying in my heart: "From Thee, O Lord, from Thee!"

Of this spirit of Humility—the truthful attitude of the soul to its Creator and its Father—the grand safeguard is Obedience. "The first degree of Humility," says St. Benedict, "is prompt Obedience."[2]

---

[1] *Philip.* iv. 13.   [2] *Regula*, cap. v.

He is here speaking, not of the interior spirit of Humility itself, which he afterwards describes in the Twelve Degrees of the famous seventh chapter of the Rule. He is referring to external Humility; and he intends to lay it down that there can be no such thing as true Humility of heart without its manifesting itself in Obedience. For no one can be humble, in the way just described, without at least obeying God. But obedience to God involves not a little obedience to His ordinances and to His ministers—obedience which must be visible to all men. And this is the least that true Humility can co-exist with. For the truly humble heart will not stint its obedience. It will seek out chances and occasions of obedience. For obedience will keep it humble. How does this come about? Because the human heart easily forgets to be humble; the distractions, the occupations, the enjoyments of life easily move it from its attitude of truth to its Creator, and set it dwelling upon its endowments, its possessions and its performances as if they were all its own. Hence complacency, vanity, boasting; and pride. Now, obedience powerfully checks this spirit of self-complacency. For obedience, whilst it bows the back, bends the spirit also. It is useless to object and say that the obeying a man has nothing to do with being humble before God. Let it be tried. Obedience at once recalls us to our true attitude, and enkindles that warmth which turns the heart to God. "Before I was humbled, I was a sinful man; since then, I have kept Thy words, O my God."[1] And again—"It is good for me that Thou hast humbled me—that I may learn Thy justifications"[2]—that is, that I may learn the secret of Thy dealings with Thy servants. What is true of all humiliation is eminently true of that searching humiliation of the spirit which we call Obedience. Therefore the wise have sought out the paths of obedience. Not only to receive safety in their ignorances, and to be sure of prudent direction and reasonable consolation, but most of all to keep themselves humble, have the servants of God in all ages striven to live under obedience. And it is for such reasons that the chief and essential vow of the Religious State is the vow of Obedience. No other vow could so surely keep the heart in its true attitude towards its God.

This, then, is the sum of our reflections: To be genuine children of our Heavenly Father we must be humble—and humble not only by conviction but also by the uniform and consistent devotion of our hearts; but such devout humility is virtually impossible without humiliation lovingly accepted; and to make sure of continuous humiliation, continuous Obedience is the sovereign secret.

There are other advantages in Holy Obedience; but they are virtually included in that deep and fundamental spiritual effect here described. The masters of the spiritual life insist on the *sacrifice* of Obedi-

[1] *Ps.* cxviii. 67.   [2] *Ib.* 71.

ence; the sacrifice of self-will, which is the most thorough sacrifice the human heart can make. We sacrifice ourselves in the "continuous martyrdom" of Obedience because we wish to give Almighty God all that we have, and to keep back nothing. But why is He so well pleased with the odour of this sacrifice of the will and heart? Not precisely because we thereby curb a heart which is inclined to sin, or chasten a will which has so sadly gone astray. Even from the pure and the innocent, God delights to receive the holocaust of their will. Why? Because the more they immolate their will, the more they strain out pride from their natures; in other words, the more they admit His fulness and His sovereignty into their inmost beings. Hence Holy Obedience begins by subjecting the heart to rules and ordinances which lead it to keep God's commandments better, and to advance from virtue to virtue. But this is only the beginning. Obedience can never complete its work whilst there remains the least danger of forgetting what God is and what we are; and that danger will be with us until we breathe our last breath. O my soul! Look thus on Holy Obedience! For Obedience is not order, or edification, or good sense, or even mortification. It is, indeed, all of these things. But if thou wert most perfect in all outward observance, most exact in the fulfilment of every rule, most edifying in the submission to superiors, and most perfectly mortified in things painful and humbling, yet Obedience has still greater things in store for thy spirit. Foolish indeed thou art to look upon Religious Obedience as a matter chiefly for novices and beginners! Blind art thou to wish to lessen the pressure of the yoke, and to withdraw thyself from observance as thy years lengthen out. The spiritual heart, as it grows more enlightened, will long with greater fervour for the continuous touch of that sovereign force which has power to transmute its service into deeper and purer acts of union with its God.

The Saints call Obedience a "short cut" to Perfection. (It is the phrase of St. Teresa.[1]) For the essence of perfection is the maintenance of the heart in union with God, undisturbed by self and by creatures. Now obedience not only teaches us how to heal our blind and wounded nature, but it elevates the struggle into the atmosphere of Divine love. How many persons in the world, and sometimes in the sanctuary and the cloister, mortify themselves and restrain themselves with no higher feeling than that it is right to do so! But mere self-restraint is no virtue. To be a Christian virtue self-restraint must unite us with God, by the act of the heart. Obedience, by softening the heart, helps to effect this. How many Christians, again, pursue "virtue" as they call it, out of mere routine, or indeed to please themselves—being all the while very cold to God and very hard to their neighbours? But obedience

---

[1] *Foundations*, ch. v. The whole chapter should be read.

cannot exist in company with self-complacency, or selfishness. Thus, to the obedient, "virtue" becomes genuine goodness of the heart, and no longer a mask of self-love. Moreover, the special gift of *success* seems to be attached to obedience; so that whatever one undertakes through obedience, whether it be external work or work upon one's own soul, is blessed by God. On the other hand, neither anger, nor discouragement, nor sensibility, nor vanity is ever successfully fought against unless there is obedience at the same time; and the ancient monks used to say that brotherly unity and stability in the community could only be increased by humble obedience.[1]

Look into thy past history, and ask thyself before God whether thou hast or hast not the spirit of obedience. Neither the duty of obedience nor its value is confined to the Religious State. All have to obey the Church and the law; many have parents and superiors; and there is no one with spiritual insight who does not strive to obey in as wide a field as possible. Thus we read that St. Anselm, when archbishop, obtained from the Pope a master who might order his personal life. But perhaps, in thy tepidity, thou art one of those who make light of obedience. Perhaps thou art one of those who draw distinctions and say: In important matters we are all ready to obey; but as for little things, the ordinary rule, the numerous precepts of superiors,

---

[1] Cassian, *De Institutis Renuntiantium*, lib. iv. cap. 8.

there is not much chance of committing sin by disregarding them. Hast thou considered that to live without obedience is to live out of the air and sunshine of God? And beware how thou flatterest thyself that thou escape sin. As often as the rule is broken, even in the least point, through sloth, sensuality, vanity, or temper, so often is there sin. And, what is more, it is possible that by a life of long-continued indifference to rule and obedience, thou mayest one day arrive at the point of gravely culpable neglect of the means of salvation. Further, he who is indifferent to obedience, be he priest, religious, or layman, is like a wolf among the sheep. Nothing spreads the deadly passion of spiritual indifference so effectually as the easy contempt for rule and authority manifested in the lives of professed spiritual persons. Is there not a point when such example as this becomes a mortal sin? O Divine Saviour! Lover of Obedience! save us from thus blighting Thy Kingdom by our blind folly!

Points for Mental Prayer.

1. Turn the eyes of thy soul on Jesus, in His Obedience. Behold Him lying upon the straw of Bethlehem, a Victim sent to redeem thee and all mankind; at Nazareth, subject to Mary and Joseph; on the Cross, fastened not by the Nails but by Obedience. *Adore* thy God, Who thus, in His sacred Humanity, deigns to draw thy heart towards Him. Draw into thy being the *humility* of which these things are the sign, saying: My Saviour, the very sight of Thee thus and thus, does not preach humility to me, but burns it into my spirit like a strong fire! Burn yet more, O Lord, yet more, that I may grow somewhat to be humble of heart! Bow thy head to receive the deep spiritual *lesson* of Obedience. Say: O my Master, what dost Thou teach me? Infinite Wisdom and Almighty Power combined humble themselves to men, to sinners, to ignorance, to brutality! Why, O Lord? Thou tellest me that it is for a spiritual end; it is that Thy Sacred Heart may glow with some brightness of sacrifice not otherwise attainable. Make me wise, O my Jesus, that I may understand this! O blessed Obedience, I long for you, I embrace you, that you may heat my cold heart till it burns with love of my God!

2. Lament before God the *imperfections* of thy Obedience. O Lord Jesus Christ! I confess to Thee my blindness and my sloth. How habitually have I procured exemptions! How difficult have I made it for superiors to give me orders! How indifferent have I been in keeping rules! How unmortified, and how wanting in alacrity, good temper and cheerfulness! How have I scandalised and done evil to Thy little ones by my bad example and my tepidity! My Saviour, canst Thou pardon me? Yes, O Lord, Thou canst, and Thou willest to pardon me, for Thou inspirest me with sorrow, and with the resolution to live for the future in the enlightened love of Obedience in all things, to my dying day.

3. But, most of all, O Saviour of my soul, I am smitten with sorrow for the *evil pride* which has made me undervalue Holy Obedience! For I have habitually judged and criticised superiors; I have made my obedience a human affair, as if my superior were not Thy representative; I have joined others, and influenced others in criticism and bitterness; I have without compunction ravaged the Kingdom of Thy Holy Spirit and even banished Him from the hearts of my brethren by my innumerable words of rashness, of folly, of unkindness, and even of wilful misrepresentation! Canst Thou suffer me to live any longer in Thy fold? Canst Thou bear with me,— Thou Who hast called me to Thee, and Whom I have treated with such ingratitude? Pardon me, O my Saviour, by the merits of that incomparable obedience by which Thou didst say to Thy Heavenly Father, Behold, I come! Pardon me! Pardon me! Give me light! Give me humility! Give me wisdom!

Reflection on Obedience of the Judgment.

Many devout religious experience great difficulty in conforming their judgment to that of their superior. They know that the saints teach that it is not enough to obey in *act* and in *will*, but that we must strive to see the thing as our superior sees it. Now this seems in some cases to be impossible, as the thing ordered may sometimes be ill-advised and clearly foolish.

The first observation to be made is, that a religious should be careful not to dwell on the reasons which seem to show that the matter in question is imprudent or useless. Every reasonable mind must be well aware that a superior has many advantages in forming a judgment which subjects have not. A humble heart will seek to persuade itself that a superior may, in spite of appearances, be right. Moreover, the reasons which our judgment perceives against the superior's decision are very frequently either invented, or at least aggravated, by ourselves. We should accustom ourselves, in the spirit of those who desire to sacrifice their inmost self to Jesus Crucified, to deal calmly with these temptations towards criticism; we shall then perceive that all we have to allege does not amount to much; that if it were the case of a third party we should probably say the superior was possibly quite right; and that what is pricking us is not the reasons themselves so much as the effect of the decision on our own pride, vanity or laziness. Thus we shall be encouraged to do what is in most cases the wisest thing to do— *viz.*, resolutely to turn our thought from all that appears to make our superior's wish seem imprudent. "In a beginner," says St. Bonaventure, "Obedience should not attempt to be prudent; there should be no endeavour to understand the why or the wherefore of what is commanded."

The difficulty, however, as regards obedience "of the judgment" is not so much with beginners as with those who are more advanced in years and even in virtue. Experience and responsibility, whilst they lay heavy burdens on the back, bring also the capacity to judge and criticise; and with the capacity, the temptation. Simplicity in Obedience is very hard to mature minds. Hence the mental attitude of too many is, "I know it is foolish, but it has to be done". Now this is not the way that the Saints and the Fathers obeyed.

It is certain that it is not always in our power so to control our judgment as not to see reasons against what we are ordered. Superiors are human, and subject to error; and their mistakes are sometimes perfectly plain. In these circumstances, we are not only permitted, but sometimes bound, to represent the case. If the thing commanded is very hard, or if contradictory commands are issued, or if our own good or that of the community would suffer, then we should lay the reasons before the superior. This should be done, as St. Benedict says, "patiently and at the fitting moment";[1] and Father Alvarez de Paz adds that we should always on such occasions pray to God with earnestness that we may have light to see whether it is proper to speak or not.[2]

But if in spite of what we can say the superior persists in a foolish order, St. Ignatius would have us not only obey, but think the superior's wish to be "the

---

[1] *Regula*, c. 68.
[2] *De Adoptione Virtutum*, Lib. v. Part 3, cap. 13.

right thing".[1] This may be accomplished in two ways. First of all, we are perfectly justified in considering that obedience in this particular point, however useless or even damaging it may promise to be in itself, is beyond doubt "the right thing" *for ourselves*. It is here supposed (as it is needless to say) that there is nothing sinful—nothing against God's commands, against justice, against the Church's law, or the rule of the order—in the superior's command. This being so, we cannot be wrong in acquiescing in the superior's decision as "the best thing, here and now, for myself". But we may go farther. No one who is acquainted with the lives of the Saints is ignorant that God's Providence frequently brings success out of foolishness, when the foolishness is the holy folly of Obedience. This may happen either when the act of Obedience, though calculated to do harm as regards its proper object, has a very different result in some wider and much more important field; or when, by God's wish, the very thing which the act of Obedience seemed bound to defeat is promoted and made to succeed by it. Thus a religious who is ordered to cease teaching, or to teach a particular manual, or to teach only at a certain hour—commands which, we will suppose, are clearly detrimental to the persons taught—may and probably does by simple Obedience contribute to the education and profit of souls over a

[1] *Epist.* xix. See also the words of St. Theresa: "Our Lord has given me the grace to think that my superiors are always right".—*Foundations*, ch. xxiv. 2.

much wider area than his own class-room. An incident in St. Theresa's life shows how Obedience may benefit the very thing it seemed likely to ruin. She was ordered by Divine revelation to make a foundation. On speaking of the matter to her confessor, he refused to allow her to act. She acquiesced, and humbly obeyed. Some time later, the confessor gave the required permission; and God revealed to her that the foundation would now be a much greater success than if she had undertaken it at first; although, let it be observed, it was He Himself who had inspired her to act.[1] Thus God *always* crowns Obedience, though the obedient soul may not know at the moment, nay, may never know,—in what direction the success is to be.

[1] *Life*, ed. by Manning, p. 251.

XX. POVERTY.

IN our contemplation of that virtue which St. Francis of Assisi calls the "queen,"[1] let us begin by thinking of our Blessed Lord and Master. "Poverty," says St. Bernard, "was not to be found in the heavens; on earth it abounded, and man did not know its value; therefore the Son of God, being smitten with desire of it, came down from Heaven to make Poverty His own, and to teach us how precious it is."[2] The Poverty of Jesus and of His blessed Mother was extreme, and, we may say, excessive. That is, to all appearance, He carried it much further than was necessary in order to accomplish any visible purpose. He chose to be in want of the commonest necessaries. He was born, not in a house or cottage, but in the stall of a beast. He laboured with His hands. He was often in want of sufficient food, as we gather from many passages of Scripture and from the words of the Saints. To worldly prudence it would seem as if His work would have been better advanced had He chosen to possess more of the world's goods. And let us further ob-

[1] S. Bonaventura, *in Vita*, cap. vii.
[2] Serm. i. *in Nativ. Dom.*

serve that He practised Poverty not merely to edify others—that is, to enhance His character in the eyes of the Jews, or to attract souls to Him. He practised it consistently, from the Manger to Calvary, in all things, in secret as in public, with an evident choice and preference. This proves that Poverty has some Divine effect upon the acts of the heart. For the mere fact of being in need or want is no virtue, but often a temptation to sin. Thousands of the poor are made worse by their poverty; and the first step towards bringing them nearer to God is to lift them out of their sordid indigence. What, then, is the effect of Poverty such as Jesus practised?

Consider, first of all, certain evil effects of affluence or possession. First, it causes attachment—binding the heart and will as with fetters to the things of the earth. A heart which is attached to earthly property gives itself with difficulty to Jesus Christ. Next, it causes anxiety; occupying the mind, filling the heart with trouble, taking up time and attention. He who has possessions is solicitous about them, and not very solicitous about God. Thirdly, it causes pride and vanity; the man who is an owner or proprietor feels a security, a sense of power, a flattering superiority, which lifts him up in self-satisfaction. Such vanity and self-content are directly opposed to the child-like humility of the Gospel, to the docility of faith, to the acknowledgment of sin, and to filial abandonment to our heavenly Father. Hence the hearts of the well-to-do are generally hard; whilst a man's thorough conversion often results from his losing everything he has. This is what St. Paul was thinking of when he said to Timothy that the rich "fall into temptation and the snare of the devil, and many unprofitable and hurtful desires, which draw man into destruction and perdition".[1] Blessed be my holy vow of Poverty, which frees me from these entanglements, and makes it easy for me to press near to my Saviour's path!

Next, reflect upon some of the advantages of Poverty. First, it removes many temptations; not only such temptations as we have just considered, but temptations more remotely connected with money; such as dishonesty, sensuality, impurity. The poor man, if he love his poverty, is sheltered from the troubled atmosphere where the devil has his own way; the occasions of sin pass him by; grievous incitements to betray his God rarely visit him as they visit his brethren in the world. Next, holy Poverty casts the soul upon its God, in loving confidence. This is a most precious result. Virtue is not virtue unless the heart is united with its God. But nothing so effectively turns the heart's affection in confiding simplicity towards God as the sense of having nothing in this world. "Now," said St. Francis when he despoiled himself even of his clothing in the presence of his friends,—"Now I can say with truth, Our Father Who art in heaven!" O

---

[1] 1 *Tim.* vi. 9.

happy rest of the heart upon its God! O Lord, I am needy and poor; but Thou art solicitous for me! Thou art my helper and my protector! O Lord, make no delay! Thirdly, Poverty is a painful thing to bear, and, like all painful things, duly accepted, it intensifies the acts of the heart in spiritual intercourse with God. As St. Chrysostom says, "Poverty is the modern substitute for the fires of the persecutor."[1] It makes a holocaust of our bodies. With its accompanying hardships, its manifold sting, its searching humiliation, it is a continuous and lifelong mortification of the flesh. "Why," says St. Bernard, "is the same promise made to the poor as to the martyrs, except that voluntary poverty is a species of martyrdom?" O my Jesus! make me fear to trifle with my vow of Poverty! It is heavy—heavy and painful; but that is what Thou hast ordained, that so it may draw me to Thee! If I fail to accept its pressure—if I seek to escape from it—if I use every opportunity to evade its holy rigour—should I not tremble, O my Master? For by Poverty I must either grow into Thy likeness or fall away from Thy company. My brethren in the world may moderately enjoy their possessions, and yet not turn their backs upon Thee; but not so with Thy vowed servants! Their act of renunciation overshadows them every moment, and it either lifts them up or casts them miserably down.

---

[1] *Hom.* xi. *ad Hebræos.*

We may here, then, enter into our past and present life in the spirit of sorrow and of desire of amendment. First, we have not unfrequently allowed ourselves to *regret* our vow of Poverty. For example, we have behaved in a very unspiritual way under certain exterior humiliations brought upon us by poverty; or we have been impatient that our monastery or congregation could not have a better house, a better church, a better table. Or, if we are superiors, we have been hurt to be forgotten by benefactors and by the world generally. Next, we have had many inordinate attachments even in our cloister; attachments and preferences for lodging, clothing, books, and various objects. "The smaller the thing is," said an ancient Bishop and Monk, " the hotter is the unmortified man's rage for it.[1] Many a religious is prepared to work and pray with exemplary industry, but will make it very unpleasant to a superior who attempts to change his cell, or to take away his books, or even to deprive him of a favourite inkstand. Such a spirit of attachment destroys the virtue of Poverty at its very root. The rich of this world who are not attached to their riches are more truly poor than the religious who is inordinately attached to a pen, or a needle, or a little print or image of a Saint. Thirdly, have we been careful to have nothing superfluous? Superfluities are such things as a religious keeps beyond

---

[1] S. Eucherius *ad Monachos*.

what is authorised by the custom of spiritual men, men of delicate and God-fearing conscience, in his own order or congregation. The word, therefore, need not be taken too literally, so as to exclude even the least thing not strictly necessary—as, for example, one or two books, a common image or two, a second penholder, a desk, or a paper-knife. Even spiritual men, ardent in the pursuit of perfection, make no scruple as to having such things. But anything more would be a "superfluity"—such as too many books, valuable objects, curious things, specially convenient belongings, pretty useless things, souvenirs, more clothes than needful, odds and ends such as one gathers and does not like to part with. To retain things of this kind, even if the superior permits, and one is prepared to give them up, is contrary to religious Poverty. No superior has any valid right to permit such things to be retained—except, perhaps, when he is afraid that some poor religious will otherwise be driven to insubordination or melancholy. And as to being prepared to resign them, that, no doubt, is something; but it does not prevent them from being superfluities. What we ought to do is not only to be prepared to give them up, but to give them up in reality. Fourthly, we have to accuse ourselves of many words and signs showing how unmortified we are in things of daily life, when our vow of Poverty makes itself felt. <u>St. Vincent Ferrer,</u> speaking of the power of gaining souls, says that a religious will never succeed in this unless he in all sincerity trample on worldly goods and practise genuine Poverty; "and," continues the Saint, "he must not be afraid to suffer unpleasantness for Poverty's sake; he must love Poverty and bear the destitution of Poverty (*inopia paupertatis*) for Christ's sake. How many boast of their profession of holy Poverty, and yet cannot bear to be in want of anything! They call themselves friends of Poverty, but Poverty's true friends and companions —hunger, thirst, contempt, and lowliness—they avoid with the utmost care!"[1] Would it not seem, to judge from our murmurings and complaints, that we had entered the religious life in order to have all our wants supplied and to live in comfort? Is this holy Poverty? Is it not rather hypocrisy and dishonesty? Is it not very often, perhaps, even self-deception? "To desire to be poor," says St. Francis De Sales, "and not to feel any of the inconveniences of Poverty, is to wish for the honour of Poverty and the advantages of riches." Thus it is with us, who, in a certain sense, cling to our vow, and yet spoil the practice of it by unmortified grumbling. And how much harm is thereby done to our brethren around us and to the work of the Holy Spirit in their hearts! O my Jesus, give me greater love of Thee! O Holy Spirit, send into my heart one ray of Thy heavenly fire that I may feel my baseness, and may arise and grasp Thy gift of holy Poverty!

[1] *Tract. de Vita Spirituali.*, c. 1.

For the better understanding of the state of our heart, let us reflect on certain degrees of religious Poverty. The first step on the ladder of Poverty is to accept or to hold nothing without permission. We are here concerned with the matter of the vow. Of mortal sin, however, it is not intended here to speak. Let it suffice to say that a religious who truly loves his holy vows will be far from wishing to confine himself to what is strictly necessary in order to escape a grievous fall. In one word, a good religious is filled with the *spirit* of Poverty; it is part of his character, not from nature, but by grace and practice. He therefore strictly keeps such rules of his order or community as regulate the acceptance or retaining of money and other things. He uses money as if it did not belong to him, handling only what he must handle, expending it only as directed by the well-understood order or wish of his superior, jealously stinting himself in matters where there is some liberty, accounting for all to the last farthing, and feeling glad when he is rid of it and once more without purse or scrip. As he deals with money, so must he deal with everything else; although it is money which most imperils the soul of a religious. But even as to his very clothing, he should be studious to ask permission and to beware of putting pressure upon his superiors. This is the spirit of Poverty.

The second step on the ladder is to have a great love for the Common Life. The common life of religious congregations is that equal distribution of things needful for life, which, in imitation of apostolic times, is the distinguishing feature of the religious life. The common life may not be a very severe life. It is certain that there are tens of thousands of poor people around us who fare worse and are worse lodged than a lay-brother in the strictest of religious orders. But a man is no nearer to God merely because he starves or is housed like the beasts. The common life of religious, whilst its frugality and austerity differ in different orders, is always frugal and austere. But it is not only by its severity that it enables the soul to advance in spiritual progress and to draw nearer to God; it is much more by the spirit of obedience, self-effacement, and mortification of the will, which the faithful following of it entails. To live, to eat, to be clothed and lodged, as other people prescribe, in the same fashion as others, every day—this is no small trial to the egotism and pride of the spirit. Hence the good religious, as being one who has entered religion to make of himself a holocaust to his Saviour, is especially devoted to the common life. He dreads exceptions. He will have nothing better than others; he will never, if possible, be absent from the common table, where sweet reading with tranquil silence and the company of brethren dear to Our Lord transform the refection of the body into a spiritual feast where Christ presides. Whatever his age, his dignity, or his services, the true religious wants to have nothing more than the youngest or most ignorant brother.

And he is just as much on his guard against singularity. To withdraw from the common life even for the purpose of living more austerely is rarely without danger. Human pride and self-love will undergo many inconveniences for the sake of their own gratification. To conquer one's humour for separateness and solitariness and to force one's self to play one's part in the ranks of the community, is an admirable exercise of that mortification of the spirit which so effectually leads the soul to God. This is the secret which St. Francis de Sales imparts in his often repeated phrase, "To ask for nothing and to refuse nothing". Humbly and gratefully take what the rule offers, or the superior prescribes, and sanctify yourself by directing your intention to God's greater glory. But abstain as far as you can from asking for anything more. It is in sickness that such a practice as this becomes more necessary, and also more difficult. A time of sickness is a time of great danger, both for the sick person and the community. If the sickness of a religious is slight, or if it recur frequently, or if there is a long convalescence, then the holy strictness of rule and discipline is in much peril; for the infirm person is likely to become self-indulgent and soft. If there is much sickness in a community, common life is almost suspended, silence suffers, easy-going habits are contracted, and the rules are broken with but little remorse. And this cannot be altogether prevented; for superiors are bound to be kind, solicitous and even indulgent in all that concerns the sick. But, this being so, there is the greater obligation on the religious whom God visits with sickness to remember his vow of Poverty and his obligation to follow his Saviour. Sometimes even solid and mortified men and women become strangely soft and pitiable under sickness. Do thou remember, O my soul, that when pain and weakness come, thy duty is to use them for thy profit. Embrace, therefore, the hand of God; seek not for special care, unusual remedies, expensive advice, or perfect nursing. Think of the vast number of poor who have none of these things—nor even the comfortable room and bed, the kind attention and the sufficiency of all things which thy brethren secure to thee. Murmur not if thou art at times forgotten, or carelessly treated, or badly understood. Remember that thy Lord opened not His mouth. Dispense not thyself from thy prayer or thy practices except by obedience; and continually, as far as possible, convert thy pain, thy weariness, and thy desolation into acts of love and resignation. Be simple with thy superiors; state and explain, as if a third person were in question, whatever it seemeth that he should know; and then leave all to him. Or rather, leave all to thy Heavenly Father. For it is thy privilege, as one of the poor of Jesus, to expect all things from His hand. "Cast thy care upon the Lord, and He will feed thee!"[1] This was the promise, and it must needs be fulfilled.

[1] *Ps.* liv. 23.

The third step in Poverty is to be content with, and even to love, what St. Benedict calls "the worst of everything".[1] This is the spirit of the Saints. To practise it requires the illumination of the Holy Spirit. This illumination we gain by affective prayer and the practice of the common life, and by the observance of humble obedience to superiors and directors. But oh! what peace, what contentment, what joy, is the reward of those who are truly needy and sincerely love to be so! Let us meditate on the prayer of St. Francis: "O Lord Jesus, show me the ways of Thy beloved Poverty! Most truly, O Lord, is she the Queen of virtues; for Thou, leaving the dwelling of the angels, didst come down to earth that Thou mightest espouse her. And she clung to Thee so faithfully, that she began her service even when Thou wert in Thy Mother's womb. At Thy birth she received Thee in the manger and the stable; during Thy life she so stripped Thee of all things that she would not allow Thee even a stone whereon to rest Thy head. In the conflict of Thy passion she alone stood by as armour-bearer; when Thy disciples fled, she did not leave Thee, but fearlessly adhered to Thee with the whole band of her princes. In her strong embrace Thou didst breathe forth Thy soul. O my most poor Jesus, I ask this favour for myself and children for ever, that for love of Thee they may never possess anything of their own, and

---

[1] *Reg.*, cap. vii.

that they may suffer Poverty as long as they live in this miserable world! Amen."

Points for Mental Prayer.

1. Contemplate Jesus, as St. Francis contemplated Him: poor in His birth, in His home, in His life, in His surroundings, in His disciples, in His death on the Cross. *Adore* Him as your God, your Master, your Judge. *Compassionate* Him as your most dear Brother and Redeemer. *Long to imitate* that most poor, unworldly, detached and divine life.

2. Think upon that noble and excellent vow of Poverty which has placed you in the company of those who follow your Lord. Say to Him: O my God, I choose Thee! Of all the things which my eyes covet and my hands might grasp, I choose Thee, and Thee alone! Thou art my inheritance! Thou art my portion! I choose, deliberately and with all my reason and will, to be destitute (as far as it may please Thee) of earthly possessions, comforts and resources; and as deliberately do I throw myself upon Thy Providence, as a child upon the breast of his mother! "Father and mother have abandoned me; but the Lord hath taken me up!"[1] I accept Poverty with all her attendant humiliation, pain and inconvenience. As with Thee, O my Jesus, so may it be with me!

3. At Thy feet, O my Saviour—at Thy feet,

[1] Ps. xxvi. 10.

weary and sore as they are in seeking me—I cast myself to ask pardon for my sins against holy Poverty, and the spirit of Poverty! How shall I atone, O Jesus, for my tepidity, for my repining, murmuring and refusing? How shall I obtain Thy forgiveness for my comforts, superfluities, perhaps even luxuries? How shall I make up for the years I have lost in ignorance and blindness, not understanding, not valuing holy Poverty? And canst Thou ever forgive me for the harm I have done to others by my reckless words and my miserable unfaithfulness to my vow? Oh! may I enter into myself! May I repent! May Thy Spirit lead me to reform—to live less unworthily of Thy Saints and of Thee!

XXI. PRAYER.

The command of our Lord, that we should "pray always," far from being a precept of extraordinary and unusual perfection, is really nothing more than a loving injunction to live up to the end and purpose for which we are made. It is true that it is seldom we find these words of our Saviour literally fulfilled, or fulfilled with anything approaching to real continuousness. But no one can live as a Christian, much less as a religious, who does not lift up his heart in Prayer with a certain frequency; because we are made to love and serve God, and made, therefore, to commune with Him by understanding, will and heart—which is what is meant by Prayer. We are made to worship Him; we are made to love Him; we are made to petition Him and to thank Him; we are made to ask His pardon for our transgressions. Therefore, Prayer is so absolutely needful—not at every moment of our life, but all through our life—that we turn our back upon our last end if we do not pray. And the more continuous and intense our Prayer, the more perfectly do we fulfil the end of our existence.

A Christian in the world is advised to use frequent vocal prayer, and to be regular in Mental Prayer at least once each day. If regularity can be secured a certain continuousness is secured. The more fervent the Christian, the more frequent will be his times of regular prayer. The rules and customs of religious are adapted to make prayer and spiritual occupation so regular and frequent as to turn the whole day into a more or less continual prayer. First, there is the Divine Office; next, the hour or more of meditation proper; then Holy Mass, visits to the Blessed Sacrament, examinations of conscience, and various vocal prayers in public or private; and lastly, running through the day, from the moment of awakening to that of falling asleep, there is the habitual practice of recollection and ejaculation. These various practices, like the channels of water which irrigate the land in every direction, distribute holy Prayer over the whole of our waking hours; and if we are faithful in them, our life may be truly said to be a continual Prayer. "Seven times in the day have I uttered Thy praises."[1]

We are now to direct our thoughts, as is most proper in a time of retreat, to the subject of Mental Prayer. Although every kind of Prayer is holy and profitable, nevertheless our progress, and even our salvation, depends in a great measure on our Mental Prayer. For not only does Mental Prayer mean an intimate and real converse with God, which vocal prayer, being composed by others, and being for the

---

[1] *Ps.* cxviii. 164.

most part formal and without variation, can probably never bring us to, but our vocal prayer will remain words and nothing more unless we practise Mental Prayer. And the more we attend to that exercise of the soul's powers, to that stirring up the will, to that directing of the intention, and to that intensifying of the affections, which constitute Mental Prayer, the more habitually and the more effectually shall we be in union with God in all our acts, words and thoughts.

Hence the hour, or half hour, of Mental Prayer, is of extreme importance in the life of one who would strive to follow Christ. It is the hour in which the soul lives; that is, lives its true life, and rehearses for that life of eternity, in which Prayer in its highest sense will be its rapture. It is the hour of its intensest discipline, when acts are produced which vibrate long afterwards through the hours of the day, through the spaces of life. It is the hour of speaking to God in His Holy of Holies, where the soul finds insight, and strength, and endurance. It is the hour of calm, when the thronging elements of a man's personal life are ranged in order and marshalled to obedience, so that the will may aim at one thing and one thing alone. It is the hour of the kindling of that precious fire—the fire of Divine Love—which must burn through every pulsation of life, or else life's deeds can never be borne to the heavens, but must drop like leaves to wither on the earth. It is the hour when the continual presence of the awful

Sovereign of the creature is, in a certain sense, made actual and real; when the heart speaks to God, and —what is of infinitely greater moment—when God speaks to the heart.

One of the principal purposes of a retreat, therefore, ought to be, to make sure that we are faithful in the practice of Mental Prayer, and that we have an intelligent appreciation of its purpose and method.

No more salutary advice can be given to a soul than that the daily Mental Prayer should be faithfully taken, whatever the difficulty may be. There are some who neglect Mental Prayer through mere sloth or spiritual indifference. Such souls are in extreme danger and danger of mortal sin; because such a disposition leaves the soul defenceless before temptation of every kind—as defenceless as a sleeping man would be against a murderer. Others are irregular in Mental Prayer because they have no sufficient knowledge of what its purpose is, or how they should set about it. Many religious among the active orders are most insufficiently instructed in this respect; and, in consequence, they pass their lives, which are full of works of charity and devotedness, without really drawing near to Christ, and therefore without acquiring anything like the merit unto life everlasting which might easily have been theirs. Again, there are too many devout persons, whether priests, religious or seculars, who give up Mental Prayer under the stress of occupation. They have learnt to pray, practised prayer, and loved prayer; but as they advance in years and come to have more to do, they are led to think that work will supply for prayer. They ought to understand that no one has any right to be so overwhelmed with work, however excellent such work may be, as to be prevented from taking his hour or half hour of Mental Prayer. There may be a day now and then when the formal or precise half hour must be omitted. But even obedience does not excuse, in a religious, the *habitual* neglect of the prescribed time for meditation; because such time is ordered by the rule, and therefore no superior can dispense from it, except rarely and for an urgent reason. In truth, it is a pernicious mistake to suppose that any one can work for God while neglecting Mental Prayer. Our work in itself is of no efficiency whatever. True, we may have certain duties to perform, which it would be wrong to neglect; but our words and acts, of themselves, and except so far as God co-operates, are of no more power to move the hearts of men or build up the Kingdom of God, than the strokes of a church bell. And there can be no doubt that a very large amount of the activity of pastors, preachers, and other labourers in the vineyard, is barren and unproductive precisely for the reason here named—that God withholds His co-operation from the unspiritual man. Hence, half an hour's prayer, so far from interfering with work, may be the very condition of the success of our work. "An interior man," says a profound spiritual writer, "will make more impression upon hearts by a single word animated by the Spirit of God, than another man by a whole sermon which has cost much labour and is full of excellent ideas."[1] Now, no man can live an interior life without Mental Prayer. And although there may be some who are so advanced in recollection as to be able to elevate their heart to God at all times without the necessity of making a regular meditation; yet even these would be in the position of men who tempted God unless they did what their rule and the ordinary Providence of God prescribed. As for those amongst us who live in constant distraction, with only a passing good thought or a transitory ejaculation here and there in the day, what can we expect to do for God, unless we go apart awhile with our Master, and spiritualise our very human lives? For success and self-sanctification are one and the same thing. O my Jesus, make me faithful to regular prayer! Fill my heart with a burning desire to be near Thee—to study Thee—to transform myself into Thy likeness! Strengthen Thou me against sloth and indifference! Let me hear the summons to Prayer as if it were Thy own voice! Permit me not to be deceived by the devil, and by my own folly or vanity—but draw me, by the sweet example of Thy Mother and Thy Saints, to see that no time is more valuable than the time spent with Thee—no occupation more absolutely

---

[1] Lallemant, *La Doctrine Spirituelle*, v., ch. ii., art. 2.

certain of results than the activity of the heart in communing with Thee!

As to the purpose or end of Mental Prayer, it is not necessary to say much. I have generally avoided calling it "Meditation," because there is real danger of its being thought to be a mere exercise in thinking. It seems absurd to say so, but it is true that the name "Meditation" does incline people to this idea. The more or less long and elaborate expositions which one usually finds in books of meditations also tend the same way. Now, all spiritual writers insist repeatedly that the purpose of Mental Prayer is not to think, or reason, or learn, but to make Acts, or to elevate the heart to God.

It follows, therefore, that we have to think, or reason, so far as may be necessary, in order to set the heart or will in motion. Hence, the Mental Prayer of one soul will differ considerably from that of another, and the same soul will pray differently in different stages of spiritual advancement. Some minds cannot think much; others are helped a great deal by thinking. Some find their hearts very slow to take fire; others almost naturally begin to make devout Acts as soon as they find themselves on their knees.

For beginners, and indeed to a very great extent for all of us who are ordinary persons, there must be a good deal of thinking, or we shall lose our time and get no further forward. In other words, we must have a kind of programme ready when we get upon our knees, and must more or less follow it out. This programme may be either found in one of the regular books of Meditation, or it may be made up by ourselves; or it may be partly one thing and partly the other, as when we use a book, but note on the margin certain Acts which we propose to make, or when we use a passage in Holy Scripture and mark out the various words on which we propose to found spiritual elevations. Such a programme should be prepared over night; briefly, however, and without labour or strain, so that it may be fresh when we take it up in the morning. After we have made a few preparatory Acts, such as an act of the Presence of God, an act of loving humility and trust, and a prayer for the grace of the Holy Spirit (not forgetting an invocation of our Lady and of such Saint or Saints as we may desire), we begin with our prepared programme, either reading it in the book or recalling it to memory. There seems no doubt that all should be allowed to use a book during Mental Prayer; for although there are some who will take advantage of this and only *read* (without praying), yet these can be corrected; and, on the other hand, nothing fixes the wandering attention like a book (or paper), which at once suggests thoughts without the fatigue of trying to remember. When Affections begin to come, we have (for the time) reasoned enough. The principal Acts which we should try to make are Adoration, Praise, Faith, Preference, Humility, the Offering of ourselves, Resignation, Thanksgiving, Confidence, and (when meditating on the Incarnation) Desire to imitate, or to be transformed, and Compassion; but the most important Acts of all, which must be repeated over and over again in all our prayers, are Love of God, and Sorrow for sin; and we must by no means neglect Petition. We shall find such Acts suggested in the manuals; or we might have them briefly indicated in our notes. It is better to leave the exact words to the impulse of the Holy Spirit during the course of the Meditation. Even if we use forms of Acts already printed, it is well to make them our own by emphasising, repeating, or analysing the words before us.

When we have exhausted a point, or when it seems no longer to afford exercise for the mind and heart, we can pass on to another. There is no necessity to take all the points we have prepared; happy they who find enough occupation in one! But neither should we scruple to leave one set of thoughts for another when we seem dry or unable to get forward.

As to the subject of our Mental Prayer, the only general rules seem to be two: first, that the life of our Lord, and more especially the Passion, will be nearly always useful for most, and must not be entirely neglected by any; and, secondly, that when, by advice, we have taken up a definite line of subjects—whether it be the Attributes of God, the Virtues, the Four Last Things, or the Life or Passion of our Saviour—we should not abandon it too soon or too lightly, but give it a fair trial. For although it is true that we are right to adopt for Mental Prayer the class of subjects which suits us, rather than one which does not seem to be useful, yet we must not follow mere whim or obey the humour of a day or an hour, but be slow in changing what we have deliberately taken up.

One of the most important lessons that a servant of God can learn in the practice of Mental Prayer is not to be discouraged by distractions. Let him be concerned about them, and take such means to obtain recollection as prudence may suggest; but he must not allow distractions to make him lose heart; for, in the first place, he will have them to the end of his life, and, in the second, a very little earnestness will prevent them from spoiling the precious minutes of Mental Prayer. The secret to be learnt is this: That (putting out of the question how far we are the guilty cause of distractions by what has occurred *before* the hour of our Prayer) no distraction is sinful until it is noticed by the mind. How, then, have we to act? Simply, the moment we *notice* that we are distracted, to turn quietly once more to God. If we do this without hesitation, as soon as the distraction is perceived, no harm whatever is done by that distraction. Nay, the humble, sorrowful, and loving conversion of the heart to the presence of God, being performed with the more fervour from the very fact of our becoming aware of the distraction, is itself a most excellent exercise of Mental Prayer. And if the whole of the time of Prayer were spent in the repetition of this exercise, it would be a time well spent and meritorious. St. Thomas says: "A distraction which is involuntary does not take away the fruit of Prayer".[1] And St. Francis of Sales says that if in Mental Prayer we should do nothing but banish distractions and temptations, the Meditation is well made.

Points for Mental Prayer.

1. Place before thy eyes the image of Jesus in prayer, upon the mountain side, at night. He Who is the Object of all Prayer—He in Whose hands are all the issues of Prayer—even He deigns to pray, and to pray during long, silent and solitary hours. O Lord and God, Who hast come to seek me and to save me, I worship with all my being Thy sovereign Majesty, hidden under the human form of one who prayeth! O most loving Master, most solicitous Teacher, I long to learn of Thee! Thou teachest me that there is no divine work, no divine life, without unceasing Prayer! Thou biddest me to "come apart" with Thee upon the mountain, however heavy the day's work, however anxious the crisis, however importunate what still remains to be done! Open my eyes, O Jesus, that I may see the truth and necessity of this! Above all, let me feel

---

[1] *Summa*, 2ª, 2ᵃᵉ, qu. 83, art. 13.

that the moment of Prayer is the moment of coming to Thee—to my only true Friend, without Whose guidance, and help, and love, all effort is cheerless and all work is barren.

2. Study with affection thy Saviour's fashion and way of Prayer. Observe, first, His Reverence. My Jesus, Thou dost bow Thy head, and prostrate Thy body; Thou dost seek the solitude; Thou dost guard Thy senses from distraction; and for Thee there was no need of these things. It was for me Thou didst show Thyself in all things so reverent in Prayer, lest I, when my day should come, might be as one who tempteth God! Next, His Simplicity. Thy Prayer, O Divine Lord, was not in reasonings or subtleties or sentiment; but in lifting up of the heart direct to Thy Heavenly Father: "Our Father!" "Father, if it be possible!" "I confess to Thee, O Father!" "Father, forgive them!" "Father, keep them!" "Father, into Thy hands!" Give me the inestimable grace of simple, direct, and continued Prayer! Thirdly, His Fervour. In the Garden, O Jesus, the sweat of Blood testified to the vehemence of the acts of Thy Sacred Heart, and all generations are urged to fervour by the description of that hour of agony. But how many times, dearest Saviour, how many times, before the moment of Thy passion, had the Mount of Olives, or some other of Thy retreats in the hills of Judea or near the Sea of Galilee, been witness of physical emotion well-nigh as severe! Give me the supreme grace of fervour in prayer! And, finally, His Per-

severance. All through His life; when He was hidden, and when He was engaged in His ministry; whatever the fortune of the day might be; when things went well, and when He had to suffer; in the stress of occupation; amidst the clamour of souls for help; whatever might be the humour, condition, state, or preoccupation of His human nature;—always did He pray, and pray during long hours. O my Master, grant me the grace of perseverance in Prayer!

3. Return upon thyself, and thy shortcomings in the matter of Prayer. I humble myself before Thee, O my God, and confess in the bitterness of my soul my blindness to the value of Prayer! I have received instructions; I have read the words of Thy Saints; I have seen the truth of their teachings; and yet, in my frailty, I have, all my life, again and again lost sight of the importance of Prayer, and more or less neglected it! I ask pardon, also, for my sloth, in not taking the trouble to learn how to prepare myself for Prayer, and to order my life so as to be able to pray! I bitterly regret my irregularity—my neglect of the times of prayer, my absences, my frequent omissions! I confess, with shame, that I have been discouraged, disgusted, turned away from Prayer, by want of confidence in Thee, my God! How can I repent enough of my want of faith, my want of trust, my want of heart, towards Thee Who alone art my Father and my Friend!

Note on the Remote Preparation for Mental Prayer.

It is only by living a recollected life that we can ever attain to true interior Prayer. The fervours of our youth and of our beginnings are precious graces of God. But in order to be, in our maturity, men or women of Prayer, we must have attained habitual mortification of the senses and of the intelligence. We can never be, in Prayer, more than what we are out of Prayer; that is to say, for any considerable space of time. This is insisted upon by the Fathers in many well-known passages. See, for example, Cassian (*Collationes*, ix. cap. 7). He bids us, first, to cast away all solicitude for earthly things in general; next, not to trouble ourselves about our occupations, but to learn to be able to banish them even from our thoughts; thirdly, to be very careful about idle or sinful habits of talk; fourthly, to beware of all mental disturbance of the nature of anger or annoyance, which is fatal to recollection; and fifthly, to purify our hearts of carnal thoughts and of the love of money.[1] Father Alvarez is very strong on the subject of talk and of work. We must, he says, get rid of superfluous meetings, that is, such meetings as are not rendered really necessary by business, temporal or spiritual; of idle conversations, such as neither piety nor charity calls for; of unnecessary discussions, taken up chiefly

---

[1] *De Oratione Mentali*, part. 1, cap. 2.

to relieve *ennui* or to recreate ourselves; and of frivolous or needless occupations, such as are not altogether in accordance with the true spirit of our vocation. Any one who thinks that habitual levity, curiosity, the pleasures of the senses and bodily indulgence, are compatible with the gift of Prayer and the enjoyment of divine consolation, is self-deceived, and will speedily find out his mistake.

Interior recollection and supernatural views depend very much upon what the mind habitually feeds upon. The *reading*, therefore, of those who aspire to Prayer is a matter of the greatest importance. As to this, we should observe the following rules. First, we should never read for mere pleasure; if lighter books are sometimes read, the time given to them should be carefully and on principle limited. Secondly, books of a sensual cast, it need not be said, should be solicitously avoided. Nothing defiles the imagination more than erotic reading. Those who live apart from active occupation should be particularly on their guard in this respect. Thirdly, interior souls should not even pursue literature for the sake of literature; because the literary temper is one of criticism, fastidiousness and superiority, and therefore altogether opposed to the simplicity of Prayer. But literary, historical, or scientific studies which are necessary for purposes of teaching, or which are really prescribed by obedience or by one's office, are much less dangerous to Prayer. Fourthly, the reading of free-thinking, "liberal," and non-Catholic literature should be avoided as much as possible. Such reading spoils the freshness of Catholic faith, and by saturating the mind with natural, animal, and diabolical wisdom,[1] hinders it from lifting itself up to God in the spirit of revealed truth and of divine grace. Hence, we should renounce the intellectual and recreative gratification of reading the anti-Catholic, anti-Papal, anti-Christian, and anti-spiritual literature, of which there is so much that is clever and well written at the present day. God will reward us for our abstinence by giving us true recollection in Prayer. "Behold, I will wean her, and I will lead her into solitude, and I will speak to her heart."[2]

[1] *St. James* iii. 15.   [2] *Osee* xi. 14.

XXII. THE DIVINE OFFICE.

The Divine Office is not only one of the most considerable occupations and grave duties of Priests (and of others), but it holds a most important place in the dispensation of the Incarnation. As Christ came to save us, and to draw us to Him, so He came to pray—in all the senses of the word Prayer. He came to be the representative of the human race in its perpetual and obligatory work of worship, praise, thanksgiving, satisfaction and petition. Now that He has come, and has undertaken this work, it is perfectly and consummately performed. But—as in everything connected with the Incarnation—although Christ does all, and does all perfectly, yet we also must do, in our way, all the things which Christ does. He expiated our sins; we must expiate. He draws us to Him by word, example and grace; we must carry on this ministry. And so, if He prays, sovereignly, perpetually, His body on earth and its members must also pray, not indeed without many imperfections, but yet without ceasing. This duty of constant praise and petition lies constantly on the Church as a whole. In union with Christ's Prayer the Church's Prayer is a well-pleasing homage to the Heavenly Father. Therefore on the part of the faithful, in their union with Christ and with one another, there ought to be, and there is, a perpetual public official prayer, ascending to Heaven from the ministers of the Church, who represent the whole Church. Therefore, the Divine Office, though it is far from constituting the whole of that sacrifice of praise which the redeemed world must offer to God, and which it does offer, nevertheless forms an authorised, sanctioned, official and most fruitful portion of the world's homage. "Let my prayer, O Lord, be directed like incense in Thy sight."[1] The Divine Office is the incense offered to the Eternal Throne by the heart of humanity. The thought of that perpetual and universal homage recalls the picture in the nineteenth chapter of the Apocalypse, where the homage of the heavenly multitudes is described. We hear first the voice of the vast assemblage of the redeemed crying out, "Alleluia! Salvation and glory and power is to our God!" Then the four and twenty Ancients (the hierarchs of that Church) and the four living creatures (under which name is expressed the Angelic Host) fall down and adore God sitting upon the throne, saying "Amen!" "Alleluia!" Next, a single voice "out of the throne"—no other voice than that of Christ, as man—sounds through the vault of Heaven. "Give praise to our God, all ye servants, and you that fear Him, little and great!" Finally, once more up rises the voice of the great

[1] Ps. cxl. 2.

multitude, "as the voice of many waters and as the voice of great thunders," saying "Alleluia! For the Lord our God the Almighty hath reigned!"[1]

That which is to go on for all eternity, with delight and with ravishment, we begin to practise on earth; painfully, imperfectly, interruptedly, yet lovingly, zealously and fruitfully.

Let us consider the excellence of the Divine Office.

First, it is the public Prayer of the Church, and therefore the Prayer of Christ Himself. Joining my poor and unworthy voice with this grave symphony of worship and petition, my feeble breath becomes a part of that which is mighty and divine. The purpose of my life is only to give myself, as intensely and as continuously as I can, to my God. How fitly and beautifully does this task of Prayer, recurring "seven times in the day," distribute the loveliness of Prayer over the whole of my poor life!

Next, it is a public Prayer—with Christ, therefore, in the midst of those who pray. Even the priest who says his Office in private shares in the fruit of the public Choir, because he is associated in it by the ordinance of the Church, in whose name, even when he is alone in his small presbytery, he utters the Psalms and the Prayers of His office. In Choir, the Office is more of a sacrifice, because it involves obedience, order, greater or less inconvenience and even pain. In Choir, moreover, the contagion of

---

[1] *Apoc.* xix. 1-6.

numbers usually increases fervour, voice helping voice, and heart inspiring heart. But the solitary priest may make his recitation resemble the choir of a cathedral, by his punctuality, his reverent formality and his attention to little things. He who unites in one the voice and heart of the Choir is Jesus Christ, present in their thoughts. Let the priest imitate the Venerable Curé d'Ars, who used invariably to recite his breviary at the foot of the Altar, pausing frequently to gaze up at the tabernacle where Jesus was; so strongly was he borne to unite his Prayer with that of his Saviour!

Thirdly, reflect upon those inspired words and forms which it is thy privilege to use in the Divine Office. The Psalms, the words of the Saints, the words of the Church! All may be said to be inspired —not all in the same strict sense as the words of Holy Scripture, but all as being at least the indirect utterance of the Holy Spirit. *Voces Spiritus Sancti* —this is what St. Bernard calls the Divine Office. There is something which inspires awe in the thought that, in reciting the Psalms, we are uttering forms of Prayer dictated by the Holy Spirit Himself. Nay, more; those august words of praise and petition are not only divinely inspired, but they are the utterances of our Lord and Saviour Jesus Christ. The Fathers of the Church all agree with St. Augustine when he says, Christ was in David; in David Christ was prefigured.[1] When the Royal

---

[1] Serm. ix., *De Verb. Apost.*

Psalmist speaks, it is Christ who speaks. The Psalms are His instrument, His voice. He speaks, sometimes in His own person, as our Head, sometimes in the person of His mystical Body, that is, of us and of His Church. And as we follow Him, and our lips reverently repeat these sacred forms, they readily express our own emotions and desires, just as if they had been written for ourselves. It is natural that this should be so. For Christ our Lord took upon Himself all our infirmities, always excepting sin and concupiscence. Hence when He prays, it is as if poor human nature prayed; for He is truly Man; and He even deigns to express the sense of sinfulness, speaking as a sinner because He is the Brother of those who are all sinners. O blessed words of the Psalms, which the Apostles and the Martyrs have used, in which the Saints of all ages have lifted up their hearts to God! O blessed and fruitful words, in which the servants of God have praised God ever since Christianity began, and which at this moment are continually resounding day and night all the world over, in emulation of the unceasing song of the Angels and the Blessed! May I join myself to this holy choir in joy and reverence! May the opening of my breviary be to me as the signal for uniting my voice to the voice of my Saviour and of all His army of devoted servants! For there is no sentiment of my soul which does not find expression in the Psalms; if I am joyful, the Psalm is joyful; if I am sad, the Psalm mourns; if I would worship God, the Psalm has phrases which man's heart could never have found; if I would repent of my manifold sins, the Psalm wails and implores and clings to the mercy of God; if I would ask for grace, the Psalm pleads for every good and perfect gift; if I suffer, I find the Psalm filled with utterances which are none other than those of Christ, in the Garden and on the Cross; and if I would pray for my friends, living or dead, the Psalm has petitions for blessings and for length of days, and has also sighs from the depths for those who can now no longer help themselves.

Fourthly, the Divine Office furnishes our hearts with a continual food for prayer; because it presents us with daily thoughts of our Lord Jesus Christ, of our Lady, and of the Saints. Each season of the year, almost every day, has its liturgical picture. We have our Lord and Saviour in His coming, His birth, His manifestation, His sufferings, His death, His glorious resurrection. How fresh and how joyful are the various festivals which succeed one another from Advent to Advent! How profitable a way to keep ourselves near to God is it to enter with devotion into each feast as it comes! How the Psalms seem to adapt themselves to the spirit of the liturgy! How the calm and pregnant sayings of the Fathers and Doctors throw their light into the depths of our own spiritual life—as they have done for a thousand years with every generation of Christian hearts! With Jesus comes Mary. Her festivals place before us the thought of her who is not only the Mother of our King, but who reflects, reiterates, and (if we may say it) amplifies the spiritual effect of the life of Jesus. Each Saint, coming in his turn as a star in the firmament of God's Kingdom, does the same thing in his own degree. The Saints are the illustrations of the Divine Book of the Gospels. In most Holy Mary and in the Saints we not only read what Jesus said and did, but we see His own features, His own winning attractions. Thus, every day the Divine Office is for us a fresh inspiration and a new stimulus to give our whole heart to God. O my Lord Jesus Christ! Enlighten me to find Thee daily in my breviary! Give me the grace to appreciate the holy liturgy! Let me make more account of Thy daily service than of any worldly occupation!

Fifthly, we may encourage ourselves to love the Divine Office by reflecting on the pious and stirring associations which are connected with it. The Office (not to speak of Old Testament days) goes back to that "hymn" which our Blessed Saviour said with His disciples after the Last Supper. Many such hymns must they have said together—and many of those Psalms must they have recited, in which He Himself is prophesied and described. It goes back to the public prayer of the Cenacle, before the Spirit was given; to the breaking of bread before the Apostles separated; to the psalms which accompanied the great liturgies of Rome, Alexandria,

Antioch, Constantinople; to the days of the thousands of monks of the Syrian and Egyptian deserts. It was in the great Churches of Rome and Milan that it seems to have taken something like the shape that it has now; and St. Benedict, in ordering the Office of his Monks, frequently uses the expression, "as chants the Roman Church". With the missionaries of Rome and the monks, the Divine Office spread itself over Europe. How pleasing it is to think of the innumerable Cathedrals, Monasteries, and Collegiate Churches of the ages of Faith! To think of the daily and perpetual Office; of the splendour of the great festivals; of the Saints, who loved to assist at Matins, Lauds, Vespers; of the thousands of simple hearts who nourished themselves upon psalm, and antiphon, and lesson and responsory! To think of St. Gregory with his clergy, St. Augustine of England with his monks, St. Columba in his rude choir amid the Western seas, St. Cuthbert dying in his hermitage whilst Matins were going on in Holy Island, St. Stephen with his first Cistercians in their oratory of branches and straw, St. Bernard storing up during the midnight Office that honey which he afterwards dispensed in the Chapter-house, St. Dominic assisting at Lauds with Holy Mary and the Saints, St. Felix of Valois, on Christmas night sharing the same privilege, St. Charles Borromeo in the choir at Milan, St. Francis of Sales at Annecy; or, again, among holy women, St. Hilda at Whitby, St. Etheldreda at Ely,

St. Clare at Assisi, St. Walburga, St. Gertrude, St. Mechhildis, surrounded by their bands of holy nuns! O blessed Saints, who found in the Divine Office your sweetness and your union with God, pray for me that I too may find it sweet to occupy myself with it, and that it may draw me always nearer to my Saviour!

Having thus reflected on the excellence of the Divine Office, let us consider how we may best discharge our duty in performing it.

The great idea of the Saints and spiritual writers seems to be—to attend to the presence of God; to begin the Office, continue it, and end it as if we were always in the sight of God and His angels. In the Office, attention is nearly sure to bring with it devotion. St. Charles Borromeo used to urge his priests to concentrate their attention carefully *at the beginning* of their recitation. He himself used to spend a quarter of an hour in Mental Prayer before beginning Matins and Lauds over night; and he advised all to renew their attention every time they said *Deus in adjutorium*. It will help us much if we accustom ourselves to make an effective act of the Presence of God whenever we begin to say Office.

For the purpose of keeping up attention during the progress of the recitation, we may make use of various means. We are not to be scrupulous about minute attention. If we read the words reverently, place and circumstances being such as to subject us to no unnecessary cdistration, and our thoughts being gently constrained to union with God, it is enough to satisfy obligation. But the more actual devotion we can put into it, the better. Thus, we may take the words, or the general sense, of psalm and responsory, and apply them to the Feast, or the Mystery, of the day; or to our Lord's Passion; or to God as our Father and Last End; or to the Blessed Sacrament; or to our Lady or the Saint of the day; or to our sins, our wants, our resolutions. *Cibus in ore, Psalmus in corde sapit,* says St. Bernard. The Divine Office is the food of the heart. O my Lord Jesus Christ, can it be because my heart is so occupied with worldly things that Thy sweet psalmody awakens no relish in me? Perhaps I ought to study more than I have hitherto done the meanings and purposes of Thy sacred Canticles. "*Psallite sapienter,*" Thou sayest by Thy Holy Spirit. I must sing with intelligence; understanding something at least of the wealth and abundance of significance which there is even in the shortest phrase or word of Thy inspired song. "He who understandeth," says St. Thomas, "findeth food and refreshment for mind and for heart; but he who understandeth not is without all refreshment."[1] Let us imagine how this angel of the Schools, or how St. Augustine, must have lifted up the heart as he used these divine words! Listen to St. Augustine: "Oh, how fervently I uttered my service to Thee, O my

---

[1] In *Epist.* 1 *Cor.* xiv. 14.

God, when I read the Psalms of David—those songs of faith, those breathings of piety! How I was set on fire by them; and how I burned to have them recited throughout the universal world, that they might bring the human spirit to Thy feet! . . . How I wept over Thy hymns and canticles! The words of them streamed into my ears, and with them came the truth into my heart; and piety grew warm within me, and tears flowed, and it was very well with me then!"[1]

To a religious, the Divine Office should be his principal vocal prayer—a prayer which indeed may well render superfluous almost all other vocal prayers. Not that a religious should not say his rosary, or little prayers for special intentions. But, otherwise, is not the Divine Office sufficient? What is there that we do not pray for in the Office? What intention is there that cannot be expressed in the words of the Psalms, the hymns, the responsories, or the collects? If you wish to pray for yourself, or for your friends, for the Church, or the Holy Father, for the monastery, for final perseverance, for any virtue or against any habit or temptation, for the conversion of sinners or of the country, for the faithful departed, you cannot fail to find forms of prayer in your Office every day. If you would indulge in devotion to the Holy Trinity, the attributes of God, the Holy Ghost, the Incarnation, the Passion, our Lady, St. Joseph, St. Benedict,

---

[1] *Confess.* ix. cc. 4—66.

your angel guardian, you have only to use your breviary. The truth is, that when the Divine Office is deliberately, solemnly, and devoutly performed each day, then each day is fairly filled up. To take up extra vocal prayers is to make it probable that the Office will be more or less put into the background—either through hurry, or through fatigue, or because such extra prayers divert our attention from the great prayer of all. If we feel called to pray more, let us respond to that call, not by hurrying through the Office in order to have more time for prayer, but by saying the Office more carefully, with more comprehension, with greater deliberation. This is the true monastic spirit.

There are three defects or faults which we must carefully avoid in reciting the Divine Office in private. The first is irreverence of place. We should be ready to pray in any place and in every place. But, when we can choose, we should prefer, for our Office, a place apart from noise, business, and distraction, where we may quietly kneel, or walk, or sit, and give our thoughts without interruption to God. "Dismissing the multitude, He went up alone, to pray."[1] This is the pattern given us to follow. Next, we should avoid unsuitable times. All times are fitted for prayer. But here again, when it is in our power, we should choose our time for the important duty of the "Opus Dei". It is the laudable

---

[1] *Matt.* xiv. 12.

practice of priests who fear God to recite Matins and Lauds over night; and for this, the longest portion of our task of love, we should have a fixed time—either in the middle of the afternoon, or late in the evening, according to our duties and habits. The day hours are best said either before Mass—if we can also get in our Mental Prayer—or very soon after breakfast. Vespers and compline might be said on occasion of a mid-day visit to the church. To trust to casual chances for getting through our breviary, or to cut up our Office into minute portions, or to thrust it in between noisy occupations or amusements, or to put it off till it has all to be crowded into the last lawful hour, when weariness and sleep make it almost impossible to attend to what we are doing—all these things are infidelities to our Divine Master, which ought to trouble us and afflict us. Lastly, in our recitation we should avoid unseemly haste. "Haste is the ruin of devotion;" this is the expression of St. Francis de Sales. How often do we find plenty of time for sleep, for sitting at table, for unnecessary talk, for amusements—but allow ourselves to rush with indecent haste through the task of our breviary! This, if persisted in, is certainly nothing less than mockery of God.

Points for Mental Prayer.

1. Place before thy eyes our Lord Jesus Christ, after the Supper and His divine discourse, singing a

hymn with His disciples before He went forth to Gethsemane. Observe His sense of the Divine Presence—all His bodily powers absorbed in the contemplation of the Godhead. Observe His inward and outward devotion; imagine His immaculate Heart in its purity wholly occupied with prayer and self-surrender; admire that strenuousness with which He joins with His disciples—He Who is the most holy God! O Jesus, I adore Thee Who didst come down from Heaven to take captive my heart by Thy example! Praise for ever and ever be to Thee, O my Master and Teacher, because Thou dost show me how to sing in Thy sight! Behold me at Thy feet! I desire to learn! Let faith, reverence, and love come out from Thee and transform my misery to Thy likeness! I cannot of myself acquire the spirit of Prayer! All my efforts, unassisted, must be in vain! But Thou canst teach me!

2. Consider thyself, whether thou recitest in some choir of brothers or sisters, or whether thou sittest alone with Thy breviary, to be a part and a voice in that grand universal choir in which Jesus presides. O Lord, I am not worthy to join Thy Angels and to sit in the assembly of Thy Saints! There are in this great choir minds rapt in deep attention, hearts inflamed with intense devotion, souls united perfectly to Thee! How can I dare to make my own those holy words which in their mouths are so genuine and so beautiful? My Saviour, make me less unworthy! I offer myself to Thee! I give Thee

all my powers! I dedicate to Thee my heart, my reason, my lips! I consecrate to Thee my time and all my views and intentions! I know there is nothing I can do which is more precious than Thy Office; impress this feeling, O Lord, upon my unstable heart, that I may no longer sadden Thy Sacred Heart with my unfaithfulness!

3. Consider thy defects and imperfections in the discharge of this most holy work. O Jesus, I confess my sloth and negligence! Too often have I kept away from choir, perhaps without permission; omitted even considerable portions of my breviary; exposed myself to needless distractions; given my Lord the worst moments of the whole day; hastened through my service mechanically; taken no pains to ensure recollection either at the beginning, or during the progress of my recitation; and perhaps habitually considered my Office as the least important of all my occupations! My Redeemer! is it possible that I can have fallen into this state of unspirituality—this condition of grave danger? When I think of my deliberate negligence, the remembrance of Thy judgments comes over my being, and I tremble at the curse which Thou hast pronounced against those who do Thy work negligently! Yet, my Saviour, Thou wouldst not have me despair, or lose courage. What must I do? I will place all my sins and faults at Thy feet—I will ask Thee to remember my frame and to consider that I am dust! Ah, my Lord, I know Thou dost never forget it! Accept, then, the

confession of my heart—accept my cry for pardon—accept my petition for amendment! By Thy grace I now resolve to put my whole heart (which all belongs to Thee) into my Office—to plan how I may best say it—to dwell upon all its holy features—to make it my grand task for each day—and to take such means as spiritual books advise, that I may recite it devoutly, not once or twice, but every day till my death! Amen.

XXIII. THE BLESSED SACRAMENT.

THE Blessed Sacrament is the principal means, on earth, of union with God. Therefore it is essential that, in time of retreat, we should review our attitude and our conduct in its regard. The consequence of abstaining from participation in our Lord's Body is nothing less than spiritual death—certain and inevitable death. But the effect of partaking of it is not always life; at least, not always that strong and abounding life which is meant by our Lord when He says: "He that eateth Me shall live by Me".[1] There are those, both among religious and among Christians in the world, who communicate frequently and yet do not live spiritually. So far are they from living "by Christ" that their lives exhibit a pride, a sensuality, and an unkindness which seem to prove that they live by another spirit altogether.

Let us consider, then, that the institution of such a stupendous dispensation as the Eucharistic Presence is, on the part of God, a Divine effort to be *near* His beloved children. "No other nation," as Moses so touchingly reminded the people whom he was instructing, "hath gods so nigh them, as our

[1] *John* vi. 58.

God is present to all our petitions."[1] No human idea of God, or of God's love, would have been able even to conceive this splendid stretch of power. When God took human flesh, and so seized upon man in all man's powers and faculties, He made His eternal love visible and palpable. The Blessed Sacrament is the prolongation—as far as human faculties are concerned—of the Incarnation. Those who saw and "handled" Jesus in the flesh are scarcely to be envied by us who have the Real Eucharistic Presence.

A thing may be "present" without our being aware of it or perceiving it. But we must see a thing (by sight spiritual or sight corporeal) before it can lift up our heart. God might have been contented with His revelation and His silent grace. He has not been so contented, but has wished also that our human faculties should feel Him. The Eucharistic Presence has a double power over our beings—it has the effect of physical sense, and the effect of Faith.

That the Blessed Sacrament is powerfully adapted to impress the senses need not be proved. Although we do not see or feel Christ by immediate contact with His Sacred Humanity, yet the accidents or qualities of bread, which we do see and feel, really cover Him in so true a sense that we can truly say: He is here—He is there! The moment at which

---

[1] *Deut.* iv. 7.

He begins to be upon the Altar is known to us. He comes, and He goes away; He is carried hither and thither; He is lifted up for adoration; He is delivered in Holy Communion. Lamps burn before the Tabernacle where He truly reposes. A Church in which His Presence is known to be is different from any other building. It is possible for men and women to come in where He is, to stand or kneel in His Presence, and to leave Him again when they go out. To enter a Church where that Presence is gives a feeling as if one entered the house—nay, the very chamber—of a great king, and a most loving friend. To see from a distance the tower or roof of a Church where the Blessed Sacrament is, draws the Catholic heart to holy reverence and lifts it up in devout adoration.

Yet with all this, the sense is "held"; the eyes are veiled. To invest all this sacramental ritual with meaning, there must be Faith. There must be that firm and devout clinging to God's work which, in its effects upon our faculties, surpasses in many respects even sight and touch. The merely visible and palpable soon grows common, and quickly fails to stir emotion. Any face, any scene, however beautiful, however striking, loses its stimulating power over the human faculties when they have become accustomed to it. In the Blessed Sacrament there is no human face, no human figure. But there is the Presence of the unseen—a presence that stirs something deeper than mere sense; a presence which is enforced by the most powerful of all emotional forces—the most realistic of all our methods of grasping things outside of us—I mean, the spiritual Faith of a devout Christian heart. This is the reason why the Holy Eucharist never grows common or usual; never ceases to stimulate our very senses. There is sufficient about it that is palpable to give human faculty a foothold, but the grasp is the grasp of Faith. There is sufficient that is sensible to bring it within nature's scope; but the light which makes nature realise it radiates in its intensity from a source that is far above nature, and it can never diminish either in efficacy or in abundance. For the power of the senses depends upon the condition of the body, but the power of Faith is infused by God.

But the Blessed Eucharist is not only a Presence, it is also a Sacrament. That is to say, over and beyond our own dispositions, it possesses, elevates, and strengthens our spiritual nature. It is true, preparation on our side is required; and preparation can never be too exact, too complete. But our preparation consists almost wholly in the removal of obstacles—or, at the utmost, in forcing ourselves into that devoutly expectant attitude which is described by the Psalmist when he says: "Lord, all my desire is before Thee!"[1] The inflow of spiritual energy is the work of the Sacrament. In the Holy Eucharist,

---

[1] *Ps.* xxxvii. 10.

the sacramental effect, as we gather from the teaching of St. Thomas, bears directly upon the human will. It is intended to draw and dispose the will to adhere to God above all things and to God alone. When this adhesion to God is prompt, warm, and constant, it is what we call "devotion"; so that the direct effect of the Sacrament of the Body of the Lord upon those who receive it is Devotion. Let us observe how this agrees with the well-known passage of the Council of Trent—that the Blessed Sacrament is the "antidote by which we are delivered from daily faults, and are preserved from mortal sin".[1] These words were undoubtedly inserted in view of the Calvinistic doctrine that our nature is utterly corrupt and can never produce anything but sin. The Holy Council says that the Body of our Lord is an "antidote," expelling poison and healing corruption. It delivers us from daily or venial sins by multiplying those acts of the love of God which not only occupy mind and heart in good, but burn up and cleanse away the guilt and penalty of venial sin. It preserves us from mortal sin by firmly and ardently uniting the will to God. Indeed, that word "union," which is so constantly (and naturally) used by the Fathers to describe the effect of the Holy Eucharist, includes two thoughts: it indicates, first, the incomprehensible love of our Lord and Saviour Jesus Christ in desiring to have a spiritual union

---

Sess. xiii. c. 2.

with man, which is symbolised by His making Himself our food; and, next, it denotes that very condition—that state of spiritual clinging and adhesion of man's will to God's, which is man's ideal safe and happy state on earth. We become one with Jesus. That is, we have the same "will" as He has. What He loves, we love; what He desires, we desire; what He says ought to be done, we long to do, and do; His judgments are ours; His behaviour under every kind of condition, under all circumstances of persons and occurrences, is the behaviour we are always striving to reproduce in our own life and action. Thus, it is no exaggeration to say that in the Holy Communion, Jesus Christ gives us His own Heart, taking our heart away. His Heart is the Heart of charity, of purity, of sacrifice. And these terms describe the effect of Holy Communion upon the hearts of His servants. O my Saviour! How far have my frequent Communions been from thus transforming me! What have I been doing, O my most loving Master, that I have been near to Thee so much and yet am not on fire? It is my negligence—it is my affection for myself—it is my sloth! How full of danger is my state, O Lord! How infinitely good art Thou to visit me now with Thy holy inspirations, and to urge me to enter seriously into myself!

How, then, can we best prepare so as to make good use of this greatest gift of God?

1. Our first endeavour should be to *understand* the Blessed Sacrament, as far as we are permitted to

do so. Like all the mysteries of God's loving dispensation to man, this most divine mystery offers a wide field for thought, for information, and even for study. If we are priests, we should not be satisfied until we have read and mastered all that theology teaches us in its regard; more especially what we find in St. Thomas of Aquin, whose words combine scientific exactitude with that emotional force which is so marked a feature in the sayings of the Saints. If it is not permitted us to study theology, in the strict sense of the word, we must still make ourselves familiar with Catholic teaching on this many-sided revelation of Christ's love. We must seek out what the Saints have said about it—especially St. Alphonsus. We must find spiritual books which give us details about the Church's doctrine, and about that variety of devotion of which the Holy Eucharist is the object. We must not be unacquainted with its history; and the more we read of what the Saints have thought, said and done in Its regard, the more will mind and heart become possessed by It.

2. Next, we must, in order to prepare well for Holy Communion, make a careful use of the Sacrament of Penance. In those who live a regular life, minute examination or detailed explanation to the confessor of minor faults is not required, and should be avoided. What should be aimed at is—war with deliberate venial sin (of grave sin, nothing need here be said). We should use confession as a means to

exterminate, or at least to reduce to harmlessness, those evil inclinations and bad habits which are the cause of our more frequent infidelities to God. There should never be a confession in which, by humble and ardent contrition, we should not do our best to be washed "yet more" from sin, and to present our heart, emptied of creatures and of self, to the inflow of the sacramental grace of the Body of Christ.

3. The essential part of our "immediate" preparation must be, Actual Devotion. Deep trust in our Lord's love, humble contrition, and absolute clinging to Jesus, as our only Sovereign, our only Master, our only Friend, should occupy us, with more or less continuousness, from the evening of the day before our Communion. All our usual exercises might well be turned in the same direction—our nightly examination of conscience, our offering on awaking, our Mental Prayer, the words of the Divine Office, the lessons of the lives of the Saints. No long forms of prayer are necessary; though in such prayers as those of St. Thomas which we find in the missal, there is abundant suggestion for devout aids. But every holy formulary which comes in our way will easily turn itself into an act of devout preparation for Communion.

Our thanksgiving should not be cut short; the fifteen minutes or thereabouts should be faithfully adhered to. During the time after Communion, the soul has three precious advantages: first, her acts are more fervent, and therefore more efficient in promoting union with God and merit unto life everlasting; next, she obtains more ready answers to her petitions, for, as St. Teresa says, Jesus, after Communion, remains in the soul as on a throne of grace, and says to her: What wilt thou that I do for thee? Or, in the words of St. Alphonsus, He says: Ask Me what thou wilt, and as much as thou wilt, and thou shalt be heard.[1] And, thirdly, Jesus being so near, and being absolutely united to us in the way devised by Himself, the process of being transformed into His likeness (on which all our progress depends) goes on with great efficacy and completeness; so that one often seems to rise from Communion imbued with a detachment, a spirit of sacrifice, a love of our brethren, and a general impulse toward God, which one seldom experiences at other times. O my Saviour, I acknowledge my negligence and my sloth! How often have I approached Thee unprepared, how often have I received Thee with my mind distracted, my thoughts otherwise occupied, my heart cold, my very bearing indevout! How habitually have I cut short my thanksgiving! How have I let slip those precious moments of Thy Presence! Thy patience, O my Jesus, is infinite, or else Thy grace, before this, would have been justly withdrawn from me, and I should be plunged in the darkness of sin and indifference— perhaps in heresy or unbelief!

It is of the greatest importance that the servant

---

[1] *Works*, Centenary ed.: *The Holy Eucharist*, p. 227.

of God should not regulate his Communions by the state of his feelings. No universal rule can be given as to the frequency of Communion; it is a matter for each one to settle with his or her confessor. But it is certain that, in Communion more than anything, we should act on principle and by the light of illuminated reason, and not on impulse. On the one hand, no sudden fit of fervour should carry us to the Holy Table on an occasion when we did not intend to communicate and are unprepared. On the other hand, it is even more imperative that no feeling of indevotion, no coldness, no fear, no scruple, should keep us away when we have made a reasonably painstaking preparation and are expected to approach. It is not in the feelings that devotion is situated; it is in the will, the intention, the desire. Many souls are tormented, in approaching Holy Communion, by doubts about faith, doubts about past confessions, and by the absence of sensible devotion. All these things they should boldly turn to the purpose of a good preparation. They should fasten upon them with their reason and judgment (enlightened as these are by faith and grace), and present them to Jesus as crosses, sufferings, pains and troubles. O my Divine Master, they should exclaim, I deserve to feel no sensible devotion, and I accept this from Thy hand! I have brought this upon me by my dissipated life and my numerous sins! These doubts, O my Lord, are not in my will, but in my imagination! They infest me like venomous insects, against my own desire! Reason, experience, my confessor—all tell me to disregard them; and, therefore, as I cannot rid myself of them, I offer them as part of Thy Cross which is laid upon me, to Thyself! There could be no better preparation than this.

There cannot be any limits to the effects which may be produced in the soul of men by the Blessed Sacrament. But as these effects are only largely produced when the obstacles of self-love, attachment to creatures, and habitual sin, are removed, it is principally in more perfect and contemplative souls that the prodigality of the Divine inflow can be seen. Such souls seem really and truly to acquire His Spirit—His Heart. They inhale, if the word may be used, the very breath of His being—that supernatural love of Poverty, of Obscurity, of Obedience and of the Cross, which are to Him as the very elements of His spiritual being. They learn, or begin to learn, that secret which seems so simple to state, yet is the rarest of things truly grasped—that Jesus loves them—loves them more than thought can conceive. Let this inspiration once possess a human heart, and that heart is lifted towards God as the rising west wind lifts the pinions of the dove. It is in Holy Communion that the light breaks in. O my Jesus! Not to me—not to me, alas! can there come Thy light, Thy breath, Thy inspiration!—for I am too full of myself, too slothful, too indifferent! Yet Thou, O Lord, canst change my heart!

Points for Mental Prayer.

1. Contemplate, first of all, Jesus at the Last Supper. It is night, and the world is occupied with its pleasures, its rest, its business, whilst Jesus is thinking of those He loves so much. His Heart is overflowing with that love wherewith He loves them to the end; with that desire which has brought Him to this supreme moment in His beneficent dispensation. In order to be always "near"—even when He has left them and gone back to Heaven—He exerts His infinite wisdom and His almighty power, and institutes the Blessed Sacrament. O my Lord and Master, humbly prostrate at Thy feet, I worship Thee in Thy Godhead! O Lord, how wonderful, how admirable, how stupendous, is that stretching forth of Thy right Hand which endows the human race with such a glorious inheritance! Who can praise Thee as Thou deservest to be praised? Thou Who didst lead Israel out of Egypt and feed his hosts in the wilderness, art greater here. Thou dealest here more profoundly with the nature of man, and showest more evidently Thy own great glory and the magnificence of Thy Holy Name. And it is for me, O my Saviour, that Thou dost take up the Bread and the Chalice whilst Thy enemies draw near! For me, who am so hard to stir up to a sense of Thy most sweet love! For me, who am so indifferent, so cold, and so ungrateful! Yet at this moment, O Jesus, my heart is before Thee! I take the gift from Thy

hand! I thank Thee with every power of my being—and I implore Thee to give me understanding and the power to rule my being so as to live all my life in thankfulness, and in the sense of what Thou hast done for me!

2. Contemplate, next, what is shown to thee of the Sacred Heart of Thy Saviour in the dispensation of His Body and Blood. First there is the revelation of thy God; for as the Incarnation reveals Him, so the Blessed Sacrament reveals Him more. "Behold! He standeth behind our wall, looking through the windows, looking through the lattices!"[1] The Supreme Deity is as near thee as that! Canst thou doubt any more that He loves thee? See how He would be with thee always—with thee by a bodily Presence which carries with it His Divinity; with thee by a veiled nearness which Faith causes to burn and palpitate; with thee by a sacramental effect which, on thy receiving Him, inundates thy nature and thy powers with nothing less than His own Divine Spirit. My Divine Lord! I have dishonoured Thee by doubting of Thy love! I have served Thee without affection! I have served for myself, and not for Thee! I have even feared Thee with a servile fear! In the presence of Thy Body and Blood upon Thy altar for my sake, I ask for that filial love which I see I ought to have, for One Who loves me so truly, so deeply, so unmistakably!

[1] *Canticles* ii. 9.

3. And now I will not rise from Thy feet, O my Master, until Thou hast pardoned me! Pardoned the distraction and inattention of my life, which has been passed without understanding this greatest of Thy gifts! Pardoned my attachment to certain habits of sin which have shut up against me the heavens of Thy merciful grace! Pardon my want of preparation—my want of devotion—the shortness of my giving of thanks! O my Jesus! By Thy coming—by Thy labours—by Thy Divine teaching— by the institution of this Sacrament of Thy Love, touch my heart and strengthen me to order my life wholly with reference to Thy Eucharistic Presence!

XXIV. THE HOLY MASS.

No Catholic can for a moment doubt that the Blessed Sacrament is, and must ever be, the chief "devotion" of the Church, and of every child of the Church. Devotion denotes that occupation which is the one essential occupation of human life —occupation about the love and service of God. Therefore, just as the Incarnation (which brings God near to our minds and hearts) is, next to our belief in God's existence and Trinity, the chief dogma or mystery; so the Blessed Sacrament, which keeps the Incarnate God before our senses and our faith, is the chief devotion. Because we have Him, and have Him in this particular dispensation, we naturally occupy ourselves about Him. If He has so disposed that His true Body shall remain localised on this earth, and visible to all—in the way in which the accidents do localise Him and exhibit Him to the senses—it is certainly intended that, with these senses and faculties, in our corporeal life, in our doings, in our goings to and fro, we should take into account, before all other things, Him Whom we are thus privileged to possess. "I am the Lord that dwell among the children of Israel."[1] O Chris-

---

[1] *Numbers* xxxv. 34.

tian heart! If He said this to the people of His choice when He was impressing His law upon them, how much more feelingly does He say it to us who have not only His law but His most munificent grace and His life-giving truth! Can we forget Him? Can we neglect Him? Can we pass Him by?

In a Christian land, therefore, in a Christian community, the Blessed Sacrament is first and foremost. For It great churches rise, for It precious tabernacles, costly vessels, are provided. Christian Faith lifts It up on the altar, kindles the lights around It, offers the flowers and the incense; and brings, too, that which all these things signify,—the perpetual, affectionate, and triumphant love of thronging multitudes of the faithful. The Mass is not only the daily devotion of the pious, but it is the grandest of all earthly pageants—on those occasions when, in a great Church all ranks of the clergy, all orders of citizens, with every magnificent appliance, with the poetry and music of the Liturgy, are brought together to profess faith and love. The Benediction and the Procession are rightly dear to all who would honour Him to Whom all earthly honour is less than the dust of the wayside. The open Church invites the loving soul to make its visit and its prayer where the lamp sheds its silent ray. How touching is the persistence of the Saints in seeking out Jesus in the Tabernacle! The Angels are there before them. There is a tradition that St. Michael is the Guardian Angel of the Blessed Sacrament. More than one of the Saints have said that to the great Hierarchy of the Thrones is chiefly committed Its honour and worship. St. Francis of Assisi imparted to Jesus in the Blessed Sacrament all his thoughts and plans; St. Dominic would pass whole days in the Church; St. Francis Borgia visited It seven times a day; St. Ignatius spent before the Tabernacle every moment he could obtain; St. Aloysius, who had to be forbidden to visit Jesus, would weep and lament as he felt the attraction almost too strong to resist; St. Francis Xavier preached all day and prayed all the night before the altar; St. Vincent de Paul never passed a Church without going in to pay a visit; St. Alphonsus, whose burning words so many use in their worship of the Blessed Sacrament, would spend as many as eight hours at a time in Its presence, and could only be with difficulty forced to leave It for a while. The ardour of Thy true servants, O my Jesus, in visiting Thee and giving Thee the best of their time and service, fills me with confusion. Too little have I thought of Thee in Thy greatest mystery! How ungratefully have I neglected Thee! How many days have I passed without once kneeling before Thy sacramental Presence! How often have I been near Thee, and yet not visited Thee! How often have I preferred my amusements, some unnecessary occupation, perhaps some light and foolish book, to Thy presence, Thy company, and Thy communion!

Let us reflect that Jesus in the Blessed Sacrament,

being Who He is, is the centre of all power and spiritual influence in this Christian dispensation. Not only, therefore, is it natural to Him in this mystery to sanctify those who approach Him; but He ought, if all were as it should be, to draw to Him all the sinners, unbelievers, and heretics of the world, and to convert them. Yet how often does He remain in a place for years, for generations, without any signs of such a triumph! How often does a Church remain with its doors open and its services faithfully carried out for half a century, and all the time there is hardly a conversion! Why is this? The reason is, that Jesus in this world is in the hands of His servants. As a rule, He will not act and work except so far as the devotion and sacrifice of pastors and people carry Him. As long as He is suffered to remain a mere Presence, shut up, scantily and formally honoured, perhaps neglected, He is in the world as if He were not in it. He is the Sun, but the clouds and vapours of indifference obstruct His shining. But let His people remember Him, make much of Him, frequent His Presence, make use of His great unbloody daily Sacrifice, and crowd to the Table of His communion, then He puts forth His right hand, and souls are gathered to the harvest. It is where the Blessed Sacrament is devoutly honoured by priest and people that conversions are made. O Saviour of souls! It is I who bind Thy hands! It is I who shut the door in the face of those whom Thou wouldst save!

The holy Sacrifice of the Mass, being the chief Act in which Jesus makes His Eucharistic Presence effective in the world, is the chief Act of Catholic devotion. "God Himself," says St. Alphonsus, "cannot cause an action to be performed which is holier and grander than the Mass."[1] "The effect of the Holy Eucharist," says St. Thomas, "is equivalent to the total effect of the Passion."[2] Whatever the Passion did or does, the Mass can do. We must look upon the Mass, therefore, as nothing less than the Sacrifice of Calvary, so performed as to be more perfectly applicable to individual souls. For this is the reason why the one supreme Sacrifice goes on throughout all generations—that individual souls may more effectively partake of its benefits. It is true, the price of our redemption was paid once for all, the gates of Heaven opened, and original sin counteracted, without any act of ours corresponding to the Act of Christ's Sacred Heart as Redeemer. But men may lose Heaven even now that they are redeemed. The Cross must save them still—must draw them, strengthen them, pardon them, and give them final perseverance. This is the reason why we have the Mass. It is given to us, with all the stupendous miracles of mercy which it involves, in order that the graces of the Precious Blood may be more immediately at hand to us; that every day of our lives we may be drawn to God, purified and made strong. It is

[1] Centenary ed.: vol. xiii. 291.
[2] In *Joannis* vi., lect. 6.

for this the Altar of Sacrifice stands continually in the midst of each Christian flock. It is for this that the Priest, made holy by a Divine consecration, lives beside that Altar, ready, as morning succeeds morning, to lift with pure hands the one only Victim to the majesty of the Creator and Last End. O my Lord Jesus! must I not live for Thy daily Sacrifice? If I am a Priest, must I not say Mass every day? If I am one of the flock, must I not be solicitous to hear Mass as often as I can?

For the Mass will certainly save my soul, and transform my soul more and more into that which Thy Blood was shed to make me. There are four things, O my Jesus, in the Mass: there is Thyself, there is Thy sacrifice, there is Thy power, and there is the correspondence of my own heart. Because Thou art there Thyself, it is a moment of awe, of fear, of love, of attraction; Thou makest Thy tabernacle in the clouds, and the earth is silent before Thee. That Act of Sacrifice which Thou dost here accomplish means the lifting up to God of that mighty Act of Thy Sacred Heart which is the grand cause and motive-power of all the oceans, seas, and rivers of grace which deluge the earth with bounty; that Act in which humility, obedience, and suffering (though their bodily effect is now over for ever), intensify supreme worship and supreme love. Then there is Thy power;—a power to which the conversion of the greatest sinner is a little thing; a power which is all for men; a power which bursts forth from the restraint of its own laws, as the imprisoned scents of the flowers are liberated by the morning sun; a power which knows only one obstacle and that is (not the unworthiness but) the unwillingness of men. Finally, there is the correspondence of those who assist. God has redeemed us without ourselves, but (if we possess the use of our reason) He will not actually save us or crown us without ourselves. The moment of the Mass is the grand moment for those necessary acts of the heart of man without which he cannot ever see God. It is the moment for worship, for the giving of thanks, for the asking pardon for sin, for the petitioning for grace and help. It is the moment of all moments for that speech with God, that communion with God, that giving of oneself with all that one is and has to God, which is the purpose for which we exist here below. For what happens, O Divine Saviour of my soul, when my poor acts arise from my sinful heart at the moment when Thy Divine holocaust goes up like the incense of a universe to Thy Heavenly Father? My acts ascend with Thine! My feeble offering and my weak prayer, my selfish thanks and my lukewarm appeal for mercy—all this is caught up in the whirlwind of Thy ascending flame, and borne to heaven upon its mighty breath! Never, O my Jesus, is human prayer so powerful, so efficacious, so worthy of its God, as when that prayer is made during the sacrifice of the Mass! O moment of predilection! O precious moment! O golden time!

Yet to me the Mass is too often a weariness. Too often does mere sloth prevent me from saying Mass, or hearing it. I habitually endure it rather than use it to the utmost. Seldom do I meditate upon it. Seldom do I speak to my flock—if that be my duty—upon it and upon its treasures; although, as pastor, I am bound, by a decree of the holy Council of Trent, to do so frequently.[1] My preparation is, perhaps, of the briefest; I even habitually hurry from my bed to begin Mass! My thanksgiving is too often cut down to the shortest limits. O when will priests and people understand that in neglecting the Mass they trample upon treasures, they throw away gold and precious stones, they turn their back on Jesus, and on heaven! O folly of men! O sin of those for whom Jesus Christ has done so much! O mistake, which will have to be paid for at the last accounting day! O ingratitude!

There are many ways of hearing Mass. Each one is right during Mass in praying as he feels most drawn to pray. All prayer, of whatever kind, goes to God, and if the due conditions are present is heard by God. Some find devotion in following the Ordinary and Proper of the Mass. In using this method, we are drawn to the Holy Liturgy, to the Church's feasts and seasons, and to the admirable prayers uttered by the priest, which have come down

[1] "Frequently, and especially on Sundays and festivals, (shall) Parish Priests explain portions of the Mass, and treat of some of the mysteries of the Holy Sacrifice" (*Sess.* xxii., c. 8).

from the earliest Christian times. Some like to say their Rosary. The effect of the Rosary is to place Christ's image with that of our Mother Mary before our eyes. Others, again, have various intentions or contemplations, which they choose as the spirit of piety inclines them, thus making the Mass a means of sanctifying daily life, and of enabling us to exercise the prayer of "petition," a kind of prayer which should by no means be neglected. Lastly, there are those who find it best to place the Passion before their eyes, and to follow Christ step by step from the Agony to Calvary. As the Holy Eucharist was especially intended to recall the memory of the Passion—*recolitur memoria Passionis Ejus*— it is needless to say how profitable is this way of hearing Mass, provided it be carried out with due attention and devotion. It might be suggested that it would sometimes be easier to carry it out if we considered the Mass as both Calvary and the Last Supper. For indeed it is, and is intended to be, both. It is Calvary, because there is the Sacrifice; that annihilation of Himself, which Jesus brings about by descending to the Christian altar and placing Himself under the forms of bread and wine. It is the Last Supper, because the minister and the assistants partake and do not merely stand by. Hence, there are four great divisions of the Mass. The first is the preparation of the human heart. In this, which extends from the beginning of the Mass to the end of the Gospel or *Credo*, the minister and the flock humble themselves, confess their sins, and refresh themselves with the always suggestive words of Holy Scripture. Here we might say: O Jesus Christ, I come to Calvary to be with Thee in Thy bitter agony; but I am too unworthy to stand in the shadow of Thy Cross. Fill me with the fear of Thy judgments, O Lord! Fill me with sorrow for my sins! Here I kneel low down before Thy altar! Here I beat my breast and say, *Mea Culpa*! Here I cry, O Lord, have mercy upon me! Here I give Thee glory in the highest, and cry out, O Thou Who takest away the sins of the world, have mercy on me, hear my prayers! For Thou only art holy, Thou only art Lord! Here I stretch forth my hands in a collect which implores grace and strength! And how efficacious are those words of Thine in the Epistle, in the Gospel, which Thou dost vouchsafe to me! O let me heed them! Let me catch a sound, a phrase which will urge me on like a trumpet, or like the sound of Thy own voice —urge me to know myself, to know Thee, to give myself to Thee!

The second part is from the Offertory to the end of the *Sanctus*. This is the preparation of Jesus Christ, the Victim. See He comes from the obscurity of the ages—when the bread and the wine are brought to the Altar, are held up, are offered! Men hear Him say, "O Father, behold I come!" Let me lift my eyes, as the Priest lifts the Host and the Cup, and bid Thee welcome, O Jesus, to this earth!

Welcome to Bethlehem, welcome to Nazareth, welcome to Mary and to Joseph! Welcome to the lake, the ways, the houses of Galilee; to the streets of Jerusalem, to the scene of Thy Sacrifice! Let me fill the silence with acts of adoration, of admiration, of hope! And let my heart echo the resounding words of the Preface, with its announcing voice as that of a herald coming before a King, and let me make my own that Holy! Holy! Holy! Blessed is He that cometh! Hosanna in the Highest!

The third part is from the beginning of the Canon to the *Agnus Dei*. This is the "Action," or Sacrifice. As it begins, the Priest retires into silence, with his face to the Altar and the Sacrifice. First, enter with him into that wide and grand sweep of thought which, in drawing near the great Act of Sacrifice, embraces the universal Church and the whole race of men. Christ died for all men, and especially for His Holy Church; and how appropriate it is that when he raises his hand in the *Te igitur*, the minister of Sacrifice should place before God, first, the Church with its Pontiff, and then all men throughout the world. Next, lifting his thoughts to the heavenly courts, he remembers the Saints and the Martyrs, all saved by the Blood of the Cross; and he offers the coming Sacrifice as the "oblation of the entire family" of God—of those whom It has already saved, and those who are still pilgrims towards heaven. On these latter, that is on ourselves, he invokes mercy, peace, and the grace of final perseverance. Then come the words of Consecration. O Jesus, in that act Thou dost worship Thy eternal Father with infinite worship; Thou dost offer an expiation for all the sins of the world, and, if need were, for those of ten thousand worlds; Thou dost lay at His feet the thanksgiving of the whole universe for the multitudinous gifts of creation, natural endowment, and supernatural grace; and Thou dost draw upon the whole world the rain and the dew of perpetual mercy. How can I value enough the privilege of bowing my head at this moment of Thy Divine power and stupendous condescension, and of joining, in some measure, my poor acts to Thine, in the confidence that they will rise to heaven with those of Thy most Sacred Heart! O moment of benediction! The priest goes on to commemorate the Passion; to remember the faithful departed; again to communicate with the Apostles and the Martyrs; and then, having, with profound homage, offered "all honour and glory" to God through the Eucharistic Presence, he raises his voice in the prayer of the universal Church, taught by Christ, and here uttered with deep solemnity under the most solemn circumstances. Join devoutly in it, word after word. Next prostrate thyself once more before thy Saviour, and salute Him as the Lamb of God, imploring mercy and peace.

The fourth part of the Mass begins with the prayers preparatory for Communion. Whether or no you communicate sacramentally, these prayers may be followed, for they are most admirably associated with the Blessed Sacrament. Pray, with the priest, that, through the Blessed Sacrament, you may be delivered from sin and all evil, may persevere in God's commandments, and may never be separated from Him. Pray that you may never make a sacrilegious Communion, but that this Divine food may always be your safety, your health, your well-being in soul and body. Then make at least a spiritual Communion.

Points for Mental Prayer.

1. Contemplate Christ offering Himself in the Holy Mass. Be inspired and inflamed to make a total offering of thyself to Him, with Him. Offer Him the total devotion of thy being—thy body, soul, faculties, actions, pleasure, pain, time, and all that thou art and hast. This is the great effect and result which the Holy Mass—so great and lavish a generosity—should have on each of us. This is also the grand end and purpose of our whole existence.

2. Contemplate in Jesus (*a*) His perpetual Sacrifice. From His Conception, all through His life, to the consummation on Calvary; from Calvary all through the centuries to the day of judgment. O Jesus, untiring in Thy love, inexhaustible in Thy goodness, how can my soul any longer refuse to love Thee without reserve? (*b*) His love of each of us. In the Mass, as on the Cross, He is sacrificed for me—for

me; as if there were no one else upon the earth! (*c*) His continued self-devotion to the interests of men, which leads Him to annihilate Himself thousands of times each day for their good. How different with us, who will not even use the Holy Mass for the benefit of others living or dead!

3. Regret, with loving acts of sorrow, (*a*) your indifference to the right understanding of the Mass. O Jesus, how many Masses have I heard since the days of my infancy—and have I, even yet, begun to study this tremendous mystery? (*b*) Your remissness. Lord Jesus Christ, how often I might hear Mass when I do not! How coldly and mechanically I assist at it! How little profit I derive from so many Masses! (*c*) Your wilful distractions. Saviour of my soul, I neither begin with recollection, nor take the means to occupy my mind, nor rouse myself to shake off distractions when I notice them! For all these negligences and sins, pardon me, and give me grace seriously to amend.

XXV. THE LOVE OF GOD ABOVE ALL THINGS.

It is necessary, in a retreat as at other times, to insist strongly on the advantages of frequent and fervent acts of the Love of God, and on the absolute necessity of exercising such acts.

Divine Charity is the queen of the virtues: first, because it unites the heart immediately with God as He is revealed to us in the revelation of His infinite love; and secondly, because no virtue is "virtue" in the highest sense unless it has in it the light and the heat of Charity. Charity has two states or conditions: it is a permanent "habit," that is, a power and endowment of the soul; and it is an "act" exercised by the soul, in virtue of such endowment, God's grace assisting. As an endowment of our frail human nature it comes to us by the power and operation of the Holy Spirit. In the words of St. Paul, it is "poured out upon our hearts by the Holy Spirit Who is given to us".[1] Man cannot acquire Charity by the powers of his nature, neither by any exertion of his own can he put on that Divine garment which lifts his very being into a sphere that is not of this earth. Sanctifying Grace and

[1] *Rom.* v. 5.

Divine Charity are the outpouring of Christ's Spirit, the Paraclete. For habitual Grace and the supernatural spiritual endowment of Charity are only distinguishable from one another as the sun's light is distinguished from the sun. Sanctifying Grace is the life of the soul; Charity is that same living force ready to burst forth into all the operations of the supernatural life, and chiefly into actual love of the Source of all its life and beauty.

For just as breathing, motion, and speech are the manifestation and the embodiment of physical life, so the acts of Charity are the expression and the realisation of the supernatural life of the immortal soul of a man. This life is the only life which it is worth while to endeavour to live. Our physical life we are bound to care for, because God has placed us where we are; our intellectual life we must cultivate according to circumstances. But we should breathe, and act, and move, with a view to the intensifying of the spiritual life; we should study, and learn, and recreate ourselves only that we may love God the more. This is not to say that we must retire into a desert, or neglect those who depend on us, or drop our duties. To what extent this may be lawfully done depends upon many circumstances; there are many degrees of renunciation before we come to the Saints of the Desert. But whatever we do must be either love of God, or for the sake of His love. The love of God must work upon our whole activity, just as the whole movement of the sea on a sunny day sparkles with the radiance of the sun.

All this is more or less elementary, and is well understood by every one who seriously attends to his salvation. But what is not so clearly seen is, that one of the most important occupations of a Christian life is the exercise of direct and explicit acts of love. For what purpose, O child of the Heavenly Father, wert thou created? was it not to give thyself wholly to Him, in order that He may give Himself in overflowing abundance to thee? But it is not by thy hands, by thy works, by thy labour, or by thy kindness to others, that thou canst wholly give thyself to Him; it is only by the act and intensity of thy heart. This act of the heart we call an "elevation," because by it the whole being lifts itself to God; we call it "speech," because the intelligent nature of man, assisted by grace, can form as it were words and sentences—independent, indeed, of all physical utterance, but formed with greater or less distinctness, imprinting themselves more or less vividly on the imagination, rapidly succeeding each other as the sparks fly upwards from the forge. *Eructavit cor meum verbum bonum.* My heart uttereth a good world! Oh! how good, how profitable, how sweet is that "word" of the pure and mortified heart which is addressed throughout the hours of the day to its Lord and Father! In mental prayer this "word" is fervent and continuous; it is the very essence of all prayer, to which all thought, all consideration, all imagining should lead, as the heaping of dry branches is the preparation for the fire. In actions of liturgical worship, during the time that is spent nigh the Altar (which carries the Body of Christ, and which is itself the Body of Christ), if the " word " of the heart ceases, worship and service become mere formality,—only the outward activity of the hands and the lips. But the servant of God knows how, in Office and Liturgy, to sanctify the Lord Christ in his heart.[1] His heart seizes every word that sounds forth, every rite, every detail of ritual, of place, of posture, and lifts itself to its Lord, as a little bird flies swiftly up towards the sky when it has found its morsel of food upon the lower earth. From choir to choir, in the sight of the Angels, the psalm passes, and the sound of holy words makes sweet melody; but sweeter far is the melody of the heart which transforms the sacred sounds into acts of worship, of adhesion, and of petition,—which pass, not from one choir to another, but to the very roof and the firmament, to the gates of heaven, even to the throne of God. As the day goes on, the labour of the hands is accepted, offered, consecrated; not passively or indifferently, but with loving effort, which results once more in liftings of the heart. For just as the infirm and the lame will hurry forth with heavy step to see their prince pass by, so the servant of God will make the effort to worship and

---

[1] 1 *Peter* iii. 15.

love his Heavenly Father in all that he does from morning till night. An effort perhaps it must be. For as yet, whilst in this mortal body, the heart does not always find it easy to lift itself to God. But the very effort adds fuel to the flame of Charity. When we love God easily and promptly, it is too often because of mere sensible feeling—at least, in the beginning of our conversion. But when we have to conquer the resistance of sense and feeling, then there is fervour and merit. Thus, whether we are with others or alone, we shall always be most of all with God. When we have to spend many hours of the day in the company of others, in labour, in ministration, in business, or even in moderate recreation, the "word" of the heart must never cease for long. To forget God may not always be to offend Him; but to forget God is to waste so much of one's life and to forfeit so many degrees of His communication in the life to come. Happy are those who can find solitude, and who learn to value it! In the midst of silence, God seems more near, and it is more easy to speak to Him. Then one can live one's true life—the life which directs all its powers and acts towards Him Who is the Last End. Even when the mind is employed in study or work, it need never be far from an act of love or adhesion. How many fail in the attainment of knowledge of Divine things because they do not look for light in the right direction! Light is streaming upon the soul, at all times—light from Him Who enlighteneth every man that cometh into the world.[1] The gifts of wisdom, of understanding, of knowledge and of counsel are part of the retinue of Divine Charity. They seem too often to be obscured, or as it were paralysed; but why? Because the heart does not make that recognition of them—that acceptance of them in faith and humility—which sets their activity free. When the heart says, O Holy Spirit, it is Thou and Thou alone that canst enlighten my blindness!—that is all that is required to put in motion the most stupendous of all forces, a "gift" of the Holy Ghost. When, in study or perplexity or in practical difficulty, we mingle our solicitous efforts with acts by which we suppliantly and confidently invoke the Source of all wisdom and prudence, present in a special manner in the souls of all who are in Divine grace, how can it be but that light must come and direction must be given? Thus are study and labour and administration at once sanctified and promoted. And when there is trouble, or difficulty, pain of body or sadness of mind, then more than ever must the heart speak to its Creator continually in ejaculations of love. For suffering and annoyance either sting us to impatience and so separate us further and further from God, or, if accepted, they inflame charity as no other stimulus can. Unhappy are those who miss their chances when the sacred visitation of suffering comes upon them! But how

[1] *St. John* i. 9.

blessed is the heart which lifts itself to God in resignation, in devout acceptance, in contrition, in adhesion, in love, whenever the flesh suffers, or the nerves are jarred, or the feelings hurt, or pride touched, or vanity wounded, or the spirit filled with anxiety and bitterness! Then is the moment for God to be made all in all. It is His moment; He made it, and sent it; He watches its effect. O my God, in my hours of sorrow and suffering, whom have I in heaven or on earth but Thee? It is Thou Who sendest me annoyance and pain, that I may turn to Thee! Thou art jealous, O my Heavenly Father, of my attention to things other than Thyself! Thou wouldst have my thoughts and my love. Thou hast said by Thy prophet, "The Lord is nigh unto them that are of a contrite heart";[1] and, "In tribulation I am with him".[2] And because Thou longest to be with me, Thou promptest me with suffering to invite Thee to come to my aid! O my Jesus, give me to understand how full of Thy love is every day of my life! How every breath that buffets me, every creature that hurts me, every pang that troubles me, is only a messenger of Thine to make me lift my heart up out of the mists of worldly existence to Thee Who art my All, for ever and ever!

Such are some of the active effects of the most royal and august endowment, Divine Charity, which

[1] *Ps.* xxxiii. 19.   [2] *Ib.* xc. 15.

is the gift of the Holy Ghost the Sanctifier, sent by Jesus in the efficacy of His poured-out blood. When that endowment falls from heaven upon the spirit of a man, it is God's free gift. Yet even in its infusion it is, in a manner, dependent upon our dispositions—dispositions of aversion from sin, faith, and initial love. It is to these acts that sinners should be exhorted—for when any mortal being does what lies in himself, God is never wanting in doing what He alone can do. Once infused, Charity grows and increases in proportion, as the will becomes more and more subject to its influence, and more and more actuated by it. Every act of charity disposes the soul towards the increase of charity; every fresh act makes the heart more ready to break forth into a further act; and as this exercise becomes more and more habitual, there is every now and then an act of special fervency and perfection which, like the ninth wave of the advancing tide, definitely and permanently carries the Divine flood to a higher mark in the heart of the servant of God.

Seeing that the growth and increase of Charity means greater nearness to God, greater friendship with Him, greater merit and higher glory in heaven, it is certain that the Christian who serves God in earnest should take every means to increase Charity in his soul. Spiritual writers give us four principal means of promoting the growth of Charity. The first is, to strive for a more perfect knowledge of God. It is just this "knowledge of God" which makes the "Charity" of the blessed in heaven so full and overflowing. We come to know God better by using our minds, under the impulse of grace and the guidance of piety. Worldly people, and especially non-Catholics, whose studies, pursuits, and interests lie in matters of business, pleasure, science, art, and literature, can no more take a warm interest in God than they can in any other mere name, when little or nothing but the name is known. Catholics who are brought up from childhood in familiarity with the mysteries of Faith and the Life of our Lord, acquire a very precious and lasting knowledge of God. If, in more mature years, they read constantly, and think out the marvellous views which are suggested in such overwhelming abundance by Catholic doctrine, on the Trinity, the Incarnation and the rest of our revelation of God, they cannot but be occupied and moved by such ideas; and this is but a step from the exercise of Divine Charity. Professional theologians, above all, are fortunate in being able to devote themselves to Divine knowledge. *Quantum bonum plenius cognoscitur*, says St. Thomas, *tanto magis est amabile.*[1] The good is more lovable in proportion as it is better known. And this is especially true of that one only and infinite Good in Whom, however deeply we penetrate His essence, no drawback can be discovered of any kind whatever. O my God! give

---

[1] In 3 Lib. Dist. 27, qu. 3, art. 1.

me light to know Thee, that I may love Thee the more! May my reason, my intelligence, my thought, my imagination, and all my powers occupy themselves with Thee—and, as far as possible, with Thee alone! May I drink in Thy holy word in the Scriptures, at the altar, and in books! May it dwell in me until all its sweetness passes into my own heart! I am ignorant, O my Saviour, and slow of heart; but the heart can penetrate where the reason is sometimes at fault; supply my deficiency with Thy holy gifts, that as Thy light groweth in me Thy love may daily more and more increase; until my path, growing lighter and still more light, lead me to Thy perfect day![1]

The second means of increasing Charity is to strive for greater purity of heart and detachment from creatures. As St. Augustine says, *Augmentum charitatis est diminutio cupiditatis*,[2]—the more we diminish "cupidity" or the love of created things, the more we grow in the love of God. Pride, vanity, carnal desires, sloth, and all serious preoccupations which dispute our heart with God, are fatal to progress in Charity, as long as they are unresisted, or only feebly resisted. Hence the necessity for continual mortification of evil inclinations and war against bad habits. But it should be carefully observed, that, in order to love God, and to grow in Charity, it is not necessary to be *freed* from these evil inclinations; it is only

[1] *Proverbs* iv. 18.   [2] *Ep.* 177.

necessary, by resisting them, to form a good and strong habit of never yielding to them. When we firmly resist, that resistance, though the struggle may trouble us, only makes our Charity the more fervent. O Jesus! help me or I must fall! Give me strength to overcome my love of the world, of the flesh, of myself, by the most pure love of Thee!

The third means is the gradual purification of our love of God itself. St. Bernard distinguishes three states of love. First, there is *the child's love;* when we love our God because He is so good and love-worthy, but at the same time are not well able to do without consolation, internal and external; fervent feelings, pious friends, devotional services, sympathetic confessors, peaceful and joyous companionship, and the like. The second is *the son's love;* when we truly love God, but dwell too much on the rewards of heaven and the delights of life everlasting. The third is *the spouse's love;* when we think more of God Himself than of all His rewards. In urging ourselves, however, to greater purity of love, we should by no means force ourselves to a higher degree of "purity" than we seem to have light and grace for. Above all we must never try to put hypothetical cases; never ask ourselves if we could love God supposing there were no heaven, or if He condemned us to hell. Few are capable of using in their own behalf those sayings of some of the Saints which are so heroic. When we are recalled to "disinterested" love, that call will carry with it the light to understand what it means. Meanwhile let us pray that we may love our God more and more for Himself alone.

The fourth means is the frequent *exercise* of Charity. Of this we have already spoken. Love groweth by love. Life becomes stronger by the exercise of loving. Observe the numerous Acts of love in the Psalms; in the *Confessions* of St. Augustine; in the writings of St. Bernard; in the lives of all the great Saints, most of whom have left their characteristic sayings behind them, as that of St. Francis, *Deus meus et omnia*, " My God and my all ! " In the treatises of Blosius will be found a very large collection of every kind of Acts of love. But, indeed, no great variety of Acts is required. Oftentimes the greatest devotion is experienced in the use of a single phrase, repeated again and again. "Oh ! the love of God, the love of God ! " said St. Paul of the Cross. "O Jesus, the God of my heart ! " said St. Francis Xavier. St. Ignatius, whenever the clock struck, used to raise his heart to God and say : " Give me, O Lord, Thy love and Thy grace " ! St. Leonard had that ejaculation which is so well known: "My Jesus! Mercy ! " Those who are in the habit of reciting the Psalms can never be at a loss for a fervent act of love and union. It was the expressions of the Psalms that the Saints themselves chiefly used and made their own,

Points for Mental Prayer.

1. "What is God?" says St. Bernard. "He is the Almighty Will, Beneficent Power, Eternal Light, Unchangeable Intelligence, the Supreme Beatitude; He creates men to give Himself to them; He fills them with life that they may feel Him; He moves their hearts to desire Him; He enlarges their hearts to receive Him; He justifies them that they may merit; He stirs them up to good purposes and gives them the fruit of good deeds; He guides them in the observance of His commandments, illuminates them with His teaching, makes them kind and merciful, gives them strength to serve Him, and visits them with His consolations; and it is He Who will flood them with His knowledge, give them everlasting life, satiate them with all happiness and keep them safe with Himself for ever!"[1] Dwell on one or more of these attributes of Him Who is good to those who trust in Him, and to the soul that seeketh Him.[2]

2. Consider that thy life is made up of the elements of time, thought, labour, interest, duty, recreation, pleasure and pain. Make, then, Acts of this kind: My God, I dedicate to Thee every moment of my time; especially that instant in which Thou foreseest I shall draw my last breath! I dedicate to Thee henceforth all my thoughts, and every Act of my intelligence! May I never work or labour any more except for Thee! Turn all my interests, pre-

[1] *De Consideratione*, v. 11.   [2] *Lamentations* iii. 25.

occupation, and solicitude to Thee, and Thee alone! Let all my duty be done for Thee and Thy love! Grant that recreation and amusement may never take me away from Thee, or make me forget Thee long! May I renounce pleasure and the satisfactions of the body and the delights of the mind, unless they unite me to Thee! May I bear with patience, nay, welcome and seek, crosses, hardships and sufferings, that so I may be drawn the closer to Thee Who art my only Father and my portion for ever!

3. Consider with sorrow thy deficiencies in thy past life, and thy neglect of Acts of Charity. O my Heavenly Father, how little have I cared to have Thee in my daily life! What hours, what days, what weeks have I spent with hardly a thought of Thee! What blank and distracted meditations! What wandering and mechanical recitations of the Divine Office! What purely human solicitude in work and duty! What fears and hopes, what anxieties, what enjoyments—all, all without reference to Thy will or Thy love, have made up the greater part of my life! What good works have I spoiled, what numberless imperfections and venial sins have I fallen into, because I have never lifted my heart to Thee! How have I missed the opportunity of drawing near to Thee when Thou didst send me crosses and pain! How have I wasted my life and neglected my preparation for eternity! But, most of all, how have I forgotten Thee, my only Treasure, my dearest Friend, my Father and my All!

XXVI. THE LOVE OF ONE ANOTHER.

The second great commandment of God is like unto the first. The love of one another resembles the love of God; because the very spirit and essence of the love of our neighbour is the love of our Divine Master. Why must I love my neighbour? What is there in my fellow-beings which claims my interest and my affection? Natural feeling is mere nature; and although it is good and right and virtuous to follow the impulses which prompt us to love a parent, a child, a husband or wife, a friend or a benefactor, yet this is not the highest kind of virtue; it is not the virtue which merits life everlasting. Christianity, revelation, the law of the Gospel, point to something more Divine. Unless in my neighbour I can see my God, I cannot give to my neighbour a love that is supernatural. Unless in my neighbour I can see the interests of my God and the will of my God, my neighbour can never be loved with a love "like unto" the love that I owe to my God. But this is just what I can see, and ought to see. For what is my neighbour? What are all these beings who people the world and among whom my life and my lot are cast? They are, before everything else, immortal souls, created by Him Who created my soul, redeemed by the Blood of Jesus, and destined for the bliss of the beatific Vision. Now I know that my God loves me, guards me, and guides me with the anxious solicitude of a father or a mother, so that I may belong to Him at the end of my probation and never be separated from Him. It is thus also that He loves and deals with the souls of all other men and women. They are dear to Him, as I am; some of them much nearer to Him than myself; but all dear. What is dear to my God, how can it but be dear to me? If it is not, then I do not love my God as I ought; for I do not will what He wills, and work for that which He desires. O my God, how far am I from living up to this idea! How have I failed —how do I at present fail—in understanding how precious in Thy sight are all the immortal souls which Thou hast created! My eyes have looked upon others with kindness (it may be), but not for Thy sake; with interest, perhaps, but for worldly, earthly, human reasons; with indifference. too often, standing proudly aloof, heedless what might happen to "strangers," as I have called them; too often, must I confess, with feelings of spite, ill-temper or even hatred, which have led me on even to scandalise and hurt those whom my Heavenly Father longs to bring nearer and nearer to Himself!

The philanthropy of the day, which has no motives higher than this earth, is not a "Christian" virtue. Its radical defect is that it does not love men and women as God loves them. God loves their souls; philanthropy loves only their bodies. God wishes them to have His Holy Faith to guide them to Him; this philanthropy despises faith and extols religious indifference. God would prepare them for the next world; this philanthropy would make them content with this. God would have them live in the practice of that religion which alone can strengthen them to gain the eternal Kingdom; this philanthropy would substitute for definite religious duties a vague and shallow sentiment, of little more moral value than health or good spirits. It is true that suffering, poverty, and misery of every kind must be met and relieved without inquiring as to the spiritual state of those who are in need; this is a first and primary duty. But it is a duty which can only be made into Divine love by being done for God's sake; and the relief of the pressing need of the body is indeed, as a rule, an essential preliminary to the saving of the soul; for excessive poverty and suffering, taking the world as we find it, interfere with all religious duty. But the works of mercy spiritual are higher than the works of corporal. To instruct the ignorant, to provide spiritual help for the poor, to bring as many as possible to the Sacraments, to lessen the occasions of sin and its chances—these things are what the true Christian, after he has ministered food, clothing, shelter and consolation, must aim at carrying out, for thus only can he love men and women as God loves them; thus only can he save immortal souls. It is thus, O my

Jesus, that Thou didst set an example of love for men and women; Thou didst heal their bodies, but Thou didst also save their souls. Thou didst say, Arise, thou art made whole; but Thou didst also say, Thy sins are forgiven thee; go and sin no more! Give me Thy holy grace, that no false delicacy, no human respect, no sloth or indifference, may prevent me from promoting, in due season, the spiritual good of my neighbours.

Nevertheless, it must be well borne in mind that simple kindness—bestowed indeed for God's sake, bnt not necessarily having any direct reference to the saving of your neighbour's soul—is a most blessed Christian virtue; a virtue blessing both him that gives and him that receives. To give peace and serenity to the heart of another is to prepare the way for God's grace; for God cannot come into a heart that is tossing with passion or seething with unwilling pain. Kindness has the effect of balm; it soothes suffering, softens pride, dissipates selfishness, and exorcises bad temper. Most of us are not kind enough. Perhaps we may be dry and hard by temperament; perhaps we cannot easily enter into the troubles or pain of another heart; perhaps we are austere " on principle," thinking it more wholesome for every one concerned; or again, perhaps it is mere selfishness and self-concentration which withhold us from exerting ourselves to be kind and sympathetic. O my sweet and gentle Saviour! How often might I have won a soul first to peace and next to union with Thee, by placing myself at that soul's service! By Thy kind words, by Thy kind actions, give me light and grace to help my neighbour!

But kindness to others is not only beneficial to those to whom we are kind, but it also has a marked influence upon our own spiritual state. There are times when kindness costs very little; when suffering, innocence or goodness, or all three, unseal the fountains of our sympathy;—kindness is then very sweet; but, in this case, if it is to be of any spiritual profit to us, we must with some care purify our motives. Especially must we look into our conscience if we find that we habitually practise kindness as a gratification and a luxury. Such a feeling is by no means evil; nay, it is pure, elevating and helpful; but, to a spiritual heart, it is not enough. Like all other human activity, it must be offered to God for His own sake, or it will not be accepted at the gates of Paradise. Moreover, if it is too thoughtlessly indulged in, it may do us great harm; we are thus unfitted for the time which most surely will come, when kindness is against the grain of our poor weak and wounded nature, and nevertheless is a duty. These occasions are far more numerous than the others. The soul to whom our kindness is owing may be uninteresting, despicable, not "nice," even repulsive. Nature rebels; yet our duty is clear. The priest with his poor, the religious with her disagreeable sister, any man or woman with troublesome and irritating children or relations, or unpleasant neighbours,—to all of these, kindness is a duty, but a hard duty, which the flesh would shirk if it could, and which will never be fulfilled without supernatural motives and clear spiritual views. But to force oneself (with God's grace) by the gentle pressure of divine motives to the saying of a kind word when the occasion arises, to the doing of a charity in a really kind way, or to the devoting of time, pains and means, with patience and sympathy, where these are required,—is to bless ourselves as much as those we help. For nothing draws us nearer to God than the effort of the heart to trample on self; and except when we have the grace of bitter personal suffering, this effort of unselfishness is never more effectively made than when we strive to be kind to others. For example, let us take the simple kindness of ministering to another's recreation. The hour comes when we meet our religious brethren or sisters, and when it is a duty to "take recreation". The mere feeling that "recreation" is a duty of the moment is enough, with some people, to set their nature against it, and to make them shrink up into self and moroseness. Yet this sort of meeting is useful and necessary. It is required to cement union, to keep up community life, to cheer the ordinary soul, and to exercise every one in certain most essential virtues which can by no means be exercised in the cell, or the choir. For example: you come into the recreation-room in a sour and selfish temper; your nature prompts you to keep apart, to resent every effort to amuse you, to despise innocent gaiety, and even to break out into unkind and cutting words. You are in a condition fruitful of venial sins; a condition which, were it to be unreformed and to become habitual, would finally make you turn your back on God. But it is very probable that your state is not your usual one; it may arise from various circumstances, and even from physical reasons. It is none the less a danger and an evil. Let us suppose that you have the grace to enter into yourself and to say: "My God, what am I about? These souls here present require my aid and my co-operation; each one has its own troubles, its own pains, its own sorrows; each one is dear to Thee, Who at this moment art solicitous for its profit and advantage; and here am I, nursing my pride, hugging my selfishness, as if there were no one but my miserable self in all this universe! I will arise; I will put pressure on myself; I will act in spite of my repugnance; I will enter into the hearts of those about me; I will even exert my powers, such as they are, to console, distract, brighten and encourage these souls whom God loves." This does not mean that you are to pour yourself out in vapid, tactless and aggressive recreating talk or laughter;—very little need be said or done; the good, kind, unselfish spirit is everything. But observe what happens. The moment you have, by God's grace, aroused yourself, shaken off self, and begun to think how you can help your brother or sister, that moment the cloud lifts from your own brow, the weight is removed from your own heart; and you receive that precious peace and innocent joyous heart which those ought to have who serve God in full earnest. Who is more blessed by your self-conquest—your neighbour or yourself? These reflections are of much wider application than to the recreation-room of a community. They may be applied whenever a parent has to do with a child, a master with a pupil, an employer with an inferior, a priest with his people, or any man or woman with any friend, acquaintance or neighbour. Cultivate this habit of thinking how by word or deed you can help every one you meet, and you cultivate the habit of trampling on self; and you thus make it easy to give yourself wholly to God.

In order to practise to the utmost of your capability this most sweet virtue of fraternal charity—whether in the monastery or in the world—three things chiefly are required: the first is Intelligence; the second, Devotedness; and the third, Restraint of the Tongue.

Intelligence is not only required that we may thoroughly take in the reason why we must love one another. This we have already considered. Intelligence must accompany our love of our neighbour at every step. It is needful to insist on this, because we constantly encounter a false and dangerous fraternal charity which does incalculable mischief.

It is the fraternal love which is grounded on sentiment, and which increases or diminishes with every change in our feelings or our fancy. We meet with it most commonly among women; among school-girls, fellow-workers, and even in religious communities. But it is by no means unknown among men also; and the sign of its presence is that (equally unreasoning) coldness and unkindness towards many which is sure to accompany it. *Da mihi intellectum, ut discam mandata Tua!* Give me intelligence, O my God and my Teacher, that I may learn Thy commandments! We must understand, then, that the least of our neighbours, brothers, or sisters, is an immortal soul, with the Blood of Jesus signed upon it, with a title to a kingdom in the future far beyond earthly kingdoms, and with a zealous Angel guarding it day and night. We must understand that, whatever appearances may seem to show, that soul has qualities, gifts, aspirations, virtues, nobility and dignity. Thy friends, O Lord, are become honourable exceedingly![1] If Thou dost honour them, O my Master, who am I that I should not imitate Thee? If you bring your understanding thus to bear upon your brothers or sisters, you will see also that you must use it in order to treat them aright. They are not units of clay or wood, that you can regard in the mass and have done with. They are very individual—in their qualities,

---

[1] *Ps.* cxxxviii. 17.

histories, successes, failures, joys and sufferings. You have to be considerate to them; that is, to bestow upon each, and in proportion to each one's nearness, sufficient study and consideration, in order that you may do the good that is possible and avoid all harm. How many sins will those have to answer for who are without considerateness? There is a verse in St. Paul which we may render thus (looking at the peculiar force of the original word): "In brotherly love be ye tenderly affectionate one to another, in honour being beforehand with one another, in prompt and zealous alacrity not slothful."[1] It is that "preventing one another with honour" which here chiefly concerns us. The whole passage clearly has in view an intelligent considerateness which each one should have for his neighbour in all the concerns of life. Such considerateness will also lead a man to turn his eyes upon himself, and to try to suppress, correct, or mitigate in himself anything that may be offensive, scandalous or distressing to those about him. The root of true Christian politeness is personal humility; but the quality which comes next in importance is considerateness. Humility, considerateness, and the suppression of what may be disagreeable in ourselves—these are the elements of that "politeness" which the servant of our Lord substitutes for that worldly courtesy which is too often only exterior; which seldom hesi-

---

[1] *Romans* xii. 10, 11.

tates to wound, and which, at the very best, is of no moral value to him who practises it.

Next, our love of one another should be marked by real Devotedness. That is, we must be prepared to make *sacrifices* for our neighbour. We must give our time and pains according to our circumstances, to the poor, the sick and the old. We may not be able to emulate the heroic devotedness of a St. Vincent de Paul, a St. Peter Claver or a St. Joseph Calasanctius. But there is seldom a day in which we may not help some one near us who stands in need of help; nay, in which it is not our positive duty to do so. The Saints would kneel down and kiss with burning countenance the wounds of the poor, because in doing so they seemed to kiss the wounds of Jesus Himself. This devotedness is especially the duty of superiors. They should never be weary, never be sour-tempered, never be impatient. "Come to me," St. Catherine of Bologna used to say; "come to me, dearest daughters, by day or by night; wake me up if I am asleep; fear not; we must share our tribulations, and share our consolations!"

Thirdly, our love of one another must be characterised by Restraint of the Tongue. All who know anything about religious communities are aware that the practices which come nearest to ruining them are criticism of superiors and uncharitable discussion of one another. It is with the latter that we are here concerned. O my soul, look into your own habits and practice! Are you not one of those who report conversations, colour facts, and sow discord? Have you never turned the very goodness of another into evil by your sneers and insinuations? Look how often you have been meanly jealous, and said everything you could to lessen the credit of others! Think of the ignoble tittle-tattle in which you have indulged, spreading reports, magnifying small secrets, and setting people by the ears! Moreover, have you ever scrupled to sacrifice your brother or sister to your wit or cynicism, saying words which bite and stick, words which divide hearts for many a long day? How true is the word of St. Bernard that the tongue which talks without the restraint of charity is the tongue of the viper!

Points for Mental Prayer.

1. Contemplate Jesus, before His agony, praying for the flock that He loved so much. "Father," He said, "make them one—even as Thou and I are one!" As far as the power and the gifts of Jesus go, are they not one? All of them are immortal souls, with the power to know and love God, with the Blood of Calvary upon them, with the same bliss of eternity as their end and purpose; all loved and cared for by our Heavenly Father; all brethren of Christ Jesus. "I love them," said St. Mary Magdalen of Pazzi of her religious sisters—"I love them because Jesus loved them!" O God of love and union, give me

light to love all human creatures as Thou lovest them! Make me love Thee, and only Thee, in all and in each! Give me a holy dread of opposing Thy august designs by my selfishness, my want of restraint, or my temper! Shepherd of souls, may Thy flock never be disturbed, distressed or scandalised, poor wretch that I am, by me!

2. Trample on thyself, that thou mayest freely love those whom Thy Saviour loveth. Would that I could empty myself, O my Jesus, of myself! What is it that keeps me from Thee but my want of mortification, my shrinking from what is disagreeable, my pride and sensuality? And behold! here is the altar on which I can burn and consume myself—the altar of the love of my neighbour! He that doth a kindness to one of these, doth it to Thee! Fill me with Thy Spirit that I may humble myself to my brethren, feel with my brethren, rejoice with them and weep with them, relieve their poverty, serve their sick beds, and give them of my very best in the spirit and in the body—and that in all this I may understand how in ministering to them and forgetting myself, I am sure to find Thee!

3. Look back upon the faults and defects of thy past life. Ask pardon for thy hardness. O kind and merciful Saviour, forgive me my indifference to the souls Thou lovest! Forgive my unconcern for the poor! Condemn me not for my neglect of the suffering!—for my contempt of the aged and infirm! —for my want of consideration for the tempted, the

shrinking, the downhearted and the unsuccessful! Touch my heart with the fire of Thine, that I may not only amend but wash away with tears my faults of the past! Ask pardon for thy partiality. I confess, O my generous Lord, that even in my kindness to others I have sought to gratify myself. How many times have I done harm to souls by foolish affection! How often have I sown divisions by private friendships! How frequently have I made others jealous and bitter by my preferences! Forgive, O Lord, these sins against Thy dearly loved flock! Ask pardon for thy uncharitable speech. What do I deserve, O my loving Master, for my rash judgments, for my unkind words of others behind their backs, for my mean and unjust insinuations, for my irresponsible chatter, for my sneers and cutting speech? Alas! My guilty tongue has laboured to spoil and ruin that which Thyself hast built up and wouldst preserve—a peaceful and united community! I see my folly now, and I humble myself for my sinfulness! It is for Thee to pardon me; for Thee to change my spirit and my life!

XXVII. WORK AND APOSTLESHIP.

A GREAT part of every man's life must be spent in labour of some kind; labour with the hands or labour with the head. Work is in many cases a positive and serious duty. It is an admirable and necessary means of fulfilling the great precept of fraternal charity. It is an occupation, and thus keeps the door shut on many temptations. And it is an abundant source of that holy penance which ought to prevail in the life of every true follower of Jesus Christ.

The best kind of work is work for the sake of others. Thus the work of priests is the most holy and meritorious of all, because it is undertaken directly for the saving of immortal souls. But the work of fathers and mothers, of husbands and wives, is also most pleasing in the sight of God, because in the first place a great deal of it is directly concerned with immortal souls; and, next, because even that which is of a temporal and earthly kind is done, or ought to be done, chiefly to make salvation more secure to those who depend upon us. Religious, whether contemplatives or not, work for the bodies and souls of their religious brethren or sisters, and many of them for the bodies and souls of the poor, the orphaned, the sick, and the young. Many good people in the world, without being bound by any tie of duty, spend themselves in good works for others' sakes. Some write, some administer, some occupy public posts, some labour with the hands. All this may be, and ought to be, directed to the good of the soul, and also to the good of the body so far as this does not interfere with the welfare of the soul. If we labour for ourselves alone—as too many appear to do—our labour is rarely sanctified; because in these cases work is mostly dictated by the spirit of pride, or the spirit of avarice, or the spirit of luxury. Only in the rare instances in which the inspiration of God calls a tried heart to a solitary life of prayer is work altogether dispensed with, or reduced to the smallest proportions; for then the servant of God is called to an immediate intercourse with the Creator which is both more holy and more advantageous to the human race than any labour could be, whether of speech or of ministration. Thus the fathers of the Desert seldom interrupted their contemplation, and then only to supply themselves by labour with the small quantity of food required to keep them alive.

In order to enter into ourselves, in the presence of God, and to renew the spirit of our mind on the subject of work, let us consider,—first, Apostolic work; secondly, the work of Duty, and thirdly, Penitential work. Some work will be found to combine two or all of these characteristics.

The Saint specially raised up by God in these latter days to press upon priests the necessity of zeal in the saving of souls is St. Alphonsus. He says that in giving the spiritual exercises to the clergy, the sermon on zeal is the most necessary, and may be the most useful of all; for if one priest present resolves to devote himself to procuring the salvation of souls, God will gain not one but a thousand souls, through that priest's labours. A priest is one who, more than other human beings, has to carry out that universal and mysterious law of God—that no man can be saved except by the ministry of another man. God never, or most rarely, interferes directly (except by His invisible grace) in the saving of any soul. He leaves us to parents, to tutors, to friends, to priests. "We are the coadjutors of God," says St. Paul.[1] Priests especially may be called in St. Jerome's phrase, "saviours of the world".[2] "Behold," saith the Lord, "I will send many fishers, and after this I will send many hunters."[3] When our Lord Jesus Christ sees the men whom He has chosen to reap the harvest of His Precious Blood slack in their duty, worldly and scandalous, how would His Sacred Heart grieve, if grief could touch it now! If they are not zealous, it is because they do not love Him. This is the plain truth. "Zeal springs from love," is the phrase of

[1] 1 Cor. iii. 9.   [2] *In Abdiam.*, 21.
[3] *Jeremias* xvi. 16.

St. Augustine. The absence of zeal is the absence of love. O my Lord and Master, Thou hast tied Thy own hands, and sent me, a priest to do Thy work! Thou hast given me special graces, and conferred on me a dignity above that of the Angels! How can I think without shame and remorse of my past life—of my want of preparation, my idleness and my self-indulgence? I resolve, O Lord, to begin afresh to serve Thee as Thy minister ought!

There is nothing, as St. Chrysostom says, which is so pleasing to God, and so near His heart, as the salvation of souls.[1] St. Alphonsus relates that our Lord once appeared to a priest and said to him: "Labour for the salvation of sinners, for this is most pleasing to Me".[2] Ah! if He appeared to you, in your sloth and indifference, and spoke thus, what answer could you give Him? "If you love Me, feed My lambs—feed My sheep!"[3] This is the burthen of all His exhortations to pastors. And how grandly the great pastors of Christian history, in the strength of the Blood of Christ, have carried out this essential precept! Think of St. Charles Borromeo among his flock; of St. Cajetan dying of grief because he could not save more souls; of St. Francis de Sales amid the cold and the ice of his missionary journeys; of St. John Chrysostom desiring to be an outcast if souls might be converted;

---

[1] *In Genesim.*, Hom. 8. [2] Centenary ed., xii. 167.
[3] *John* xxi. 17.

of the great St. Martin, of St. Patrick, of St. Augustine, and the men who converted England, Scotland, and Germany—or of St. Paul himself, who was ready to become *anathema* for the souls of his brethren! O holy pastors of every century, of every land, where is your spirit now? What are we doing, while the world is perishing around us? What are our comforts, our ease, our recreations, nay our good name itself, in comparison with the value of one soul? *Animam salvasti, animam tuam prædestinasti!* Thou hast saved a soul, thou hast predestinated thy own soul! These are the immortal words of St. Augustine. Can a priest be lost who has saved souls for God? " O what consolation," says St. Alphonsus, "and what confidence shall the remembrance of having gained a soul to Jesus Christ infuse at the hour of death!"[1] My Jesus, give me grace to merit this consolation! But if I am to merit it, I must adopt the means. "Many," says St. Paul, "seek the things that are their own, not the things that are Jesus Christ's."[2] Have I not laboured in the vineyard out of human respect, for vanity, and for advancement? I confess that I have been of the number of priests who grasp after money, who are fond of applause, who lose heart if things go contrary, who seek consolation in creatures, who keep away from the poor and the repulsive! In all this, is it not clear that I have sought myself, my own

---

[1] Centenary ed., xii. 172.   [2] *Phil.* ii. 21.

glory, my own ease, and that I have been comparatively indifferent to the glory of God? How vain, how barren, how useless, is all that is done through vanity or self-seeking! No wonder my words are fruitless, and my ministry sterile; no wonder that my flock are lax and indifferent, my church badly attended, my schools unsuccessful in making pious children, and my efforts at conversion without effect. No wonder my district goes back instead of advancing; no wonder that Catholics fall away, and Protestants do not come in. It is my fault! St. Philip Neri used to say: "Give me ten zealous priests and I will convert the whole world". "A single priest," says St. Alphonsus, "of moderate learning, who loves God ardently, will convert more souls to God than a hundred priests of great learning and little zeal."[1] But I—I do not try to sanctify myself, and therefore I cannot bring God to others. I do not pray—I neglect even my half-hour's meditation; and therefore the dew of heaven falls not on my soul. I do not prepare for Mass—I hurry over my thanksgiving. I am inaccurate, unpunctual, and disedifying in my celebration; and therefore my ministry is not blessed! Pardon me, O my Saviour! Thou givest me light now to see my sinfulness—give me also the grace to amend. I resolve to carry out with exactness all my own spiritual duties; I resolve to devote myself to souls, to be assiduous and patient in the confessional, to prepare myself

[1] Centenary ed., xii. 179.

when I have to speak Thy word, to seek out sinners, to welcome those who want instruction, to mortify myself in all recreations and excursions which may take me from my people; to be kind to the poor, patient with the sick, solicitous with the dying! It is only by Thy powerful grace and comfort, O my Jesus, that I can carry out these resolutions! I beseech Thee, by that act of Thy Sacred Heart by which Thou didst accept Thy mission, by Thy Divine condescension to the woman at the well, by all that burning zeal and thirst for the good of men which rose to its height upon the Cross, make me less unworthy to be Thy minister—to be the dispenser of Thy mysteries.

Others besides priests may make the considerations here set down. The religious superior, the teacher, those whose office it is to assist the fallen, to help the aged, or to tend little children—all these have an Apostolate. So also have masters and mistresses, fathers and mothers, and frequently also elder brothers or sisters, or other relations. And this apostolate is a serious responsibility; souls depend upon it for their salvation; yes, it is not too much to say, for their salvation. And therefore, like priests, all these are bound to be good, to pray, to practise their religious duties, and frequently to examine themselves upon the discharge of their obligations. O Jesus, Good Shepherd, zealous lover of souls! how few there are who zealously give themselves to Thy dear and well-loved work!

Work as Duty has next to be considered. The chief point which must here be placed before the mind is that duty to a Christian is not the exercise of strength of mind, strength of will, uprightness, magnanimity, courage or endurance, but it is the will of God. We hear much at the present day of devotion to duty. This is very often only another name for devotion to the world. But the servant of Christ must do his duty, not to show his mettle or to do credit to his natural gifts, but only for God's sake and in order to carry out God's will. It is thus that the monks pray in the early morning of each day (when the tools of the manual labour used to be brought into the chapter-house): "Look down upon Thy servants, O Lord, and upon their work, and direct their children; and let the brightness of the Lord our God be upon us; and direct Thou the works of our hands over us; yes, the work of our hands do Thou direct."[1] O holy labour! sanctified by Christ Himself, by Mary, and by Joseph! It is God, and no one else, who imposes it upon us. Perhaps we live in the world, and have to win our bread and that of our families by some kind of work. Oh happy necessity!—for thus we become like to Christ and the Saints. How devoutly each morning in our prayers should we look forward to our labour, and offer up all our thoughts, words, and actions to the greater glory of God! What nobility does God's

---

[1] *Ps.* lxxxix. 16, 17.

holy Name shed upon the routine work, the plodding efforts, the commonplace tasks which make up our lives! "Let the brightness of the Lord our God be upon us!" In the office and the counting-house, in the shop and the market, in the fields, in the streets, in the warehouses, at the docks, on the railways, toil is made holy and noble by that effulgence from the Heavenly Father's throne; for there falls upon the labour of His servants the brightness of the Divine will and the brightness of the Divine love. If we belong to a religious community work seems even more to come to us straight from the hand of God. When we work for our community, for the little ones, for the poor, it seems so easy to believe in those words of Jesus: "When you do it to these My least brethren, you do it to Me!"[1] O blessed labour of the religious life! Labour begun in obedience, carried on in joyous cheerfulness, and completed in humility of heart! St. Francis of Sales said, writing to a religious: "If I were employed in anything, or had an office given me, I *would love it*, and try to fulfil it duly".[2] This is the grand instruction for all labour in a community; love it. Love it because it is the sweet yoke of Christ, because it is obedience, because it is fraternal love, because it is the imitation of the Holy Family. And if you love it, you will carry it out, as St. Benedict advises, with confidence, with promptness, and with

[1] *Matt.* xxv. 40.
[2] *Letters to Persons in Religion* (Mackey's Translation), p. 894.

devotion.[1] Observe that he places holy confidence first; because one must *believe* in one's work and in the superior who orders it. Toleration, more or less contemptuous, will not do; there must be the spirit of faith; and we must believe, or incline ourselves to believe, that what we are doing is the very best for the time, place, and circumstances. Oh how much merit we lose by allowing ourselves to say. This is useless, or this is foolish, or this is a mistake! Obedience (where there is no question of sin) never makes a mistake. And it is no matter how lowly or unimportant is the work we have to do. St. Francis of Sales said to an out-sister of the Visitation: "It is a great honour, my daughter, to guard the doors of the monastery; there is nothing small in the service of God".[2] O Jesus, grant me clearness of understanding, and root out of my heart the spirit of foolish pride, that I may rejoice in work for Thee, and rejoice the more in proportion as it is humble work like that which Thou Thyself didst choose!

But the work of Jesus was more than lowly: it was penitential; it led up to the Cross, and partook of the Cross. Of suffering we have already spoken; but let us here remind ourselves that we may not shrink from work because it is penitential. No doubt, all work is, or becomes in time, more or less penitential; and it is this which makes so many murmur

---

[1] *Non trepide, non tarde, non tepide* (*Regula*, c. 5).
[2] *Letters to Persons in Religion* (Mackey's Translation), p. 217.

and grow weary. But let us remember this—that it is the Cross, and the Cross alone, which is the test of our love of Jesus Christ. No one can remain near to Christ in love and obedience to His will who does not embrace what is hard to flesh and blood. And this is doubly true of work and duty; for there is a special bond between the work imposed by obedience or duty, and nearness to Jesus. It was to His Apostles that He said, "You are those who have remained with Me in My temptations"— that is, who have stood by Me in My Apostolate, and shared in the labour and contempt which have been My lot; "therefore hath My Father disposed to you a kingdom, that you eat and drink with Me at My table;"[1] that is, the Heavenly Father's grace hath made you My intimate companion, here in this life and hereafter in the life to come. Think of these words, O priest, who art discouraged by the sin and indifference of men! Then is the time to stand firm to Christ; to remain faithful to one's spiritual duties, and to be resolute in every detail of duty. Then is the time to offer one's body and one's intelligence, one's time and one's fatigue, to Him Who shed His Blood for thee and for all men. Then is the time to redouble one's mortifications, to sacrifice rest, recreation and pleasure. It is no matter if thou gainest no one, nor appearest to have saved one single soul. Be assured that thy painful labour is not in

[1] *Luke* xxii. 28.

vain; nay, it is all treasured up, beyond the hand of the thief or the attack of the moth, one day to produce its fruit in the conversion of sinners and the perfection of the just; for just as not even the smallest act of the Sacred Heart is thrown away, so neither is the smallest act of any servant of God, done in the spirit of love and penance. Therefore, rejoice when duty brings the Cross. Rejoice when flesh and blood neither see success nor feel confidence and courage. Work on, work on! Use all thy resolution; keep thy unwilling powers to their task; shrink not from the path of thy Saviour! Thy work, as mere work, is of little value; even for the gaining of bread and shelter it is feeble without God's special blessing. But done in Christ, done in Christ's way, directed and sanctified by Christ's rules, purified and intensified by Christ's Cross, it is a great power; for the spiritualised labour of Christ's servants is the greatest human force in the moral universe.

Points for Mental Prayer.

1. Place before thy eyes the Holy House of Nazareth. Behold Jesus, Mary and Joseph at their labour. The Sun of Justice stoops to manual occupation, to household service, to the toilsome winning of bread. Oh, infinite condescension! Yet, it is not condescension, so much as infinite love. For really there is here nothing humiliating, nothing degrading. But thou, my soul, didst not know this. To thee,

and to the foolish judgment of men, this occupation is unworthy and base. The truth is, that it is neither noble nor ignoble, but indifferent; and it takes its character from the heart, which directs the hand. Not a movement of the God made man but was lifted up to infinite worth and dignity by the act of the Sacred Heart, which directed it and went with it. I adore Thee, O my Saviour, and I thank Thee for this teaching, prompted as it is by Thy infinite love of me! I know not how to sanctify my labour! I see now how precious may be every action of my hands! I am feeble in prayer, and poor in the things of the mind and spirit; but I will work, O my Lord and Master, I will work! I will devote myself to the souls and bodies of Thy brethren; I will imitate Thee, and I shall share in the dignity and the value of Thy most holy labour!

2. Consider that Jesus spent Himself for souls, whilst He did not omit anything which could comfort and do good to the bodies of those who approached Him. So it should be with me. O my Master, make my work *pure;* let no worldly preference, no self-gratification, be the motive of my labour or my sacrifice. Let it be all for Thee! In the poor, in the ignorant, in the sick, may I ever behold Thee— even Thee! Preserve me from preferring to help those who can make me a return for what I do! Guard me from merely following my likings and my feelings! Cure me of only caring to do what is agreeable to me! Give me firmness, moreover,

when my duty bids me hurt that I may heal! But always incline me to mercy and compassion that I may comfort and console all Thy creatures, bodily and spiritually, during all my life.

3. O Lord Jesus Christ, I crave Thy loving forgiveness for having so sadly wasted my life! I have been busy, but without profit for eternity! I have laboured, studied, preached, instructed, administered —but were I now to awake from this world, and to open my eyes upon eternity, how empty would be these hands which have been so active all this time! For I have been negligent in offering my work to Thee; and it is charity which makes labour of value in Thy sight! I have followed my own will; sometimes, yes, too often, absolutely sinned against obedience; frequently neglected my clear duty through sloth and self-love! And how have I turned my back upon Thy Cross! How have I dreaded Thy thorns, Thy scourges, Thy nails! Forgive me, O Jesus, that I have refused to accept from Thy hands the most sanctifying of all crosses—duty that is painful, obedience that is hard! Pardon me, and give me Thy grace to amend!

XXVIII. OUR LIFE AND ITS SURROUNDINGS.

We live in a world of persons and things. No one can escape having to do with those about him, or dealing in some way with temporal matters—money, business, social life, politics, and what happens in one's own neighbourhood. Yet to love and serve God is all we have to attend to. To reconcile actual life with this grand principle which ought to rule it, has always been the great trouble of the servants of God in every age.

Let us lay down certain rules or tests by which, in our retreat, we may judge whether we live for God alone, or not. It will appear, from our examination, that the best solution of the difficulties and uncertainties which beset us, is to live in community. Those, therefore, who have the happiness to be called to a community life should use this meditation for the purpose of esteeming it the more and of clinging to it the more fervently and the more faithfully.

1. There are things which are *necessary* for us; such as food, clothing, lodging, etc. The rule in regard to these is, that the servant of God should take or use no more than is necessary. If we are poor and straitened, and find ourselves frequently unable

to obtain even what we ought to have, such a condition of life is not in itself blessed; because, if we do not accept and embrace our poverty, it is to us the very reverse of a blessing. But how happy are we to have the opportunity of imitating Jesus, Mary and Joseph! With what fervour should we clasp to our hearts this holy state of want and need! There is no condition of life which more surely leads the heart of the truly wise straight to the Heavenly Father. O Jesus! The poor and the needy shall praise Thy Holy Name![1] Would that we understood this Divine truth! When losses come upon us —when the world uses us hardly—when our projects fail and we are ourselves friendless and forsaken— then how near are we to God, did we but know how to embrace His merciful visitation!

Those who live in community can often enjoy this privilege of feeling the sting of poverty. It may happen that the community is poor—perhaps very poor. Then, how sweet it is to offer up the hardships felt by flesh and blood, in union with the poverty of the Holy Home of Nazareth—in imitation of the poverty of the earliest gatherings of those whom St. Benedict drew into the wilderness, or whom St. Dominic gathered round him, or whom St. Francis taught to depend upon the care of their Heavenly Father!

But if it be that real poverty seldom makes us feel

---

[1] *Ps.* lxxiii. 21.

its pinch, then we must first of all feel humbled that we, who perhaps profess poverty, should feel it so little; or that we who boast of being followers of Jesus should be so unlike Him. Next, we should strive to be satisfied with what is more or less strictly necessary. Whatever we can do without, that we should do without. Such a rule, it may be admitted, is not always easy of application. It requires the light of the Holy Spirit to draw the exact line, and to see what we can prudently do without, in food, lodging or dress. Beginners should be cautioned not to be solicitous and anxious in details; for such solicitude causes more evil to the spirit than it brings advantage. What we should do is this: from time to time in our prayer, or at least with earnest thought, we should review the circumstances of our life; we should examine if we are living too luxuriously, too easily, too lavishly; we should scrutinise our habits, and discover whether there is anything which we can really do without. Then we should make resolutions in accordance with the great principle of using necessary things only so far as they are necessary. These resolutions should be based not only on fervour, but on prudence; and it will be a part of our prudence not to place on ourselves burdens which we cannot bear. But these resolutions, once deliberately made, must be our *rule*, until the time comes for reviewing them again. We should neither increase our strictness nor diminish it on the impulse of the passing moment.

In small matters, such as are not affected by our resolutions, we should refuse to hold discussions with our own conscience or feelings, but should act with Christian freedom. "Bring up sacrifices," cried the Psalmist, "bring up sacrifices and come into His courts!"[1] A life so regulated, though it may seem at first trial weary and repellent, is nevertheless a true sacrifice to the Father to Whom we would give our whole hearts. It will intensify in a marvellous way our love and our clinging.

In a community we find rules to this effect already made for us. All we have to do, therefore, is to conform ourselves with exactness to what is the rule. "He that keepeth the law multiplieth offerings," says the wise man; "it is a wholesome sacrifice to take heed to the commandments."[2] . . . "The oblation of the just is an odour of sweetness in the sight of the Most High."[3] How sweet in God's sight is the fervour of a community that loves community life; whose members rejoice in the regularity, the measure, the simplicity, the equality and strictness of conventual usage! What numberless offerings ascend to God's throne from the hearts of such happy religious!

2. There are many things which are not necessaries of life; which do not appear regularly in our life; and yet which it is prudent to use sometimes. To exercise a wise decision as to such things, and

---

[1] *Ps.* cxv. 7. [3] *Ecclus.* xxxv. 1, 2.
[2] *Ib.* 2.

as to the time and manner of using such things, is a great spiritual act. Some of these matters are very important, such as the choice of a state of life; but in everything which regards occupation, work, reading, recreation, friends, etc., etc., there is need of solid Christian principles. So far as we are free to choose, and have no special duty to discharge, the rule on which we should act should be this: Whatever draws us nearer to God, in so far as it draws us to Him, we should prefer; whatever interferes with our complete devotion to Him we should dread and avoid.

This rule is not so very difficult to apply. In the persons and things which surround us, we can without difficulty see certain attractions, occasions, or dangers which plainly lead the heart of a man either to God or away from God. If our work, our amusement, our book, and our friend dispose us to piety, to prayer, to self-restraint, to recollection, to the practice of religious duty, let us by all means make as much use of them as possible. If, on the other hand, they present occasions of sin, if they tempt us to offend God, if they dispose us to reckless liberty, if they make prayer difficult, and keep us away from the Sacraments—then there is nothing for it but to give them up. Here, O my soul, behold again the opportunity of that life of "sacrifice" which all must lead who desire to follow their Saviour! To renounce and avoid everything, be it what it may, which does not in some way lead us to God—this is what the Psalmist calls "the sacrifice of justice,"[1] which he constantly calls upon us to make. For is it not mere justice? Is not God everything to thee? What is any creature to thee, except so far as it brings thee to Him? What is any person or thing to thee, except so far as thereby thou art made to know God, to love Him the more, to serve Him the more faithfully, or to repent more sincerely for thy offences against Him? Turn thine eyes, then, upon thyself. Is there nothing that thy heavenly Father even at this moment calls upon thee to renounce? Is there no person who is to thee an occasion of sin? Is there no habit or practice which prevents thee from giving thyself wholly to God? Be sure that thou canst not begin to lead a spiritual life—or even the life of a Christian—until thou hast given up that which stands between thee and thy Lord.

3. One thing which we must aim at in ordering our life is, the faculty of seeing Christ in every person and in every thing. The sense of the perpetual presence of God, which we shall perhaps never fully attain, should nevertheless be desired and striven for; and as Jesus Christ came to reveal God to us, so the effort to see Christ in our surroundings is a more successful way than any other of keeping God before our eyes. Hence no servant of God should be content with his life, unless it tends to foster this habit of seeing Christ. What is meant by seeing Christ in creatures? It means that, whatever

[1] *Ps.* iv. 6.

happens, we are to disregard the apparent cause or agent, and to say, with devotion : This is His doing! This is His holy will! This is His love! In this it is He Who is trying me—He Who is teaching me! In painful things we must see His desire to turn us away from creatures to Himself; in things consoling and pleasant, we must recognise that love which would attract us by easy ways again to Himself. In work, we must have before our eyes Him Who laboured at Nazareth. In amusements, we must behold Him drawing souls at the feast and the banquet. In dealing with persons, we must recognise that we are dealing with souls for which He died. In the poor, we can hardly choose but see Himself, Who came as a poor man and a servant. In our equals, or those whom we meet in daily intercourse, we should behold those who require, quite as much as the poor, our compassion, our help and our prayers —remembering that what we do unto them, we do to Him. In superiors, we should recognise that authority which is of God, and to which therefore we bow, not with outward respect only, but with interior homage, as to our Lord Himself. There is no occurrence, no act of intercourse, which does not either present to us Jesus in person, or at least recall some circumstance of that most holy and divine human life, upon which only to look is to feel the effect of His salvation.

Unless our life, then, leads us to this spirit, it is most unsatisfactory. But it cannot do so unless it is a life of much recollection, of considerable prayer, of serious reading, and of attendance at the Church's functions. For we can only see in creatures what we ourselves put into creatures; and we can put into them nothing supernatural, nothing that savours of Christ, unless we first have the light and the knowledge of Christ in our own hearts. "In Thy light we shall see light."[1] These words are applied to the Beatific Vision, but they are also applicable to the life of grace. Why is the world so blank, so unsuggestive, so merely sensual or base, so limited and confined to space and time, as it is even to men of great mental power—except that their minds have not taken in Jesus? "O Lord God! Open Thou my eyes, and I will consider the wondrous things of Thy law! . . . Thy testimonies are my meditation!"—that record of Divine testimony which I find in the New Testament, telling me of the marvels of the Sacred Humanity. "I turned my feet unto Thy testimonies"—yes, I thank Thee that from my early years I have been accustomed to think upon that blessed Life! "I have purchased Thy testimonies as an inheritance for ever!"[2]—for nothing will draw me nearer to my last end than these thoughts on Thee, and Thy words and acts.

In a community, the regular prayer, the Divine Office, and holy reading, dispose the heart with happy persistence to the perpetual vision of Christ;

[1] *Ps.* xxxv. 10. [2] *Ib.* cxviii. 18, 24, 59, 111.

whilst the order of obedience, the serene authority of superiors, and the silent eloquence of the holy habit, make that sacred presence almost felt. Blessed are they who "turn away their eyes from vanity"[1]—that is from all human motives and impulses—from likes and dislikes, jealousy, vanity, criticism, murmuring—and see in superiors, in brethren, in every assembly and in every rule, only the voice and the hand of Jesus.

4. Another point to strive for in our daily life is the facility of rising from our faults. We cannot hope to avoid venial sins and negligences. It is, therefore, of the utmost importance that we should quickly repent of such hourly offences, and that none of them should harden into a habit. Moreover, a prompt return to God by humility, sorrow and love, frequently brings to the soul more spiritual profit than was lost by the fault itself. How little adapted is the ordinary life of the world for enabling us to rise from daily sins! The absence of serious thought, the preoccupation of business or pleasure, the outpouring of continual conversation—these things form an atmosphere in which our innumerable offences are hardly noticed by us. The result is that by degrees we grow indifferent, lax and cold, and pass under the dominion of sensuality, passion, pride, and human impulses; and it is no wonder if we constantly imperil our very salvation by mortal sin.

---

[1] *Ps.* cxviii. 37.

To counteract this tendency towards settling down into the lamentable state of forgetfulness of God, three elements are necessary in our life: regular times of examination, leisure for prayer, and (if possible) the voice of some one to warn and reprove us. In other words, we should examine our conscience every night, and also (in regard to particular faults) in the middle of the day; we should foresee (in our morning prayer) and provide for certain occasions of sin; we should never omit our prayer, vocal and mental; and we should strive to find a pious, learned and firm confessor.

Above all, we should form the habit of prompt and loving return to God. It is not enough to regret or feel annoyed at the sin into which we have fallen. Such emotion is frequently nothing more than that personal pride which is hurt by a delinquency which seems unworthy of us. Devout conversion to Jesus, humble acknowledgment that our fall is just what might have been expected, and then a loving cry for forgiveness—how valuable and profitable it is to attain a facility in making acts like these! "Return to Me, saith the Lord, and I will receive thee."[1]

In a community, we have all these advantageous conditions;—leisure for prayer, examination of conscience, the watchfulness of superiors, and the constant prompting of holy times and employments. A

---

[1] *Jeremias* iii. 1.

thousand times in the day will God "receive"—lovingly, ungrudgingly—the soul who is happy enough to understand how her very faults can be made so many steps to draw nearer to Him.

5. Most profitable is it, also, to lead a life which fosters humility, and gives opportunity for mortification and penance. On this subject, two remarks may be made. First, although it is the disposition of the heart and not the outward act that is valuable in God's eyes; yet it is morally impossible for any one to be habitually or deeply humble, or to practise satisfactory self-restraint, without external occasions of humiliation, on the one hand, and of self-denial on the other. Secondly, a life in which there is a routine of humiliation and mortification may come to be very profitless unless the heart constantly rouses itself to accept such occasions. The poor have great opportunities, through their privations, of drawing near to God; but how few bear them with resignation—accept them—much less give thanks for them!—and how few, therefore, profit by them! It is the same with too many religious. That most precious community life, with its obedience, its self-effacement, and its hardships—how rarely is it used to the utmost! "Israel, a vine full of branches!—a vine full of fruit!"[1] How few sit under these branches—how few know the goodness of that fruit!

[1] Osee x. 1.

Points for Mental Prayer.

1. Form acts of regret that thy whole life has been hitherto given up to creatures, and not to thy God. O my Father in Heaven! my thoughts and powers have been taken up all the day long with everything except with Thee! I have occupied myself with persons, with things, with actions, in which Thou hast had but little part. I have desired money, honour, ease, profit. I have aimed my life at objects which had little to do with heaven and eternity. My study has been myself, my pride, my passions. When I have rejoiced it has been in things of the flesh; when I have been sorrowful, it has been because of worldly trouble or selfish disappointment. My pride has separated me from Thee. My humiliations have only embittered me or hardened me, closing my heart against Thee, my only Friend! Pardon me, O my God, and receive back now to Thy embrace one who has found out how truly all creatures without Thee are husks of swine!

2. Lift thine eyes to the mountains whence thy help must come. Behold Jesus is there, in the Sion of His holiness! From Him streams the light which illuminates the world, and which changes all creatures into incarnations of Himself. O Jesus! give me grace to see Thee everywhere; in my labour, to elevate me; in my recreation, to moderate me; in my intentions, to purify me; in my success, to

kill my pride; in my trials, to draw me to Thee; in my neighbours, that I may serve Thee; in my children, that I may honour Thee; in the poor, that I may minister to Thee; in my superiors, that I may obey Thee; in my pastors, that I may recognise the bounty of Thy supernatural grace!

3. Make practical resolutions as to a rule of life. This ought to include the following points: Morning and night prayer; regular frequentation of the Sacraments; examination of conscience at night, with fervent acts of contrition; mental prayer, or devout reading, for a quarter of an hour, half an hour, or an hour daily, according to our state of life, our capacity, and the advice of our director; the regulation of our food, clothing, and lodging; the renunciation of this and that occasion of offending God; the hearing of Mass, not only on Sundays, but also, when possible, on week days; the Rosary and a few (not too many) vocal prayers; membership of some Association or Confraternity for our profit and that of our neighbour; and special resolutions must be made in regard to the duties of our state of life, as pastors, parents, employers, traders, workers, teachers, etc., etc. "Forsake it not, and it shall keep thee; love it, and it shall preserve thee."[1]

[1] *Proverbs* iv. 6

XXIX. LITTLE SINS.

Sins which are not mortal may be classed under three heads: first, those which are deliberate; secondly, those which are habitual; and thirdly, those which are from human frailty—sudden temptation, surprise, slight laziness, or levity.

Deliberate sins, even if they are "venial," are very lamentable and very dangerous. Let us observe how easily a deliberate venial sin passes the boundary and becomes mortal. This is especially true in such matters as slander, detraction, tale-bearing, and levity in regard to the sixth commandment. In religious, the criticism of superiors may often be a grievous matter, on account of the harm done thereby to the community. On all occasions where the only doubt is whether full consent was given, an easy temper about venial sin is extremely unsafe, and is sure, sooner or later, to land the unfortunate soul in a deadly offence against God.

The poisonous element in deliberate venial sin is the sinner's contempt of God. It is not formal contempt, or else it would be mortal sin. But it is a "constructive" disloyalty and disobedience; and in truth the soul is sometimes only saved from mortal sin by want of appreciation of what is being done.

The extreme danger arises from this,—that the soul gives itself away to its pride, passion, or sloth, not utterly, or formally, but like one who is more or less reckless. To give the reins, even to this extent, to our fallen nature is to unmuzzle a wild beast; the next thing will be a deadly wound. The will becomes accustomed to yield, the judgment grows lazy, faith is weakened, and a fatal indifference spreads round the heart, like the air of a pestilence. As soon, therefore, as our examination tells us we are becoming hardened to deliberate sin, *however small the sin may be*, we must turn quickly to our Heavenly Father, or else it is a mere matter of time that we shall offend Him mortally.

Habitual venial sin has special dangers and difficulties. For if one deliberate sin in a small matter disposes the heart so effectually to the gravest offences, what must be the effect on mind, will, imagination and spiritual energy when a habit of this kind of sin has been formed? There are persons who are habitually and without making any contrary efforts, ill-tempered, untruthful, slothful in religious matters, free in speech, careless of their neighbour's reputation, dishonest, and lax on the point of charity. Any one of these habits is a millstone round the neck. No one is safe for a moment who remains easy under such a habit.

One of the effects of a retreat ought to be a new

sense (or a revived sense) of the unfaithfulness to God of a soul thus given to a tepid life. Such a soul can hardly call God her father. If our whole life ought to be a happy trust and confidence in God and a sweet intercourse with Him, what must be said of a soul which is deliberately mean with Him, deliberately deficient, deliberately grudging, deliberately attached to what He denounces, deliberately persevering in a danger of losing Him altogether? O my Lord God, no wonder that Thou dost punish venial sin with temporal death! What evil of this earth can be compared to it?

The grand character of the dealings of Jesus Christ with the soul is generosity. He exhausted every means of benefiting us, and He poured out for us the last drop of His precious Blood. There is no way of responding to such generosity except by being generous; let us be generous, and we are not only safe but happy. On the other hand, a life of cautious indulgence—for that is what venial sin comes to—dries up holy Charity. It drives the grace of God from all the outposts of the spirit—from the imagination, the feelings, the human motives, the natural springs of energy. It does not destroy or kill divine Charity; but, as St. Francis de Sales says, " Charity is sometimes weakened and depressed in the affections till it seems to be scarcely in exercise at all, and yet it remains entire in the supreme region of the soul. This happens when under the multitude of venial sins, as under ashes, the fire of holy love remains covered and its flame smothered, though it is not dead or extinguished."[1]

O my Lord Jesus Christ, what is that is thus paralysing my heart—which ought to be alive, and to burn with fervour in Thy service? I love Thee, yet I love thee not! I have not rejected Thee; yet, like the Ephesian, I have fallen from my first charity! What is it that drags me so dangerously near the abyss? Is it my softness, which makes me afraid to mortify myself? Is it my vanity, which dreads the least rebuff? Is it my ostentation, which spoils all my good actions and hides Thee from my sight? Or is it some base desire, some prompting of carnal passion, that I do not vigorously resist, but unworthily trifle with? Or is it something in my natural temperament that I have never really attempted to check and correct—unkindness, temper, jealousy, or despondency? Or perhaps it may be my neglect of prayer, my want of preparation for Mass, my absence of attention in saying it, hearing it, approaching Holy Communion? My omission of morning and night prayers? My omission or cutting short of meditation? My distracted haste in the Divine Office, or in my vocal prayers? Enlighten my eyes, O my Saviour, that I may find out what habitual sin (venial though it be) has taken hold of me. But grant me more than this; give me also the strong impulse of Thy grace that

---

[1] *The Love of God* (Mackey's translation), book iv. ch. ii.

I may shake off these fetters, and be once more free with that freedom wherewith Thou hast come to make us free! Give me, O Lord, a generous heart! Let me learn at the foot of Thy Cross, that it is only when I give Thee all that I am safe! Rebuke my mean indulgence with the grandeur of Thy magnanimity! Make me ashamed of following Thee in so half-hearted a fashion, after the revelations of Bethlehem, Nazareth and Calvary!

Consider what are the consequences to the soul of habitual or deliberate sin, however light the sin may be. First of all, the very least sin is a detestable evil, greater and more to be dreaded than any evil or suffering in the temporal order. Pain, torture, death, annihilation, are slight compared with the least offence of Almighty God. Oh that we had something of the sensitiveness of the Saints! Next, we must remember that venial sin disposes to mortal sin—and therefore to the turning of our back upon our Creator—and that in three ways: first, it withdraws to a greater or less degree the soul from the influence of sanctifying grace—grace remains in the innermost fortress, but the outworks are in the enemy's hands; secondly, it superinduces the dangerous condition of laxity, indifference, tepidity, self-gratification, pride—a condition which varies according to individual character, but is always most dangerous; dangerous, because it is like a malarious atmosphere, in which one may at any moment catch a deadly sickness; and thirdly, because in such a state we cannot count upon the help of the actual grace of God, partly because we do not ask for it, partly because by our preoccupation with self and creatures we interpose obstacles, or, in other words, "resist the Holy Spirit". [1]

Further, there can be no doubt that venial sin is most severely punished. Even if there were nothing else, the impurity and perversity of our powers of mind and body would have to be remedied and removed before we could enjoy the Face of God. Only fire will serve for this—either the fire of Charity or the fire of Purgatory!

The third description of venial sin is that which is not habitual nor deliberate, but rather the effect of surprise, frailty, temperament, levity, or curiosity. No one on earth can be without sins of this kind. Our Lady was free from them, but no one else—not even the greatest Saints. In none of them have inordinate emotions been completely extinguished; of none, even at the end of their career of self-discipline and of generous love, can it be said that they were not liable at least to slight sins of surprise. Such liability to sin is by no means incompatible with true and genuine "perfection"; for it does not exclude a love of God above all things, intense, extending to every kind of duty, abhorring even the least sin, always seeking that which is more pleasing to Him, ordering all the powers of the soul in His service, and never

---

[1] *Acts* vii. 51.

forgetting Him for a single waking hour. A Saint may possess such a love as this—a love which is justly called perfect—and yet will be found to fail in little things, at times. We may be quite sure, then, as regards ourselves, that we shall produce a plentiful crop of small sins, and that as long as we live. Every time we go to confession we shall have to blame ourselves for our frailties, our weaknesses, our partially deliberate shortcomings and our negligences; and these will generally run in the same lines week after week and month after month. It must be noted, however, that although these trivial sins constantly recur over and over again, yet they do not come under the description of "habitual" venial sins. In one sense, doubtless, they are habitual, because they recur; but it would be more correct to call them "natural" or "instinctive" than habitual, because what is habitual has been acquired by our own act or negligence, and these sins really spring from our fallen nature. Hence we should not be disturbed because they are constantly repeated.

At the same time, it would be a very dangerous thing to acquiesce in them. It would be very bad if we said to ourselves: "These falls are inevitable, therefore I will pay no heed to them". They are unavoidable considered *en masse;* but there is not one which, singly, might not, and should not, be avoided, if we corresponded fully with Divine Grace. Moreover, these small faults, thus left with us and not taken away by God's powerful assistance, have a special part to play in the work of our perfection—as we shall presently consider.

How, then, are we to treat our indeliberate sins?

First of all, we are to keep them well before our eyes in our daily examination. It is melancholy to see how many good people never suspect their little failings. Some have no turn for self-inspection, or self-consciousness. Those who have reason to suspect their character to be of this kind should ask questions sometimes, of a confessor or superior. Others, having fought at one time against their failings, have now grown accustomed to them; have ceased to be afflicted by them, or have grown disheartened. We must never let our daily sins slip out of our daily memory.

Secondly, we must look on ahead, and take precautions. As these small sins come from temperament, surprise, levity, etc., and as every reasoning creature has a certain power (with God's grace) to repress inordinate feeling, to guard against surprise, and to take levity sternly to task, we must rouse ourselves to attend to this in our daily life; and an excellent means of doing it is to direct ourselves to it every morning, renewing the necessary resolutions for the day.

Thirdly, we must habituate ourselves to mortification, and even to penance. An enormous proportion of our little sins come from self-indulgence or self-love. To be habitually on the side of self-repression is to be always prepared for temptation. Mortification may without any insuperable difficulty be made to pass into an instinct. A more invaluable instinct a servant of God could not have; for the instinct of always pausing whenever we feel that a thing is pleasant to sense or self, is adapted to protect the will in every occurrence of daily life.

Fourthly, whenever we notice that we have fallen into any fault, we must immediately return to God. This cannot be too strongly insisted upon; for this, indeed, is what the loving Providence of our Heavenly Father intends; this is the good which He desires to draw out of the evil and misery of our daily falls. But this turning to God should be tranquil, humble, and filial. It should be tranquil; for, as St. Aloysius used to say, "He who gives way to annoyance and discouragement when he falls, proves that he does not know himself, and forgets that he is made of a soil which can only grow thorns and thistles".[1] It should be humble; that is, the servant of God should acknowledge that this fault or unworthiness is precisely what might have been expected of so weak and poor a creature, who has in him nothing that is good except what comes from the grace of God. And it should be filial; the heart should try to feel that a loving Father has been slighted, a dear Friend made sorrowful, a beneficent Lord checked and thwarted; and sorrow and love will lead to humble trust and renewed resolution for the future. Any one who thus turns to God after committing a fault

[1] *Petits Bollandistes*, 21 Juin.

may easily draw down by his repentance more grace than he deserved to lose by his fall, and be nearer to God than he was before.

Fifthly, both on each single occasion and in our general devotional life, a valuable means to correct natural weakness is to cast our eyes upon the Sacred Humanity of Jesus. Of this, something has already been said. How profitable it is, when we have fallen by weakness, blindness, laxity or curiosity, to take refuge near to Jesus, and to draw out from Him that marvellous strength, that alacrity in holy things, that strenuous devotion to God and that contempt of the earth, which His most blessed Human Nature was formed to shed like fragrance upon His servants!

Sixthly, as we have already said, the disposition of soul which, more than any other, makes all sin (even the least) impossible, is generosity. This is only another name for loving God with the whole heart. To have a great desire for whole-hearted love is a most efficacious way out of the miseries of constant petty sin. True, a desire to be completely generous is not the same thing as the attainment of this happy disposition. But to keep constantly before one's eyes this, the only worthy and adequate Christian spirit, to long for it before God, to excite ourselves to live up to it, and to convince ourselves that in no other way can we ever please God or enjoy true peace of heart—these are means which will carry us far towards giving ourselves wholly to God.

Points for Mental Prayer.

1. Seek out our Lord Jesus Christ, offering Himself wholly for the salvation of sinners, of whom thou art the chief. Find Him, first of all, at His entrance into the world. At that moment all the angels of God adore Him,[1] as their God and sovereign Lord; do thou join thy poor welcome with theirs. But He, longing to begin His work, says to His Heavenly Father, "Behold, I come!" He is ready to give all, to do all; to humble Himself, to become obedient, to be annihilated, to suffer the Cross. O my Saviour! I also am ready! I wish my life, by Thy grace, to be nothing but Thy love, Thy will, Thy service! My being, my powers, my acts, words and thoughts—they belong to Thee and Thee alone! Find Him, next, in the moment of the Last Supper, when the hour of greatest generosity was at hand. What more could He do which He has not done? O Jesus, by Thy greatest of gifts, Thy true sacramental Presence, I pray Thee to make me generous in my turn! By Thy welcoming of Thy bitter passion, give me strength to make my life a continual bearing of the Cross! And find Him, once more, on the Altar of His supreme Sacrifice, when He opens His arms so wide and cries with so loud a voice that "It is finished!" O my Redeemer, let the hour come when there shall be nothing left in my heart or my life that I have not surrendered to Thee!—when no

---

[1] *Heb.* i. 6.

affection, no desire or view, no self-indulgence, no pride or vanity, shall any longer keep me from living for Thee and Thee alone!

2. Weigh well the danger to thy soul of Venial Sin. O my Father, how near have I been to the edge of the abyss! How recklessly have I played with fire! How barely have I put in jeopardy Thy sovereign friendship! O detested tepidity! O unworthy hankering after what is wrong! O blindness of my fallen nature! Alas! my forgetfulness of eternity! Alas! the meanness of my bargaining with my generous Creator, my lavish Redeemer, my munificent Sanctifier!

3. Represent to thyself that to "resist" and to "contristate" the Holy Spirit is a very great evil, and that those who are doing so must end in driving Him away, unless they quickly enter into themselves. Why, O Divine Spirit of Jesus, hast Thou poured of Thy abundance into my poor being, except to draw it to live wholly for Thee? Thou wouldst have me devout, full of alacrity, strong to act and to endure, spiritual, detached from things below. For this Thy sevenfold Gift is given; for this Thou makest my heart Thy temple; for this Thou takest up Thy abode even with my wretchedness and poverty. Yet I continue to resist Thee! My indifference keeps Thy presence inactive; my attachments, my likings, my humours (unresisted, uncorrected) deaden the play of Thy gifts, chill the Divine heat of Thy promptings, and so hinder me from making that

progress in Divine love, in holiness and in edification, which Thou dost intend. How long, O patient Master, wilt Thou have patience with me? How long wilt Thou suffer my negligence—how long wilt Thou await my complete conversion? I see, O my God, how foolish, how unworthy, and how dangerous it is to correspond so badly to Thy innumerable graces. I will rouse myself; I will be in earnest; I will give Thee my whole heart! But it is only Thou, and Thy grace, that can lift me out of my tepidity. Look upon me, have pity on me, and draw me to Thee!

XXX. SPIRITUAL READING.

To be spiritual by fits and starts is not enough. Our endeavour should be to invest life wholly with spirituality. Spiritual ends, spiritual motives, spiritual views, spiritual thinking, speaking and acting—this, and nothing less than this, is what should be the character of the whole of our rational life. To succeed in this is a long process, and a long labour; but to be content with anything less, would be to be content to be no true follower of Christ. Still, although the work is not easy, we are not obliged to do impossibilities. Let us spend each day with the prudence, the foresight, the self-denial and the leaning upon God to which we are bound as God's servants, and we shall "grow" into the likeness for which we long. One of the most effective aids in making each day of our lives truly spiritual is the reading of spiritual books.

Spiritual Reading is the listening to the Voice of God. That voice we hear in many ways. We have it in our own hearts, if we practise recollection and prayer. We have it in sermons and other instructions given by the living voice of men. But books, even if they are not so personal to ourselves as the interior speech of our Heavenly Father, nor so stimulating as certain discourses of God-fearing men, yet they have many advantages of their own. They are always at hand; they are the fruits of the labour of Saints and learned men; they offer great variety, and some of them cannot fail to suit our most special needs. Nay, when the book is Holy Scripture, it is God Himself Who speaks, and Who has left, in those inspired pages, what He knows our heart requires to hear.

That Spiritual Reading is necessary for us is easy to understand. First of all, we must have instruction. Possibly we seem to ourselves to be already sufficiently instructed. Yet how many there are who have had only the briefest and most superficial course of Christian and Catholic teaching! No one can be devout who has not a deep knowledge of the mysteries of faith. A wide or extensive knowledge may not be needed for all; but even the poorest and the rudest, if they are to live an interior life, must obtain, by teaching or by infused light, a firm and penetrating hold on the great truths of God, of redemption, and of salvation. Now, such knowledge is not acquired, generally speaking, except by sustained application and continuous attention to teaching. "Incline thy ear and hear the words of the wise; and apply thy heart to My doctrine."[1] And the Psalmist thus prays: "Give me understanding and I will search Thy law; and I will keep it with my

---

[1] *Proverbs* xxii. 17.

whole heart."[1] Perhaps the most effective sort of spiritual instruction (in the English language) is good sermons on doctrinal and moral subjects. To read such sermons is to feel the greatness, the beauty and the glory of that kingdom of God on earth which neither nature nor the institution of men can rival.

The Venerable Blosius enumerates the advantages of Spiritual Reading thus: "The mind of a good man derives many admirable gains from spiritual doctrine. It is kept pure from sin; it ceases to be ignorant; it obtains tranquillity; it is illuminated; it is nourished; it is stimulated; it is strengthened; and it is rendered beautiful."[2] You will observe that he speaks of "ceasing to be ignorant," and of "illumination". It is not enough to be above the condition of gross ignorance. God's revelation is very wide. The best intellects of all ages have used their utmost powers in amplifying and illustrating the creeds, the mysteries and the commandments. A great book, like the *City of God* of St. Augustine, which proclaims with adequate literary power and spiritual unction the stupendous work of God for human souls, cannot fail to discover to the heart a universe which to ordinary men is more or less unknown. Oh, that God would vouchsafe to give us this illumination! Men talk of enlightenment, discernment, insight, wisdom; but the Lord should be our Illumination;[3] and it is in holy books about Him and His mercies

---

[1] *Ps.* cxviii. 34. [2] *Speculum Spirituale,* cap. 10.
[3] *Ps.* xxvi. 1.

that we obtain it from Him. Many, even of those who fear God and serve Him, do not understand how bright a light and how clear a vision of Divine things, as yet almost unsuspected, await them in Spiritual Reading.

The "purity" or "innocence" which Blosius sets down as one of the effects of Spiritual Reading is that sensitiveness to sin which is the result of dwelling upon God and His dealings with His creatures. Whatever we read, there is sure to be something in it about God's Fatherhood, about His having made these hearts of ours for Himself, about the dreadful evil of sin, about death and eternity. To read of these things is to have our memory and our imagination impressed by them. It is to be roused to the great realities of our being. It is to be freed from that sleep of death and indifference which is the unhappy condition of those who live in mortal sin. Mortal sin cannot exist with the practice of Spiritual Reading. He who reads regularly comes to regard the slightest sin with horror, and the lightest occasion of sin with apprehension.

The "tranquillity" which comes from Spiritual Reading is often dwelt upon by sacred writers. It is true that certain subjects have the contrary effect. Reading may not unfrequently disturb the conscience. This, however, is not always a matter to be regretted. No peace is possible until the conscience is really roused to contrition and good resolution. When once we have taken reasonable pains to put our conscience straight with God, then those who are timid, sensitive, or scrupulous, will take advice and avoid reading of an alarming kind. The "consolation" which we have a right to look for in this most holy practice of Spiritual Reading is a kind of delight in God as the loving, the mighty, and the all-sufficing Father of our being. We realise in reading how we are bound up with God; how good He is, how sweet, how solicitous, how rich, ample, and overflowing. We are glad to renounce the world, to mortify the flesh, to humble and annihilate ourselves. We regret nothing that we have given up; but rather, in the music of the gentle refrain which arises from the words of the Prophets, the Evangelists, and the Saints, we despise and loathe everything which is not God or related to Him. This is the "sweetness" of God's word which is so often referred to by the Psalmist, "How sweet are Thy words on my palate!—more than honey to my mouth".[1]

Further, Spiritual Reading "nourishes" the soul. This comparison of Holy Reading to spiritual food is common in the writings of the Saints. It is a very apt illustration. The result, in regard to our bodily life, of sufficient wholesome food, is vigour, muscular power, easy exertion, and a kind of pleasure in the very act of living. In the spiritual life many things may be said to produce corresponding effects, such as Divine grace, the Sacraments, mental prayer, etc.

[1] *Ps.* cxviii. 103.

But there is a special aptitude in putting them down to Spiritual Reading. For Spiritual Reading really supplies the greater part of our spiritual food. Whether it be our will, our intelligence, our imagination, or our memory, it is from reading that each faculty obtains the matter on which it can act. Grace is mighty, and is essential; but since it does not work miracles (as a rule), it will not put ideas into our heads or pictures into our imagination. The Sacraments convey treasures of enlightenment and strength; but experience shows that these great forces too often lie inoperative for want of ideas, purposes, and generous aims, to act as intercepters, and transmute force into heat and action. And is not mental prayer itself too frequently feeble, intermittent, and cold, simply because our mind and memory are empty, and we have no store of thought to set our devotion working? It is Spiritual Reading which supplies ideas, motives, views, interesting information, touching histories, useful explanation, fertile developments of doctrines, wide generalisations on God, the Church, and eternity; and this great store of material only requires prayer and grace to be turned into the precious stones which form the walls of the heavenly Sion.

As Reading nourishes, so it "stimulates" and "strengthens". Stimulation is that force, over and above mere nutrition, which is developed in the reaction of the living thing, and is its response to some kind of a call upon it. By Holy Reading both feeling and intelligence are thus stimulated to activity. A saintly preacher, a striking death-bed, the example of perfect men—these things may be more powerful. But we cannot have them always with us. Our books, on the other hand, need never be far away. Do we not know what good desires, what warmth of Divine love, what generosity of heart follow from Holy Reading? And as for " strength "—whether it be the strength to make a decisive resolution, or to break with an occasion of sin, or to give ourselves wholly to God, or to be faithful in resisting a certain temptation, or to go on persevering in our state of life and our pursuit of perfection—beyond all doubt we find it in Holy Reading.

It need not be said that of all Spiritual Reading Holy Scripture is the best and the most profitable. The reason of this is, not merely the eloquence and wisdom of the writers, or the power of the ideas—although in this respect there is no book in the world to compare with the Bible—but the force and illuminating power of the Divine inspiration. Remember that Holy Scripture was intended by its Author Almighty God, to draw us to Him. Will not His words, revealed as they are for this very purpose, effect what He intends? What does He say Himself? He says that His word is "effectual"; that it shall never " return to Him void "; that it is "truth"; that it is " fire "; that it is "a hammer"; that it is " the sword of the Spirit "; that it is " the doctrine of the Spirit "; that it is " a lamp," and "a light"; that it "converts souls" and "gives wisdom to little ones"; that it "rejoices the heart" and "enlightens the soul"; that it is "an infinite treasure to men". How happy are they who read Holy Scripture—provided that they read it with reverence, with desire for spiritual profit, and with the fear and consciousness of God! The great subjects treated of in Scripture are, first, God and His attributes; next, Jesus Christ (in the Prophets, the Psalms, and the Gospels); then the great fundamental truths of life and death, the heinousness of sin, and the various virtues and vices. The historical books are not to be read by all, or at all times by any. The Holy Gospels come first in order of spiritual profit; then the rest of the New Testament; then the Psalms; then the prophetical books, especially the Book of Isaias; then the "sapiential" books. Holy Scripture should be read slowly; there is more in every word of it than all our meditations and searchings will ever find out. It should also be read in order; that is, we should not pick out chapters at hap-hazard, but read a book or a section right through. Priests, and those who have opportunity, should study for the purpose of reading the Bible intelligently. Such study is not itself Spiritual Reading, but it forms an excellent preparation for it. More especially should we study the Gospels, the Epistles of St. Paul and of St. Peter, and the Book of Psalms. To one who has the taste for it, there is no branch of spiritual doctrine or exhortation which will not be found to be adequately treated in Holy Scripture.

The next branch of Spiritual Reading may be called *Instruction on the Spiritual Life*. Under this heading come treatises on the principles of spirituality, on the virtues and the mode of acquiring them, on sins, defects, temptations, etc. Reading of this kind is not without its necessity. The soul is much assisted by possessing an orderly view of the spiritual life. Self-knowledge is thereby much assisted; and one is reminded what to aim at, and how much there is to do. It is well to have a favourite book of the kind here described, which one can master and refer to: the *Devout Life* of St. Francis de Sales, or the *Spiritual Conflict* might be suggested to most people. Treatises more full and minute are easy to find.

The third kind of Reading is what we may roughly call *Exhortatory*. As examples of this we may take the *Way of Salvation* and other writings of St. Alphonsus, or the works of the Venerable Blosius. Reading of this kind tends to become a prayer; and whilst it is the more profitable the more nearly it approaches prayer, it is for that very reason the more difficult to keep up. In this division we may consider the writings of the holy Fathers. To those who have time and capacity for penetrating a little beneath the surface of language, and who can read the Fathers in the original or can command a good translation, there is no exercise (after Holy Scripture) which is so stimulating and so satisfying as the reading of St. Augustine, St. Ambrose, and St. Bernard—to name only three. Every word of a Father and Doctor is a sanctioned word; it has fed and formed souls; the Church has grown round it, as towns have grown up round the shrine of a Saint. The Fathers have what is called a "message" for every human heart; they lived face to face with real human nature, on the one hand; and they were penetrated with the conviction, on the other, of God's incessant work upon human nature and on its behalf. Hence they are never out of date. In the Fathers you do not find spiritual nostrums, or sentiment, or views, or loud pathos, or inadequate half-truths. You find the real, the solid, the sober and the true. And yet it would be a mistake to shun modern writers altogether. It may be said that, within certain obvious limitations, any spiritual book, whatever be its style, is a useful book if it disposes the heart to amendment, contrition, the imitation of Jesus, and the genuine love of God. To read a spiritual book whose style pleases us need not be wrong, and may be most profitable. But with books of this kind, one must frequently ask oneself serious questions and answer them frankly and in the spirit of self-denial.

The last division of Spiritual Reading on which it is necessary to dwell is the *Lives of the Saints*. Many find this, on the whole, the most agreeable of all spiritual exercises. To see an heroic soul living, acting, consuming itself, in the presence of its God, is the best of all possible exhortations to sluggish human nature. The personal interest in the life of a Saint has the power (which no amount of exposition has, and which is rarely attained by mere exhortation) of liquefying or softening those emotions which, although not virtues, are like the flux in the smelting of the ironstone—they make the iron possible; that is, such emotions as admiration, sympathy, and pity. The soul, thus moved, readily pours itself forth in acts of faith, hope and charity, in contrition, and in purposes of amendment. The feeling that the Saints were once living on this earth, that they wrought out their lives on the truest principles, that God carried them through with special grace till the moment of His summons, and that they are living still and longing to help us—this gives their histories a peculiar power over the imagination of all who attempt to serve God; and thus the remembrance of God, the thought of eternity and general interest in the spiritual world are without difficulty kept up within our hearts. The Lives of the Saints have been written in many different forms. For Spiritual Reading the devotional form should be preferred. At the same time, it is not to be denied that it is important for a life to have certain good literary qualities, such as skilful narrative, apt and vivid language, and a clear chronological arrangement. For the personality of the Saint is the powerful element which must be brought out; and into this there enter, not only the Saint's words and acts, but the circumstances of time, place, age and vocation. A life which discreetly blends devotional reflections with biography, especially if they are the reflections of a holy and learned master of the spiritual life, will generally be preferred by one who truly seeks his advantage in Spiritual Reading. But the very "story" of a Saint is profoundly effective; and it often happens that a word, a saying, an anecdote, is enough to inflame the heart, and lift it up to God. "For we are the children of the Saints, and look for that life which God will give to those that never change their faith from Him."[1]

There is only one really essential and adequate rule as to Spiritual Reading—and that is, that we seek God in it. If we seek amusement, or mere information, or matter for sermons, or vague edification, or the satisfaction of literary taste—we have no right to call it Spiritual Reading; and when we have read a book or a chapter with any of these motives uppermost, our Spiritual Reading is still to begin.

It is hardly needful to add that one of our good resolutions in a retreat should be to take our half-hour's (or our quarter of an hour's) daily Spiritual Reading faithfully and regularly.

Points for Mental Prayer.

1. Contemplate thy Saviour Jesus Christ praying to His Heavenly Father on that last night before

[1] *Tobias* ii. 18.

His Passion, and saying, "I have given them Thy Word".[1] Consider that He is the Word, and that the diffusion of the spoken and written Word of God throughout the whole world and throughout all time is nothing but the diffusion of His own presence and power. Thus, in the Old Testament, He said, "Are not My words like a fire?"[2] and in His visible life He said, "I am come to cast fire on earth".[3] O Jesus, make me love Thy Word, which is the manifestation, and, as it were, the multiplication, of Thy Sacred Heart! Thy Word enlightens me, moves me, draws me; and when I am wrought upon by it, I know that it is rather Thyself, the Incarnate Word, than any echo from mortal surroundings, that takest hold of my frailty and liftest me nigher to my last end. What are all earthly communications in comparison with the heat and the purifying force of Thy heavenly Word! O adorable goodness! O ineffable kindness! O most sweet stooping down of Thy Majesty to seek and to save a poor sinner!

2. As I desire to welcome Thyself, O Incarnate Word, so give me the grace to recognise Thy word here below in all its manifestations, and to love it. I thank Thee for Thy Holy Church, and for the infallibility which Thou hast communicated to her utterances. Her word is not hers so much as it is Thine. I thank Thee for Thy Holy Scriptures,

---

[1] *John* xiv. 17.   [2] *Isaias* xxiii. 29.   [3] *Luke* xii. 49.

written by the hand of Thy Spirit for the needs of the souls of men. I thank Thee for all the words of Thy saints, confessors, pastors, and doctors, in which the inexhaustible riches of Thy Sacred Heart are poured forth generation after generation. These things, O Jesus, let me love to read and ponder. Let me find, not the ideas of men nor the artifices of human eloquence, but the revelation of Thy will, and the efficacy of Thy Divine direction.

3. Enter into thyself with sorrow and regret. What hast thou hitherto chiefly desired to read? It is not only that thou hast, perhaps, given thyself too unrestrainedly to the pursuit of study or of information, but that thou hast wasted hours and hours of precious time in frivolous and useless reading; or, it may be, vitiated and stained thy imagination by corrupt and worldly books, wearied those powers which belong to God by idly hanging over newspapers, placed thyself in danger of temptation by trifling with the blasphemies and ineptitudes of unbelievers. O Spirit of my Saviour Jesus Christ! give me discernment, discretion, and, above all, the spiritual sense, that I may know what to avoid in my reading, and where to stop! Create in me the love of Thy heavenly utterances; foster within my heart those feeble aspirations which I have towards the wisdom of the Saints! Make me faithful to my Spiritual Reading! Open my heavy eyes to some appreciation of Thy heavenly kingdom! Grant me to hear some of the least of those revela-

tions which bring the heart captive to Thy feet! Let me feel, when I read Thy word, how near Thou art, O Lord, and how truly there is nothing worth the knowing here below but only Thou Thyself! And may thy prayers, O Mother of my Lord, who didst keep all His words in thy heart—so great a treasure in so precious a tabernacle!—obtain for me the grace to love Spiritual Reading!

XXXI. OUR BLESSED LADY.

THERE is a well-known passage in St. Alphonsus in which the Saint expresses his conviction that in Missions no sermon is more profitable or produces so much compunction as the one on the mercy and the power of Mary.[1] The reason is that, to the Catholic heart, the name of "Mary" has the special power to present God's loving kindness and the tenderness of the Incarnation in its most effective light.

The echo of a grand sound brings back that sound to the ears in softened cadences; and the reflection in the calm lake of the lovely scenes upon its shores touches the sense with sweetness and mystery. In spiritual things an echo, or a reflection, if we may use the phrase, is not only delightful, interesting and attractive, but it is even necessary. For spiritual things of themselves make an impression on the human faculties with difficulty. God and His attributes are proper objects of the intelligence; but as to the rest of man's nature—as to his imagination, his heart and his senses—they are adapted to produce only a feeble effect. Hence the need for some such

---

[1] *Glories of Mary* (Centenary ed.), vol. i. p. 24.

Divine reproduction, or translation, as we find in the Incarnation. Jesus of Nazareth translates God to man's powers. But the Incarnation itself will bear to be re-echoed, to be repeated, to be enforced, to be brought home. Even the Incarnation has to contend with human imperviousness, inattention, stupidity. Even the Incarnation is affected by distance, by the mind's propensity to neglect what is, on the one hand, somewhat complex, and, on the other, somewhat familiar, and by the inherent augustness and sublimity of the mystery itself. The Saints repeat, or embody, Jesus, each in his own way; but this is done with incomparably greater fulness and magnificence by most holy Mary.

Consider, then, how Mary repeats Jesus to us, and at the same time repeats Him with an instructiveness and a touching efficacy which result from the profoundness of the difference between them. The Sacred Heart of Jesus burns with Divine love and worship. So does the most pure heart of Mary. But in Jesus it is the Divinity which enkindles this consuming fire. In Mary there is no Divine Nature to keep up by absolute power and necessity the perpetual flame of perfect charity. In her, heavenly love is the work of the redeeming grace of Jesus. She is the chief and the grandest scene of its power and efficacy. So with her purity and sinlessness; in her, they are that of the handmaid who humbly bows before the sweep of the Divine tempest which the purity of the Divinity set in motion when it touched the humanity it had chosen. Jesus suffers, because He wishes by suffering to add an intensity to the Act of His Heart which it could not otherwise have had. Mary suffers—but her suffering is chiefly compassion for Jesus, and its effect is to draw her nearer to Him. As regards us men and our salvation, Jesus reveals God's mercy, heaps act on act to satisfy for our sins, suffers from the beginning to the end in order to make us love Him, and gives us His Heart as a pattern of purity and self-immolation. And Mary, anointed with the same unction as His most blessed Soul, is filled to overflowing with a similar love for men and women; reveals God's mercy in new aspects and in lengthening perspective; offers her good works and sufferings to merit for us with a merit that is real, yet is entirely the fruit of the Precious Blood; loves us with a human love, as Jesus loves us, but also with a sympathy of her own, arising from her being only a creature like ourselves; and gives us for our model all her lovely qualities and virtues, which differ from His as the light of the moon differs from that of the sun. Remembering that the well-being of our souls depends upon our apprehending God's mercy, God's love, and God's purity, and that the Incarnation is the Divine means for enabling us to do this, it is easy to see how the blessed Mother of Jesus repeats in her being and in her life all that Divine message, all that precious revelation. Our souls, therefore, cannot spare her. How many of us are there who are touched by the thought that a creature of God, a woman, a mother, should have been lifted up so high that her purity is absolute, her love surpassing imagination, her merit transcending all thought, and her nearness to Jesus incomprehensible; and that all this comes about by the mercy and love of God for us? O Heavenly Father, revealing Thyself in Mary, from my heart I worship Thee! From my heart I give Thee thanks that Thou dost send me so sweet and moving a message! What must be the treasure of love hidden behind Thy incomprehensible light, when this gracious vision of Thy handmaid is so beauteous and so attractive! Give me Thy grace to find in Mary, by devout meditation, nothing less than Thyself, my Father and my only Friend!

These thoughts are strengthened by another. The more we believe in, and "realise," the efficacy of the Precious Blood, the more closely we shall cling to the Kingdom of God. When we contemplate Mary, we behold such a triumph of the redeeming grace of Jesus as we could never have dared to look for. There are three great prerogatives of Mary: her sinlessness, her charity (or union with God), and her sovereignty. As to the first, it is of faith that neither original nor actual sin ever touched her; that not even the least shadow of indeliberate venial sin ever sullied her. As to the second, St. Anselm has said, *Ubi major puritas ibi major charitas.* Her love was in proportion to her purity. From the beginning she was full of grace; to the grace she had she always fully corresponded; at various epochs of her life, and more especially at the moment of the Incarnation, she received such an inflow of grace and actual love as it is difficult to conceive capable of being surpassed in a creature; her acts of perfect charity were innumerable; nay, her life was one unbroken act of pure love, uninterrupted even by sleep. Love of God was the very atmosphere of her existence; it was not her will alone which was penetrated by it, but every part of her nature; and she loved with heart, mind, and strength, wholly and perfectly. So that, at least at the end of her life, she must be pronounced to have loved God *perfectly;* excelling even the highest Angels, and all the Saints, on earth or in the heavens. Then, as to her sovereignty,—when she gave her consent to be the Mother of God, she became the Queen of the universal world. She rules over the whole of the realm of her Son—that is, over angels and men, and all things animate and inanimate. But reflect what all this means. It means that a daughter of the race of Adam, a being of frail flesh, human like ourselves, has been lifted to such transcendent glory and greatness by the power of the redeeming grace of Jesus. Behold what grace can do! Behold what human nature is capable of, without being burnt to ashes! Behold how solemnly in earnest is this Lord and Saviour of ours Who would give us a demonstration of the gifts He has come to bless the earth with, and would fill our poor hearts with admiration; and not with admiration only, but with trust, and desire, and devotion. For why has He so endowed and magnified Mary, except to prove that His redemption is "most plentiful"—that His longing wish is to pour out His grace over every creature, and to draw us all within the area where the dew falls which the heavens of His mercy drop down on this earth below? O Mary, I rejoice in thy stainlessness, in thy burning charity, in thy royalty! But it is in order that I may repent of my sins that Jesus has made thee so pure! It is to fill me with ardour in love and in sacrifice that I am allowed to contemplate thee "clothed with the sun"! It is that I may value rightly my immortal soul that He hath raised thee so high! What thou art, we may all become; not in the same degree, but in the same glorious kingdom, the same Divine dispensation! We can never approach thy greatness; but far short of that greatness there are grades innumerable—all splendid, all august, all magnificent—the lowest of which is more desirable than all that the world can give! O Mary! triumph of Jesus! stupendous trophy of the Precious Blood! May He triumph over my cold heart! May He make my soul, as thine was, the happy captive of His all-conquering Cross!

But the Blessed Virgin is not only the "repetition" of Jesus, and the triumph of Jesus; she is also the instrument, or, if we may say it, the special dispensation, of Jesus. For in the Kingdom of Grace power always accompanies position. As Jesus is not only the Anointed of God, but also the Angel (or minister) of the great Plan,[1] and the Strength of God, so Mary not only participates in the riches and splendour of Him "of whose fulness we all receive,"[2] but shares in His power and His administration. This is natural and reasonable; and it is, in the fullest sense, Catholic tradition. As Eve brought death so Mary brings life. In the well-known canon of St. Bernard, "this is the plan of the Divine Compassion—He would redeem the world, and He placed the whole of its price in the hands of Mary ".[3] The words of St. Bernardine of Siena are very remarkable. "From the moment," he says, "that the Virgin Mother conceived in her womb the Word of God, she acquired a kind of jurisdiction, so to speak, over the whole temporal mission of the Holy Ghost; so that no creature obtained any grace from God except according to His Mother's intercession."[4] In the spiritual life, therefore, Mary can never be far from any of us. As she held Jesus in her arms on earth, so now she is still His Mother. Her image stands near His altar. Her name accompanies His. The "Hail Mary" follows the Lord's Prayer. The mysteries of His life and passion are commemorated in her

[1] *Magni consilii Angelus. Consiliarius. Isaias* ix. 6.
[2] *John* i. 16.
[3] *De Aquæductu.*
[4] *Pro festo Virginis Mariæ,* serm. v. cap. 8.

Rosary. Over every Church, every religious Order, her name is invoked. The Catholic seldom kneels for devotion, prepares for the Sacraments, begins or finishes an undertaking, or resists temptation, without invoking her intercession. A childlike and affectionate trust in her mercy and her power is characteristic of the Catholic spirit. "It is not possible," exclaimed Blosius, "that an assiduous and humble client of Mary should perish."[1] "She is the hope of all our life" is the phrase of St. Thomas of Aquin [2]—an expression that is consecrated in the "Salve Regina," which is, next to the "Hail Mary," the most universal prayer of the Church to Mary.

It is possible that we may find, in our retreat, that we have become careless and indifferent in our attitude towards the Blessed Mother of our Redeemer. To those who live in a non-Catholic country there is always considerable danger of this. Our faith is undoubted, but the warmth of our hearts is apt to cool. A certain restraint has to be exercised in bringing her sweet name before those who are ignorant and prejudiced; and then, perhaps, we come to neglect such reading, meditation, and devout practice as are required in order to live up to the Church's ideal and to the teaching of the Saints.

First, then, we should, from time to time, read devotional books on our Lady, and such reading should be followed or accompanied by affective

[1] *Canon Vitæ Spir.*, c. 18.
[2] *Omnis spes vitæ.* From his *Exposition on the "Hail Mary"*.

meditation. Perhaps no better reading of this kind can be found than in the works of St. Alphonsus. Their great value is that, in addition to the devout expression of this great Saint's own feelings, they give so much of the exact words of other Saints and of the great theologians. These passages, especially when quoted in the original language,[1] are pregnant with meaning, and with suggestions that appeal to mind and heart. In reading them, one should be careful not to hurry over them, as if they were merely pious utterances. It will be found that most of them, pious as they may be in form, are impregnated with the most significant theological truth. These utterances rest on the Incarnation; they indicate the connection between the Mother of our Lord and our Lord Himself; they note how she repeats Him and amplifies (to our faculties) whatever there is in Him (His Divinity excepted); they point out how she, more than creation itself, and more than all other redeemed creatures, magnifies the power and love of God and the redeeming grace of Christ; and they extol that mercy, that compassion and that beneficence which, in Mary, are as singular in their reach and intensity as is her position of Mother of God. And, with all this, these words of the Saints place before us the Saints themselves as her humble and devoted clients, proclaiming in magnificent accord the prerogatives of Mary, and her office in the dis-

[1] As is done in the notes to the "Centenary edition" of St. Alphonsus.

pensation of salvation. O burning words of the Saints! may I have light and simplicity enough to take in their full significance! O spirit of Catholicism! may I drink it in with eagerness here, in its purest source—where I find the thoughts of those whose mind, heart and feeling were filled with that Wisdom only which is the gift of the Spirit of God!

Besides reading and meditation, we should have certain daily or regular practices which we perform in honour of Mary. These things, though small, both keep up devotion and bring down grace. The Rosary should be said daily; and we should not be content with a single decade, but should say the round of the beads—five mysteries. The effect of the Rosary is wonderful in bringing Jesus and Mary together in our thought and devotion; in causing Mary to shadow forth and echo Jesus, and Jesus to shine through the queenly magnificence of Mary; in making the soul feel that no act or suffering of Jesus is understood unless we also understand its effect upon Mary; and in filling the heart with the Catholic feeling that to salute Mary is by that very fact to draw upon us the loving glance of her Son.

Further—seeing how no one can properly take in or estimate the Incarnation without some adequate idea of the Mother of God—we should try to spread all around us a solid devotion to her, according to the mind of the Church. Priests should preach her. They should not be content with throwing out a few devotional phrases, or relating an anecdote or two;

—these things are more effective in a Catholic country, where childlike devotion to Mary is an instinct. But they should rest their exhortations on the Incarnation, and on the grand fundamental doctrines of Redemption, Grace, Intercession and Divine Love. Whenever there is an opportunity for " elucidating " her (in the phrase of the Book of Wisdom [1]) they should seize it. We should all remember that it is part of her prerogative to subdue hearts to Christ's word, to promote the Faith, and to kill heresy. St. Epiphanius, with many other early Fathers, attributes our very Redemption (under Jesus) to Mary's Faith. And it must still, therefore, be the same. O Mary, obtain persuasion for the preachers of the Gospel! By thy power dissipate the mists of prejudice, break in pieces the rocks of pride, destroy the poison of passion—that all may come to know Jesus and thee!

Finally, it is especially in moments of temptation that we should turn to the maternal heart of the august Mother of Jesus. Those who are strongly tempted by sensuality, temper or pride—whether such temptations are natural to their dispositions, or are the consequence of sinful indulgence—are bound to pray, and to ask for help when tempted. There is no form of having recourse to the assistance of God so efficacious, speaking generally, as the invocation of Mary. It is her province to help the weakness of human nature; it is her office to

---

[1] *Ecclus.* xxiv. 81.

fasten upon the smallest efforts for good which the sinner's good-will manages to make, and to foster them into strength and efficacy; it is especially her business to prevent falls into the sin of impurity. For all these things, grace is at hand when she prays. There can be few more useful habits implanted in the heart of a boy or girl than that of saying daily a prayer to our Lady for purity, and of turning to her on the instant with a familiar ejaculation whenever there arises a temptation to the contrary vice. Let us resolve, in our retreat—looking at our numerous falls in the past into sins of human frailty and self-indulgence—to be careful to invoke, at the very moment we notice we are being tempted, that Queen whose power is only equalled by her tender affection for every soul for whom Jesus died.

Points for Mental Prayer.

1. Most holy Virgin! Mother of God! Queen of Heaven! I revere and bow down before thy dignity! By and through thee did Jesus come, Whose coming is the world's happy rescue! By thee the great Counsel took shape and actuality. Thy *fiat* caused it to come about. Thy consent the Angelic ambassador asked and procured. Before thee the heavens and the earth prostrated themselves, for the God of Heaven had associated thee even with Himself in the work of His ineffable love. Thou art more than His servant, more than His

handmaid, more than His minister! All creatures are these—and it is their greatest glory to boast that they are so. But thou, O Mary, art His Mother! For ever thou standest at His right hand! For ever does His glory clothe thee! For ever does thy throne lift itself in the heaven of heavens! What can the tongues of angels and of men utter that shall be worthy of thy glorious estate? Let my poor voice never cease from praising God for thee, and from extolling thy greatness!

2. Most Holy Virgin! Mother of God! Queen of Heaven! I give thanks with all the powers of my soul to that Precious Blood which hath so magnificently triumphed in thee! What is the creation of the universe in comparison with the formation and the adorning of thy soul? O noblest work of God, except the Humanity of thy Son! O full of Grace! O full of all the gifts of the Holy Spirit! O full of Faith, of Hope, of Charity! O paradise of every virtue! How doth it stir up courage and confidence in my breast to think that my Saviour's Blood can do, and hath done, so much! Holy Mother, I offer this soul of mine to the inflow and the possession of the same grace! I know—I feel, when I think on thee, that there is nothing my Saviour longs for so ardently as to bring every soul under its power, and to intensify its work in every creature! Intercede for me that He may triumph in me, and in all men.

3. Our duties to our Blessed Lady should be carefully reviewed in time of retreat. Regular devotions

—reading and meditation—practices—the habit of invoking her, especially in temptations—and our opportunities of making her better known to the world—all should be reflected upon. And then we should say: O Mary, my Mother! I desire now henceforward to consecrate myself to thee! I may have lived long without knowing, or without adverting to thee; I may have neglected thee, as I have neglected so many other things; I may have given myself to thee in my youth and then forgotten thee. For all these things I beg pardon with sincere grief and confusion. I dedicate myself to thee now as to my Saviour's Mother—the object of His affection, the minister of His grace. I dedicate myself to thee that I may remember thee in every prayer, honour thee in every act, and recur to thee in every need. I dedicate myself to thee that I may feel every day more and more deeply how absolutely my salvation (by the will of Jesus) is connected with thy beneficent operation. I dedicate myself to thee that as my Saviour's love comes to me blended with thine, so my Saviour's image may be formed within me the more effectually because I see Him not only in Himself but also in thee! O Mother of Mercy, accept me for thy servant, for thy child!

XXXII. HEAVEN.

We have a right to meditate upon Heaven, because we have a right to look forward to happiness. True virtue must, in the very nature of things, have its reward. For virtue is the love of God above all things. But to those who love and serve Him, God gives nothing less than Himself—and He is the complete and abounding bliss of human nature. Moreover, He has promised much more than human nature, of itself, could claim or expect; for to those who are sanctified by the Blood of His Son He promises the ineffable bliss of the Beatific Vision.

We are not to serve God for the sake of reward. There may be imperfect souls who, in such efforts as they make, are much stimulated by the thought of everlasting happiness. The imperfection of this motive arises when we separate the thought of bliss from the thought of God. The true view is, that God's possession, and perfect bliss, are one and the same thing. Human nature will never be much more perfect than we know it. Therefore, the thought of Heaven, not as apart from God, but without considering God, will always have its share in inducing men and women to live a virtuous life. It is a useful thought, and true as far as it goes;

but to remove its imperfection we should accustom ourselves to reflect that God Himself is our reward.

 The Christian is sometimes reproached with selfishness, in living for the sake of heavenly happiness. But there is no " selfishness," but only lawful self-solicitude, in expecting and resolving to be finally happy. What do these objectors suppose one is to live for? The Christian believes in the world to come—a state, not of trial, but of fixed and irrevocable conditions, in which the soul ought to find its final purpose; and its final purpose must mean final tranquillity and complete satisfaction. If this is "selfishness," then Christianity is selfish. But the word "selfishness," if it be analysed, includes two ideas: it implies, first, the aiming at our own welfare; and, secondly, carelessness about the welfare of others. In the present life, narrow aims and natural satisfactions are base, because they not only, as a rule, make us careless about the welfare of others, but they prevent us from attaining to God, and in numberless ways dwarf and degrade the spirit. But this cannot be said about the final happiness of the world to come. From that happiness we would exclude no one. To aim at that happiness is to carry as many others there as possible. To aim at that happiness is to repress all short-sighted impulses, to refrain from all short-lived satisfaction, and to lift the soul from base things to things lofty and noble. Above all, to aim at that happiness is to live for God and God alone;

and whilst the Christian in this life tramples "self" under foot in order to give himself wholly to his God, even in the bliss of the other world he will be absorbed in God, and will find his happiness in that very absorption. If this is "selfishness" it is of the very essence of nature, and the most imperative command of grace. O God, my God, Who didst make my soul for Thyself, give me grace to "lose my life" in this world that I may find it in the world to come!

The Beatific Vision, although so purely gratuitous on the part of God, is, if we may use the term, the natural outcome of faith and of grace. Our period of probation ended, faith changes into Sight—grace changes into Glory. For we must consider that it would not be enough that we were granted the vision of God's Face; it is necessary that our nature be so strengthened and lifted up as to be able to look upon it. But who by mere natural power can look upon God and live?[1] No creature that ever was created; no creature that could be created. Therefore the spirit of a man must have a supernatural endowment before it can see God. Let us meditate on these words of the Apostle St. John: "We are now the sons of God; and it hath not appeared what we shall be. We know that when He shall appear we shall be *like to Him;* because we shall see Him as He is."[2] The words "when He shall

---

[1] *Exodus* xxxiii. 20.　　[2] 1 *John* iii. 2.

appear" signify the judgment and the entrance into heaven; to "see Him as He is" expresses the Beatific Vision; and the phrase " we shall be like to Him" is the Apostle's announcement, that before we can see God He must have taken possession of our own being; His glory must have transfigured our being; and we must have been so gifted that it may be as it were God Himself Who looks upon Himself. This gift is called the Light of Glory. It is beautifully referred to in a well-known passage of the Psalms: "They shall be inebriated with the plenty of Thy house; and Thou shalt make them drink of the torrent of Thy pleasure. For with Thee is the fountain of life, and in Thy light we shall see light."[1] By these last words the Holy Spirit points out how our power to look on God in the Beatific Vision depends on the light of that vision first of all being poured into our own faculty. Purify my powers, O my Lord and King, that they may be less unworthy of that glorious gift of Light! Thou hast said, "Blessed are the clean of heart, for they shall see God". Make my heart clean, that it may be a dwelling-place for Thy Spirit! May I detest all acts, words, and thoughts which would tend to stain my mind and my heart; that so by degrees Thy grace may prepare me to be lifted up and wrapped round with that Gift which even the highest of the Seraphs must owe to Thy supernatural bounty.

[1] *Ps.* xxxv. 9, 10.

I earnestly pray, moreover, for the increase in my soul of holy Faith! O blessed light, vouchsafed to us in this world, to be exchanged for that supreme light hereafter! Grant me simplicity—grant me the spirit of obedience—make me reverent to all in authority, and solicitous to think in all things as Thy Church thinks! *Sicut audivimus, ita et vidimus!*[1] As we believe, so shall we see, in the city of God! As we cling to Thy earthly revelation, so we shall merit Thy supreme revelation in Heaven! As we keep Thy word, so we shall see Thy face!

What, then, is that Heaven for which we must live, if we are wise? To say that it is "God" should be enough. Heaven means the happy and secure Home into which our only true Father receives the children that He has loved with an everlasting love. It means the pleasant and delightful Home which our truest of friends has prepared for us from the beginning. It means the Fatherland where our King can treat us as He would wish to treat us—His hand no longer held by the conditions of our probation, and His love no longer forced to hide itself under the veils of mortal existence. If we would understand in greater detail the privileges of that eternity for which we are designed, let us take the description of Heaven which is given by St. Thomas of Aquin, in that ardent prayer which is placed in the Roman Missal to assist the priest in his thanksgiving after Mass.

[1] *Ps.* xlvii. 9.

St. Thomas says that Heaven means *Lux vera, Satietas plena, Gaudium sempiternum, Jucunditas consummata, Felicitas perfecta;* that is to say, true Light, complete Satiety, everlasting Joy, supreme Pleasure, and perfect Happiness.

Heaven means Light, or Knowledge. To know God "as He is" (which is the Beatific Vision) is to possess Light such as we cannot even dream of here below. There are certain natural instincts of humanity which can only be satisfied by Knowledge; we call them curiosity, thirst for information, or sometimes (when persons and not things are concerned) friendliness or affection. God is more than the whole created universe. There is more intellectual delight to the purified spirit in the contemplation of the barest outline of one of God's infinite perfections, than there is in all that science and discovery could afford us, had we the powers of an Angel to learn and to investigate the mysteries of creation. What, then, must it be when the myriad play of the inconceivable Deity pours upon our intelligences—ever new, fresh and inexhaustible? But, moreover, God includes within His own being, not formally but virtually, all things and all persons. Any pleasure which we could possibly attain, according to our character, in science, in travels, in exploration, in reading, in discovery; or, again, in acquaintance with the most fascinating minds, or the most genial of friends—that we shall have in God; but intensified a thousand times. Moreover, we shall actually know, in themselves, persons and things in a way we could never have known them upon earth;—Nature, her laws, her wonders of every kind; the past, the present and the future; innumerable possibilities, even, which are in God's power (what a world is there!); the Angels and the Saints; our own relatives and friends who have finished their course; the concerns of our dear ones who are yet on earth. O happy country, of which the Lamb is the Light, let me long for thee! How small a thing it is to mortify on earth my curiosity, to be content with my ignorance, to submit to Thy revelation—when these things prepare me for so great a flood of glorious knowledge! Thou hast made me, O my God, for knowledge; but not merely to pursue the feeble and fleeting rays of human reason and earthly science; these things are good, and sometimes enter into my sphere of duty; but I may be joyfully content if I walk, even with closed eyes, guided by Thy hand, along that path which leads to the great door of the Heavens!

Satiety, or the satisfaction of all desire, is another character of the beatified spirit. Some human desires will, in Heaven, exist no longer: for even the body will be spiritualised, and thus its grosser cravings will cease, as the dark smoke ceases when the great factory has been pulled down. But human nature, especially when elevated and refined by grace, is full of Divine aspirations, of longings for the true, the just, and the beautiful. There are desires and wants within us which will cause everlasting misery, unless they are satisfied; for thus is man's heart made. There are aspirations which hardly awake in this mortal life, at least with the multitude of men and women. It is enough to reflect that the soul, in passing the threshold of the grave, becomes alive to its need of God—to its need of its only possible last end; and that in the Beatific Vision this supreme need is utterly, utterly satisfied! O my soul, tormented and distracted by thy desires, labour for the calm of thy heavenly home! On earth, the only anticipation of Heaven is to repress, moderate and eradicate our appetites; he who yields to them makes to himself a hell before the time. But who can conceive the pure serenity of that existence for which holy mortification prepares us, when God's abundance will overwhelm our poor little heart, and our being will be evermore as a full fountain in His presence?

What is Joy? For in Heaven we are promised Joy for ever and ever. Joy seems to be the reaction of a living nature which is perfectly happy. It is sometimes a cry, sometimes swift motion, sometimes a song. In rational natures it is that lifting up of the power of the soul which strives in some way to utter what is felt; whilst in the soul elevated by Divine grace and by the light of glory, joy is charity breaking into love, praise and worship—breaking out thus, not as a duty, but as an irrepressible emotion. This is the reason why the perpetual worship of the Angelic Hosts is symbolised by song and by the harp; this joy is figured in that passage of the Prophet: "The stars have given light in their watches and have rejoiced; they were called and they said, Here we are; and with cheerfulness they have shined forth to Him that made them".[1] We ourselves have known joy, even as we sit by the rivers of Babylon. Yet the true wisdom of the servant of God is to distrust earthly joy. There is such a thing as foolish joy, springing from a gratification which we should be better without. There is a joy which God sends to help us and comfort us on our way; but even this joy we must not rest in. It is not yet the time for us to use those harps which belong to us; they must hang still upon the willows, and we must wait for our own country in order to sing the songs of the Lord. Be patient, O my soul! One day thou shalt enter into the "joy" of thy Lord. Then shall all the glorious endowments of thy being unite to enrich thy song; then shall the emotion and the vibration of thy powers result in that supreme utterance of the beatified intelligence and will which for ever resoundeth in the presence of the Throne, and which is called a "new canticle," because it is the one operation of created nature which never grows old. Thou shalt join in the "Holy, holy, holy," of the Seraphim; thou shalt join in the canticle of the Redeemed.

Supreme Pleasure! It is difficult to conceive,

---

[1] *Baruch* iii. 34.

Pleasure is that satisfaction of the being and its powers—that feeling or consciousness of well-being resulting from bodily health, mental health, the congenial exercise of faculties, abundance, and general prosperity, which is so seldom realised. We have to transfer this idea to Heaven. On earth, we may, perhaps, for a fleeting instant, have felt pleasure unalloyed. But even if the other conditions are present, the mere onward movement of time breaks up such ecstatic moments before they have lasted more than a moment. In Heaven, there is the ocean of the Presence of God, covering us over, immersing the soul in its limitless, fathomless waters. Our nature is face to face with its Last End. "Well-being" presses upon every point of our being. Our faculties energise with ease and the keenest delight. Our state is that of rich men, nay, kings, who are safe for ever in the possession of the riches, the nobility, the activity, and the pleasant surroundings in which they rejoice. What weak words are these! The truth is that our words are too gross and material to express the serene and purified "Pleasure" of the state of Bliss. The Holy Scripture calls it a "torrent," and it uses the word "inebriation". Let these hints lift our hearts on high.

When we describe Heaven as Perfect Happiness we again make use of a phrase which necessarily cannot be adequately understood. Happiness refers to the effect upon us of our surroundings; and its opposite is Misery. We are unhappy when we are in want, in distress, in pain, in apprehension —unhappy in mind or miserable in body. On earth we cannot keep misery out. Either there is poverty, or there is suffering, or there is solitude, or there is failure—there are a score of troublesome things that will sting us whatever precautions we may take. But how different it will be in the Heaven of our Heavenly Father! For "they shall be His people, and God Himself shall be their God. And God shall wipe away all tears from their eyes; and death shall be no more, nor mourning, nor crying, nor sorrow shall be any more, for the former things are passed away."[1] Yes, my soul, look forward and believe! For Isaias said, long ago: "Lo, this is our God; we have waited for Him, and He will save us; this is the Lord, we have patiently waited for Him; we shall rejoice and be joyful in His salvation".[2] To those who live for this world only, perfect happiness is a dream and nothing more. They will admit as much; for it is impossible to deny it. But to those who believe in the life to come, it is a reality. As their Creator is the Unbeginning, as their Father is the God of infinite Love, as their Friend is the Eternal, and as their Lord is the Almighty, they believe and know that the time will come when infinite Love will take them home and when the Almighty Master will crown them with glory and honour in a kingdom which can never pass away.

But Light, Satiety, Joy, Pleasure and Happiness

[1] *Apoc.* xxi. 4.   [2] *Isaias* xxv. 9.

are not Heaven. They are only the circumstances of Heaven. They are ideas which assist us, in our pilgrimage, to dwell upon the thought of Heaven. But we should always, in meditating upon Heaven, and whenever our heart feels drawn to speculate or to pray about the future—we should always take refuge with God, our Father. We should always say: "Thou, O Lord, art the portion of my inheritance and of my cup; Thou art He Who wilt restore my inheritance to me".[1] It is sweet to think of that land as our inheritance—the inheritance from which man fell, and which Jesus Christ has won back for us. But it is sweeter far to dwell on the thought that the whole "inheritance" is God Himself. Perhaps there is but little danger of our selfishly dwelling on the idea of a Heaven apart from God. Yet such an idea of Heaven is far from uncommon among non-Catholics. And that is the reason why the more reflecting minds among them have given up trying to form an idea of the life to come which shall be at once dignified and not repulsive to common-sense. For our part it is but too true that, as in this, so in other matters, we are continually losing sight of God. To dwell on Heaven, unless that thought leads us to love, to faith, to hope, to longing, is of very little use in the spiritual life. In prayer, therefore, we must direct our attention to this. Above all, in the Divine Office, in the use of those inspired Psalms which were written for our

[1] *Ps.* xv. 5.

needs, we should observe the constantly recurring passages in which life everlasting is referred to. From the Psalms we may gather the following

POINTS FOR MENTAL PRAYER.

1. In the Psalms we are continually reminded of God's *House*. The word "Sion" whenever it occurs, or "Jerusalem," should always lift up our heart to the City that is above. In Sion God dwelleth; in Sion the Lord is great. May my soul come to see Thee, O Lord, in Thy heavenly Sion! The Psalmist sighs after the House of the Lord: the House which holiness becometh, for ever and ever; the Temple whose gates are lifted up for the King of glory; the Place where God's glory dwelleth; the Tabernacles of the Lord of Hosts, so lovely and so longed for; the Courts of the Lord in which one day is better than a thousand. Make acts of longing, in the spirit of these passages.

2. Again, you find in the Psalms a thousand utterances of hope and trust. Whenever you meet these, elevate your heart to your Father in Heaven, and try to feel that if there is one thing in which you trust Him, it is in His leading you to Himself. "My soul hath hoped in the Lord!" "Thou, O my God, art my refuge! Thou art my salvation!" "In Thee have I hoped. Let me not be confounded for ever!" When you read of "the King" in that twentieth Psalm which describes the grace and the glory of the redeemed soul, endeavour to "rejoice vehemently" in the goodness of your God. The Psalm of the Good

Shepherd (the twenty-second) should bring to your memory the "pastures" of the heavenly country: and as you recount the care and providence of the heavenly Shepherd, say to Him with great fervour: O my Jesus, it is that I may for ever belong to Thy flock and for ever live in Thy presence that I beg Thy grace here below!

3. But most fervently of all should you repeat those passages which express a direct longing for God Himself. *Deus, Deus meus!* Whenever these words, or their equivalents, occur, utter them with great devotion; for such devotion is especially adapted to making you secure of the Vision of God. When the Psalm describes the glories of nature—the mountains, the sea, the forest, the storm—apply it to Heaven. When it speaks of God's attributes, as it is never weary of doing—of His magnificence, His power, His knowledge, and His mercy—imagine that you see Him in the Heavens, prepared to reveal Himself to you when the moment comes; and aspire the more earnestly. When the Psalm pours itself out in words of expectation, of waiting, refer these expressions to that which is the end of all expectation—everlasting bliss. When you adore Him, as in the Psalm *Venite* (the ninety-fourth), imagine, as you speak of coming before His Presence, and of falling down before Him, how you will one day do this in Heaven; and rejoice, saying: "The Lord is a great God; He is the Lord our God, and we are His people and the sheep of His pasture!"

XXXIII. PERSEVERANCE.

It may truly be said that to speculate on whether or not we shall persevere to the end is both barren and foolish. What we have to do is, not to prophesy as to the future, but to make use of the present. We have to deal with the present hour, and no more; nay, the point of time which may be said to be in our power is far shorter than an hour, or than a minute. Even the past, which must always enter into our thoughts and purposes, and which, fixed and monumental as it is, may nevertheless be used and qualified, can only be affected by the aspirations and spiritual acts of the present. Oh, the precious moments of my life, that come so quickly and are gone so soon! May Jesus, Who deigned to live through mortal years, and to count mortal moments, enable me to sanctify and make them fruitful!

Although we cannot by any means infallibly merit the gift of final Perseverance, nevertheless, by means of grace already received, we may merit that gift, not as a right, but with reasonable certainty. In the same way, we can merit, or at least we can be morally sure of obtaining, the actual graces which will lead us safe through our tempted career. In proportion as we render ourselves more worthy by means of the grace God gives, we may count with certainty on receiving yet more ample graces from His loving Fatherly bounty. So that, as St. Augustine says, we can merit our Perseverance as a suppliant can. Therefore, we may trust our Heavenly Father. At every moment He is watching over us. So anxious is He to help us on, that He would gladly go through afresh all His human earthly life and all the bitterness of His Passion, to save any one of us from one mortal sin. Read over the one hundred and twentieth Psalm. He states in the plainest language, and with a reiteration that seems to show a deep and serious anxiety (to speak in human phrase of the Almighty Creator), that we may depend for help on Him Who made both Heaven and earth. "He neither slumbers nor sleeps. The sun shall not burn us by day, nor the moon blight us by night. He keepeth our coming in and our going out, from henceforth, now, and for ever!"[1] The first condition for Perseverance is to believe this great fundamental truth from the bottom of our hearts. But how few really do believe it! Living habitually out of the presence of God, and without habitual thought of Him, such a conviction as is here referred to is strange and foreign to us. We distrust our Heavenly Father as we would keep back our trust from a stranger. Even the overpowering fact of the Incarnation and Passion is not felt by us as within our

[1] *Ps.* cxx.

own lives, but has the air of a history that concerns other people. How often has God complained of this! "All the day I stretched out my hands to an unbelieving people!" Let us repent. Let us turn and hasten towards those outstretched arms. What a noble word is that of St. Paul—"I know in Whom I have believed!"[1] Yes, he knew Who it was that he trusted! He knew and felt within his inmost soul how impossible it was for God to forget him, to disappoint him, to fall short of what he required, to begrudge him any grace, after He had shown the boundless love of His being by giving him so much.

This being at its root, we may go on to consider the elements of Perseverance. The first of these is a careful performance of all the spiritual duties of the day. These spiritual duties may be enumerated as Mental Prayer, Divine Office (or vocal prayer), the hearing of Mass, a visit to the Blessed Sacrament, Spiritual Reading, and examination of conscience. Perseverance may be said to be secure if these things are secure. They, in a measure, fill up and qualify the whole day, from morning till night. If an occasion of sin presents itself, it must come in between two of these exercises—not very long after one, and not very long before another. They are our light, our strength and our good-will—for they keep all these alive, as regular meals keep up the vigour of the body. So that a rule of life, in which

[1] 2 Tim. i. 12.

these things figure prominently, and in which other things that are not perhaps of daily occurrence, such as Sacraments and periodical recollections, have also their place, is of the essence of Perseverance. The soul which does these things irregularly is absolutely in peril. Irregularity means omission, or curtailment, or hurry; it leads to the abandonment, first of one thing, then of more; and it is a blight which, when we look back, is found to have left many wide spaces in our lives blank and unprofitable, or even perhaps "nigh to a curse," as the Prophet says. Let our grand sacrifice to God, then, our primary exercise of mortification, our standing proof that we love Him with our whole heart, be to keep faithfully to our spiritual duties. No work, however holy, can excuse us from them (except in the unfrequent case of necessity). If we found that our work was so heavy or so manifold as to leave us no time to perform them well, our work would have to be modified. To keep at it would be to tempt God. No superior, whatever our state might be, could dispense us from the spiritual duties of the rule—that is to say, dispense us regularly or for long; and this applies not only to the larger part of our spirituality but to any one exercise. Let us not deceive ourselves. To persevere means to take the means to persevere. Our life consists of days, and each day has to be lived through in God's holy grace and in increasing nearness to Him. It is not difficult; but the work requires an enlightened spiritual sense and a manly resolution. Let us, with all our fervour, pray daily for this fidelity. Let us think of our falls—falls which we can trace, and can put down without risk of mistake to our giving up prayer, meditative reading, or piety. Let us look abroad, and reflect that we know of numerous unhappy examples of sin, tepidity, worldliness, or even apostasy, that have most certainly come from no other cause than neglect of spiritual duties. "He that trusteth in the Lord shall be as Mount Sion. . . . Mountains are round about it, and the Lord is round about His people."[1] O my soul, leave not the shelter of these holy mountains round about thee, which represent the protection of thy Lord! To neglect a spiritual duty is to neglect thy God and thy Sovereign Master. To neglect a spiritual duty is to turn away from the feet of Jesus and to put thyself outside the hearing of His voice. To neglect thy recollection, thy duty of Divine praise, thy visit to the Blessed Sacrament, or thy self-examination, is to pass over to the crowd, to the world, nay, to the enemies of Jesus, and to be no longer of the band of those to whom He so lovingly said, "Abide in Me!"[2]

The second element of Perseverance is to dread sin and to avoid the occasions of sin. The dread of sin grows in the soul by reflection on what sin is, by the contemplation of what it has cost our blessed Lord, and by the reading of the lives of the Saints.

---

[1] *Ps.* cxxiv. 1, 2.   [2] *John* xv. 4.

Some souls are naturally not at all particular; they are free, easy, and perhaps somewhat coarse in their tastes. Others, again, dread sin, but rather through a sort of apprehension of God's anger and vengeance. Neither of these two classes is very safe. The former easily overstep the boundary between freedom and guilt; the latter not unfrequently break down utterly, and rush into evil ways with a violence as great as their former restraint was painful. In order to serve God we must cultivate a certain refinement in acts, words and thoughts; or else we shall be like those who live too close to the enemy's ground. Reflection, piety, reserve, consideration—such habits as these should be assiduously fostered by those who wish to persevere. And as for the scrupulous, they should cling to obedience; they should try to understand what it is to act on principle and reason, and not on impulse; and they should be well looked after by superiors or friends. The increase in the number of neurotic subjects, and the tendency of such persons to some form of insanity or melancholy, should make parents and religious superiors very careful that young persons of the weaker sex who are given to piety should lead a thoroughly healthy life, with plenty of fresh air, good plain food, and an absence of every kind of stimulant. In most of the rules for religious women which have their origin in France, there is a prevailing tendency to shut out air, to discourage water, and to keep the body without movement. Real religion and devotion do not consist in these things; and at the present day, in this country, they tend to bring on a kind of nerve trouble which is fatal to holy perseverance.

No one can persevere who is not careful about sinful occasions. There are occasions to sensual passions, occasions to pride, occasions to unkindness, occasions to sloth. We are not now speaking of drunkards or the dissolute. But all have to be on their guard against certain persons, or books, which are an occasion of temptations against purity. "He that seemeth to stand, let him take heed lest he fall."[1] All have to be cautious in regard to ostentation, appearances in public, showing off, and the acceptance of charges and dignities. All have to watch over themselves when with other persons, or else there will be uncharitable conversation, unkind judgment, murmuring, and many kinds of undesirable and idle gossip. And it is necessary, not only to be watchful at the moment, but also to cut these occasions short, to try to escape them, and sometimes resolutely to shun them altogether; or else the sins against charity, the disturbing of the peace of communities, and (not least) the waste of time and consequent interference with spiritual and other duties, will effectually prevent progress and render perseverance very questionable indeed. There are few worse occasions of sin, with those who profess to avoid mortal sin, than waste of time. It may

---

[1] 1 Cor. x. 12

come from sloth in rising from bed, from friends' conversation, from newspapers, from novels, from too much recreation. It leads to an unmortified, flabby, loafing, unpunctual, unprepared, out-at-elbows condition of spirit and intellect, which is as disreputable in the sight of men as it is fatal to the service of God. Young priests should dread waste of time as the "noon-day devil".[1] A strict rule of life is here their only salvation. Those priests whose day is not filled up by their duties—or who, at least occasionally, have a good deal of leisure—should have work, or a task, to which they can devote their spare time; some branch of study, some book, some theological treatise, or, best of all, some little bit of writing, which will at once require study, give precision to thought, promote readiness and fluency in the use of language, and be a serviceable possession for the future. "Idleness hath taught much evil,"[2] says the Spirit of God. "Where there are no oxen, the crib is empty."[3] There are many empty cribs —in places, too, where, by profession, there should be fulness and abundance, for the little ones of God's flock; in places where the heart of God's servants should be unto Him as "the odour of a plentiful field," instead of exhaling themselves in weak talk, unprofitable comment, and unkind remarks. "As a city that lieth open and is not compassed with walls, so is a man that cannot refrain his own spirit in

---

[1] *Ps.* xc. 6. [2] *Ecclus.* xxxiii. 29. [3] *Prov.* xiv. 4.

speaking."[1] O my Heavenly Father, how recklessly have I laid myself open to Thy enemies and the enemies of my soul! Fill my heart with wisdom and with a salutary fear! If I am so careless about the occasions of sin, why should I not one day turn my back on Thee? Why should I not die unrepentant? Why should I not lose my soul? Enlighten me, arouse me, make me understand my danger; but first, O my God, pardon me for putting myself in such deadly peril.

The third element of Perseverance is the regular and careful use of the Sacraments; especially those of Penance and the Holy Eucharist. A Sacrament is a most precious thing. It is a loving visitation of Jesus, touching the soul with the Precious Blood itself, and bringing with it supernatural effects of which we have a very imperfect idea. The Saints saw and appreciated the effects of the Sacraments; this insight is a part of that supernatural wisdom which comes from the free play of the gifts of the Holy Ghost. All who wish to persevere should direct their attention and their prayer to this most necessary discernment—a discernment that is not beyond the power of interior recollection and union to bestow upon us. The due use of the Sacraments includes three things: to prepare for them, to bring devotion to them, and to repeat them at proper intervals. Preparation for Confession and Holy Com-

[1] *Prov.* xxv. 28.

munion has already been spoken of, so indeed have the other two points. But in thinking over the conditions of Perseverance, it may well strike us that we are only half alive to the benefits of the Sacraments. Perhaps our negligence may be best described as a want of *attention*. We may be regular in our approach; we may not hurry over our preparation or our thanksgiving; but it is possible that for weeks and months we never, in using a Sacrament, rouse our faculties to their full exercise. This is a part of our general indifference or apathy to spiritual things. But such apathy should certainly be strenuously attacked on the side of the Sacraments. We should study them; we should search out their different effects; we should keep the matter before our minds, in meditation and in reading; we should learn from the example of the Saints; and we should bring our efforts after the supernatural in general to bear on the marvellous communication of the supernatural which we find here. Our progress, our purification, and even our salvation are intimately connected with Confession and Holy Communion. These great agencies do not act mechanically. There must be conscious intelligent co-operation on our own part. Can anything be more dangerous than to approach these Divine opportunities with that undiscerning listlessness which makes such a poor affair of our spiritual life in general? Let us resolve, first, to regulate our times of approaching. Weekly Confession, at least;

Holy Communion as often as we are advised or allowed—this should be our simple rule. Next, let us make it a regular part of our spiritual occupation to read and meditate on the Sacraments, setting apart for this purpose, for example, the first week of every quarter. Thirdly, let us form the habit of recollecting ourselves strenuously before using a Sacrament. Fourthly, when we have been to Confession or Communion negligently or half-consciously, let us return hotly to God at the earliest moment, begging His patient forgiveness and praying for grace for the future. Fifthly, let us, in our striving against a particular fault, or for some special virtue, or against this or that temptation, take care that the Sacraments have the share which they justly claim; that is to say, by consciously intending them to help us and forward our spiritual purpose—and this not in general terms, but with particular and concentrated intention. By means like these we shall make the Sacraments more real to us, and attain that "life" and that quickening of life which is specially promised as their fruit.

A fourth element in Perseverance is to take in a right and proper spirit our "falls". That we shall fall, and perhaps fall seriously, is certain. Now, in a fall there are two things: first, the offence against God; and secondly (if the fall happens to a person who has made good resolutions), the rebuff to personal pride. It is not too much to say that the earliest pang of regret which most of us experience when we break down, comes from the second of these, and not the first. We are disgusted—or perhaps annoyed, or vexed, or astonished, or discouraged. It is of little consequence what we call it—but it is a fact, that we can rarely help feeling our fall as a personal matter. We expected better things of ourselves! or, we perceive that we have not taken sufficient pains! or, we are inclined to give up;—why strive against difficulties! Reflections such as these have their portion of truth and utility. But they are sadly inadequate. They make our perseverance an affair of our own instead of (what it is) an affair which is entirely of God's grace. If we could manage it, the proper way to take our "fall" would be to feel no astonishment whatever, and no discouragement; but simply to turn to God and say: Behold, O my Heavenly Father, what I am! This is what must be expected from me! This is what my nature grows and produces! If it is to be anything else, it must be by means of Thy grace alone! This point has been already treated in the Discourse on Little Sins. (Discourse xxix.) Let it be simply repeated that to accept in a spirit of humility, and therefore of calmness and even cheerfulness, our falls into sin, to offer them to God, to beg pardon, to look to His grace for the future, and so to begin again with renewed courage, is of the very essence of Perseverance. Especially must it be noted that discouragement (if acquiesced in) is an offence against God and a movement of pride. If we looked upon God as we ought, we should feel it was only God Who could prevent us from falling, and, moreover, that God was always longing to do so. The fall came from our frailty or malice; but God is always ready, nay, longing, to neutralise our frailty and malice by His grace. Then why be discouraged? Are the Saviour's fountains dried up? Is the power of the Precious Blood less? Is the Sacred Heart estranged? Has God never forgiven sin or converted a sinner before? Is our case so hard to Him? There can be only one answer: "As a father hath compassion on his children, so hath the Lord compassion on them that fear Him; for He knoweth our frame, He remembereth that we are dust".[1]

Points for Mental Prayer.

1. First, contemplate your Lord and Saviour on the night before His Passion, as they went out of the supper room, and were on their way to Gethsemane, saying to His Apostles: "Abide in me. . . . If you abide in Me and My words abide in you, you shall ask whatever you will, and it shall be done unto you."[2] To abide in our Lord is to live within the influence of all things that He has left on earth in the place of His corporal, visible presence. It is to live in the holy Catholic Church, in the reception of her Sacraments, in the frequentation of the adorable Sacrifice, in obedience to lawful superiors, in the practice of prayer and holy rules, in the love

[1] *Ps.* cii. 13, 14.   [2] *John* xv. 4, 7.

and zeal for community life. Let us be sure that to live our whole and complete Christian, priestly, or religious life, is to "abide" in Christ. O divine Christian life! Founded on the Incarnation, built on the Prophets and Apostles, made firm by the traditions of Saints, illuminated by the examples of martyrs, confessors and virgins, blessed by the presence of the Holy Spirit of Jesus! may I live this life, O Lord! may I live by my rule, in my rule, under my superiors, near to Thy altar, guided by custom and precept, helped by the example of my brethren, sanctified by the love of Thee and of them!

2. One of the grand fruits of a retreat ought to be the adoption, or the renovation, of a rule of life. This rule should embrace, first, our obligations as Christians; next, the obligations of our state; and thirdly, the special means which it seems desirable to adopt in order that no duty should be neglected —as, for example, fixed hours, methods of prayer, subjects of prayer, particular practices, examinations (particular and general), days for recollection, the striving for this or that especial virtue, the safeguarding ourselves against the sins and faults to which we are most prone. Indeed, with many of us, our rule of life need only concern itself with this third head. And, except on this head, it is evident that religious living in their monastery do not require any other rule of life than that of the community. But those souls who are more or less free, either to choose their occupations, or to arrange them,

absolutely require a definite rule : Rise at such an hour, mental prayer at such an hour, Divine Office, study, spiritual reading, visit to the Blessed Sacrament, etc., etc., at such hours. Make, then, or renew, with great fervour such rules and good resolutions as you may see by God's light and the help of your director to be necessary or advisable. Then say, with St Francis of Sales :[1] " O dear resolution, you are the beautiful Tree of Life, which my God has planted with His own hand in the midst of my heart!" . . . "I am no longer my own—whether I live or die, I belong to my Saviour!"

3. End your retreat, as you began it, with devout and loving Acts of Trust in God. "Blessed is the man that trusteth in the Lord, and whose hope the Lord is. He shall be as a tree that is planted by the waters, that spreadeth out its roots towards moisture; and it shall not fear when the heat cometh . . . in the time of drought it shall not be solicitous, neither shall it cease at any time to bring forth fruit."[2] O sweet and delightful illustration of the blessedness of a soul who has truly learnt to reckon upon God's unfathomable love! In those regions of burning sun, the tree planted by the water brook is always green and fruitful. So with thee, O my heart, in all temptations and troubles, if thou continue to believe in thy Father's love! "A man's unwavering trust," He said to St. Gertrude,

---

[1] *Introd. à la Vie dévote*, p. v., chs. xv., xvi.
[2] *Jerem.* xvii. 7. 8.

"in My power, knowledge, and will to be faithfully near him on all occasions, has so powerful an effect upon My loving kindness that I cannot withhold My favours from him."[1] O Spirit of Jesus, fill and saturate my soul with true and filial confidence in my Saviour! I believe, O Lord, that Thou art my Father and my Protector! I believe that Thou desirest with an eternal longing to save me and bring me to Thy feet! I believe that Thou wouldst, if it were needful, die over again for me! I believe that Thou art with me in tribulation—that Thou art nigh at hand in all my temptations—that Thou dost receive and repay a hundredfold all the good works which Thy grace enables me to do—and that Thou art ready every instant to pardon my sins, both little and great, and to grant me Thy constant help! I believe that I have no other Friend—no other Father—no other hope; but Thou art my riches, exceeding all that I can hope or ask for.

Most holy Mary, to thy care we have all been entrusted. Behold thy child!—frail, blind, perverse, wounded, laden with sins!—yet knowing well that it was for such that thine office was given thee! Obtain for me the grace of final Perseverance! Turn towards me those merciful eyes of thine—and show me, both now and in eternity, the blessed fruit of thy womb, Jesus!

[1] *Legatus Div. Pietatis.* iii. 7.

www.ingramcontent.com/pod-product-compliance
Lightning Source LLC
Chambersburg PA
CBHW051722300426
44115CB00007B/422